PLAYING POLITICS WITH
NATURAL DISASTER

PLAYING POLITICS WITH NATURAL DISASTER

Hurricane Agnes, the 1972 Election, and the Origins of FEMA

Timothy W. Kneeland

CORNELL UNIVERSITY PRESS   ITHACA AND LONDON

First published 2020 by Cornell University Press

Library of Congress Cataloging-in-Publication Data

Names: Kneeland, Timothy W., 1962– author.
Title: Playing politics with natural disaster : Hurricane Agnes, the 1972 election, and the origins of FEMA / Timothy W. Kneeland.
Description: Ithaca [New York] : Cornell University Press, 2020. | Includes bibliographical references and index.
Identifiers: LCCN 2019024694 (print) | LCCN 2019024695 (ebook) | ISBN 9781501748530 (hardcover) | ISBN 9781501748547 (epub) | ISBN 9781501748554 (pdf)
Subjects: LCSH: United States. Federal Emergency Management Agency. | Hurricane Agnes, 1972—Political aspects. | Hurricanes—Political aspects.— New York (State) | Hurricanes—Political aspects.—Pennsylvania. | Natural disasters—Political aspects—United States. | Disaster relief— Political aspects.—United States. | Disaster relief—Government policy— United States. | Emergency management—Political aspects—United States. | Emergency management—Government policy—United States.
Classification: LCC HV636 1972.U6 K54 2020 (print) | LCC HV636 1972.U6 (ebook) | DDC 363.34/92256097309047—dc23
LC record available at https://lccn.loc.gov/2019024694
LC ebook record available at https://lccn.loc.gov/2019024695

For my wife, Laura, and children, Adam, Aaron, Ben, and Anna,
who took many trips along the Susquehanna and listened patiently
to stories that began, "It was 1972 when Hurricane Agnes . . ."

Disaster preparedness is a task never completed.

—George A. Lincoln

Contents

Preface

The application of history to the task of understanding and analyzing public policy inspired this book, which is a study of Hurricane Agnes and American disaster policy from the top down and the bottom up. Although federal disaster assistance is crucial to mending people's lives and rebuilding their towns and cities, disasters are local affairs and the rebuilding of shattered communities is overseen and managed by local figures. Even though they are localized, disasters do not occur in a vacuum. Existing policies, political trends, and the administrative power of the federal government impact the response to, and outcome of, any disaster.

When I began this work, I was less sensitive to the importance of the local context of disaster, which is too often neglected in the literature. Nor was I then aware of how significant Richard Nixon's response to the disaster would be for national policy making. The location of a disaster, the political context for the timing of the event, and the political influence of local and state officials shaped the federal response to the Agnes disaster in ways I did not realize.

I drew several critical lessons from my study of Hurricane Agnes. First was how unprepared the people and government were for the magnitude of that catastrophe. They were caught off guard even though there was sufficient data available to all involved that a flood in the Susquehanna River Basin, which included Corning, Elmira, Wilkes-Barre, and Harrisburg, was not only likely, but in fact inevitable. Ignoring the history of past floods and relying too heavily on technological solutions promoting the myth that the federal government would warn and protect the public allowed these communities to encourage development along their rivers, which heightened the risk to their properties and their lives. Residents and elected officials relied on the idea that their dams and levees were secure from flooding and that their weather forecasting would provide them with advanced warning of a disaster, neither of which proved correct. Perhaps because they presumed that the government would protect them, they lacked a local agency of first responders that could assist in warning and evacuation in an emergency. They had no plan for recovery after the flooding and no interest in changing the very policies that had put their cities and towns in harm's way.

Working on this book from the mid-2000s through 2018 made it clear that some things had not changed since 1972. Time and again the public has been caught unaware or unprepared for devastating events such as Hurricane Katrina in 2005 and the many floods, wildfires, and tornadoes that plagued U.S. society over that decade. As I write this, scientists are predicting that global climate change will increase the likelihood of natural disasters. Although I conclude that as a nation we are much better equipped to deal with disaster than Americans were in 1972, there remains much to be done in terms of regulating the nation's floodplain. Individual property owners and their local governments need to rethink how they use their waterfront property in a society that will become wetter and where flooding will become more common. Restricting waterfront development may be a great challenge for local government, but it remains the best hope for protecting lives and property in the future.

This book is the result of the patience, support, and encouragement of librarians and archivists, participants, colleagues, and editors who generously gave their time and talents to assisting in locating material, listening as I thought aloud about it, and making helpful suggestions about the manuscript. In particular, I want to thank the Interlibrary Loan staff at Nazareth College; James Folts and the staff at the New York State Archives, the staff at the Pennsylvania State Archives; Charles Bradley and the staff at the Rockefeller Archives; David Sabo and the staff at the National Archives, which at the time housed the Nixon Presidential Materials Project; Jennie Levine, formerly the Manager of Digital Collections and Research at the McKeldin Library at the University of Maryland, College Park; and Michael Knies, the Special Collections Supervisor at the University of Scranton. More generally, my thanks go to the staff at the Carl A. Kroch Library Division of Rare and Manuscript Collections at Cornell University; the staff at M. E. Grenander Special Collections and Archives at the New York State University at Albany; the librarians at the New York State Library; the staff at the Rochester Public Library, the Buffalo and Erie County Public Library, the Southeast Steuben County Library, the Steele Memorial Library, the Hornell Public Library, and the Osterhout Free Library; and the staff at the Chemung County Historical Society and the Luzerne County Historical Society.

My thanks to Mary Lu Walker and Peter Voorheis for sharing their collection of oral histories and to those who agreed to be interviewed: Robert Rolfe, Joseph Sartori Jr., Thomas Dimitroff, Lois Janes, Donald Roth, Albert Kachik, Lars O. Feese, Michael Mark, Joel Rodney, Marvin Mandel, Amory Houghton, Thomas MacAvoy, Charles Ingraham, G. A. R. Kearney, Myron Gwinner, George Winner, and the late Dorothy and William Smith. My appreciation also goes out to all the people willing to share pictures for the book, including Bonifer Schweizer, the daughter of William and Dorothy Smith; Corning Incorporated the Rakow Research Library of the Corning Museum of Glass; the U.S. Army Corps of Engineers Office of History; the National Weather Service; the National Oceanic and Atmospheric Administration; and the Big Flats Historical Society.

A special thanks goes to Michael McGandy of Cornell University Press who read several versions of this manuscript as it evolved from 2010 until the present and to Thomas Birkland who read the manuscript and made many helpful suggestions. Thanks to colleagues in the Rochester U.S. Historians working group who read and commented on chapters in this book. Finally, a thank-you goes to Laura Kneeland, who patiently read and edited this manuscript.

Abbreviations

DEC	Department of Environmental Conservation
EOP	Executive Office of the President
FEMA	Federal Emergency Management Agency
FRTF	Flood Recovery Task Force
FVAC	Flood Victims Action Council
HUD	Department of Housing and Urban Development
IDA	Industrial Development Authority
NAWAS	National Warning System
NFIP	National Flood Insurance Program
NGA	National Governors Association
NOAA	National Oceanic and Atmospheric Administration
NWS	National Weather Service
OEP	Office of Emergency Preparedness
UDC	Urban Development Corporation

Cast of Characters

White House Officials
Richard M. Nixon (1913–1994), President of the United States
Spiro T. Agnew (1918–1996), Vice President of the United States
H. R. Haldeman (1926–1993), White House Chief of Staff
John Ehrlichman (1925–1999), White House Domestic Policy Advisor
Chuck Colson (1931–2012), Special Counsel to the President
John Whitaker (1926–2016), Deputy Assistant to the President for Domestic Affairs
Desmond J. "Des" Barker (1926–), Special Assistant to the President

Other Federal Government Officials
George Romney (1907–1995), Secretary of Housing and Urban Development
Peter Peterson (1926–2018), Secretary of Commerce
James Hodgson (1915–2012), Secretary of Labor
George Lincoln (1917–1975), Director, Office of Emergency Preparedness
Robert Schnabel (1920–1981), Office of Emergency Preparedness
Thomas P. Dunne (ca. 1913–1992), Federal Disaster Assistance Administration
Thomas S. Kleppe (1919–2007), Administrator of Small Business Administration
George Cressman (1919–2008), Director, National Weather Service
Albert Kachic (1931–2019), Hydrologist, National Weather Service
Frank Carlucci (1930–2018), Deputy Director, Office of Management and Budget
John E. Davis (1913–1990), Director, Civil Defense Preparedness Agency

Members of Congress
Hugh Scott (1900–1994), R-Pennsylvania, Minority Leader, U.S. Senate
Richard Schweiker (1926–2015), R-Pennsylvania, U.S. Senator
Jacob Javits (1904–1986), R-New York, U.S. Senator
James Buckley (1923–), Conservative-New York, U.S. Senator
George McGovern (1922–2012), D South Dakota, U.S. Senator
Birch Bayh (1928–), D-Indiana, U.S. Senator
Joseph Biden (1942–), D-Delaware, U.S. Senator
Daniel J. Flood (1903–1994), D-Pennsylvania, U.S. Representative
Joseph McDade (1931–2017), R-Pennsylvania, U.S. Representative
James F. Hastings (1926–2014), R-New York, U.S. Representative
Howard Robison (1915–1987), R-New York, U.S. Representative
Gerald Ford (1913–2006), R-Minority Leader, House of Representatives
Wright Patman (1893–1976), D-Texas, U.S. Representative

State Officials
Nelson Rockefeller (1908–1979), Governor of New York
Milton Shapp (1912–1994), Governor of Pennsylvania
William Hennessy (1927–2001), New York Natural Disaster and Civil Defense Agency
William Wilcox (1920–2004), Pennsylvania Director of Community Affairs

Local Officials

Joseph Nasser (1914–1988), Mayor, Corning New York
Joseph Sartori, Jr. (1939–), City Manager, Elmira New York
William Smith (1916–2010), Senator, New York State Senate
Jack Gridley (d. 1994), Chair, Steuben County Board of Supervisors
Frank Townend (1911–2001), Director, Luzerne County Civil Defense

Citizens

Jack Anderson (1922–2005), Syndicated newspaper columnist
Amory Houghton, Jr (1926–), Chairman, Corning Glass Works
Tom MacAvoy (1928–2015), President, Corning Glass Works
Max Rosenn (1910–2006), Chairman, Flood Recovery Task Force, Wilkes-Barre
Min Matheson (1909–1992), Flood Victims Action Council
Gilbert F. White (1911–2006), Environmental Geographer

PLAYING POLITICS WITH NATURAL DISASTER

Introduction

LOCAL DISASTERS, GOVERNMENT ACTORS, AND NATIONAL POLICY

Wolfgang H. Meybaum, the senior hydraulic engineer for the New York State flood control office in Elmira, told reporters just hours before the 1972 flood, that the Chemung River posed "no immediate threat" and that despite forecasts for more rain this was "nothing we can't handle."[1] Joseph Nasser, the mayor of Corning, recalled, "We thought we were doing all right, the night before. It was going to be just like 1935 when the [Susquehanna River] crested at 17 feet. It wasn't going to be too bad."[2] In Wilkes-Barre, Pennsylvania, civil defense director Frank Townend was taciturn, self-assured, and insular. He did not communicate with other civil defense offices along the river and remained uninformed about what was happening upriver from Wilkes-Barre, which strengthened his conviction that "the river would stay within the levee."[3] Nicholas Souchik, who worked with Townend in the civil defense office, predicted that Wilkes-Barre would remain dry.[4] Their illusion of perfect safety behind flood walls was punctured, along with the dikes, on Friday morning, June 23, 1972, the day massive flooding struck New York and Pennsylvania.

Seventy-four people died, and billions of dollars in property damage in New York and Pennsylvania was caused by the remnants of Hurricane Agnes, which swept through the region in late June 1972. The generation of residents who lived through this event cannot forget the trauma of the flood and the years it took to recover from it. Nor was this disaster confined to the Mid-Atlantic region. Hurricane Agnes left a trail of death and destruction along the entire Eastern Seaboard, from Florida to New York, killing at least 128 people and displacing tens of thousands more. President Richard Nixon declared that it was "the greatest natural

1

disaster in the history of the United States,"[5] and out of respect for the victims, the National Weather Service (NWS) retired Agnes from the roster of hurricane names.

A catalog of the devastation caused by Hurricane Agnes summarizes the national scope of the tragedy. After the hurricane made landfall in Florida on June 19, it spawned dozens of tornadoes, which killed nine people. From Florida, it moved into Georgia and North Carolina and took two more lives before it drifted back over the Atlantic Ocean near Cape Hatteras, North Carolina. The death toll was only beginning to climb. The storm gained energy from the Atlantic Ocean and returned to land in the Chesapeake Bay region of Virginia, Maryland, and the District of Columbia, where torrential rain from the storm created flash floods that killed thirty-three people. The flooding forced thousands of people to evacuate their homes and caused significant damage to Richmond, Virginia, and Ellicott City, Maryland. However, Agnes saved its most savage destruction for New York and Pennsylvania, where it killed seventy-four people and left entire cities paralyzed from the flood. The flooding was most substantial in the Twin Tiers of Pennsylvania and New York, where the storm dropped 32 trillion gallons of water over two days. The subsequent flooding forced hundreds of thousands of people from their homes. The property damage in these two states was estimated at that time to be over $2.8 billion.[6]

This book will focus on Elmira and Corning, New York, and Wilkes-Barre, Pennsylvania. These cities received the brunt of the flooding generated by Hurricane Agnes and suffered the most extensive damage. In Corning, the flood destroyed the downtown district, temporarily closed the Corning Glass Works (CGW), the largest employer in the valley, and left a third of Corning residents temporarily homeless. Flooding in Elmira left the downtown in shambles, permanently closed some of the severely damaged businesses, and left half the population of Elmira with damage to their homes. Flooding spawned by Hurricane Agnes in the Wyoming Valley of Pennsylvania nearly destroyed Wilkes-Barre and damaged or destroyed tens of thousands of homes in the outlying suburbs. Gas fires burned some buildings down to the water line. The people within these cities saw their homes destroyed, their businesses shattered, and for some, a lifetime of precious memories and accumulated wealth destroyed by a flood they had never anticipated. Meanwhile, the local government within these communities had to restore public services, replace infrastructure including roads, bridges, and sewage treatment plants, and cope with an eroded tax base. To restore services and recover, local officials joined with leaders drawn from the private sector to implement recovery and rebuilding, which took over a year to complete.

National trends influenced the federal and local response to the disaster. Hurricane Agnes struck the United States less than five months before the 1972 presidential election, and Nixon's response to Hurricane Agnes was one variable in that election, which charted the course of American politics for the next three decades. The choice of presidential candidates reflected underlying questions about whether the United States would continue to expand on the liberal ideals of the Great Society, as personified in George McGovern, or embrace the conservative values of Richard Nixon, who rejected New Deal liberalism and supported New Federalism, which sought to empower individuals and state governments.

In order to win reelection in 1972, President Nixon enacted the most substantial disaster aid package in history to that time, termed the Agnes Recovery Act, which he was convinced was the key to winning New York and Pennsylvania. To ensure its passage, he invited five hundred local officials to the White House for a summit on the legislation. Feeling empowered by the invitation and heartened by the generous assistance promised at the White House meeting, local representatives fully endorsed the act and successfully pressured members of Congress to pass it.

The 1970s were a turbulent time in American political history. In 1972 the country was divided over the Vietnam War, which shaped the everyday thinking of that generation. Proponents of generous disaster assistance, like Governor Milton Shapp of Pennsylvania, interjected the Vietnam War into their claim that the United States should fully compensate flood victims for their loss of property. Shapp and others questioned how the nation could spend billions of dollars bombing and rebuilding Vietnam yet refuse to spend billions helping its people. Based on the premise that people were victims of disaster through no fault of their own, some elected officials wanted federal disaster policy to mirror the Great Society programs. The Great Society had sought to protect the most vulnerable populations, such as the elderly and the indigent, so it made sense to liberal policymakers that the federal government should pay full restitution to citizens whose homes and businesses were destroyed by the flooding.

The idea of indemnifying flood victims met stiff resistance from President Nixon and a bipartisan coterie of conservative House and Senate members, who rejected the proposal as too costly. Conservative lawmakers also believed that the expansive welfare state had de-enervated ordinary Americans and granted too much power to bureaucrats. They did not want another government entitlement program. The victims of the disaster were bitterly disappointed by the government's failure to enact full indemnity for their losses, and many remained mired in debt for the rest of their lives.

Public anxiety over the growing federal bureaucracy and expansive power of the federal government influenced Richard Nixon's 1968 election platform, which called for restoring power to the states through New Federalism. The welfare state created by the New Deal and bulked up by the Great Society led to a vast expansion of the federal bureaucracy. New government programs spawned an array of administrative offices and officials who were not under the direct control of Congress or the president. Nixon tried to circumvent the bureaucracy by creating layers of political appointees to supervise the work of agencies such as Housing and Urban Development (HUD), but this strategy was virtually useless. Unable to control the bureaucracy, the president was nonetheless responsible for their actions. Storm victims blamed the president when administrators overseeing disaster relief in Pennsylvania seemed to unleash on the flood victims a sea of red tape that needlessly stalled necessary aid. The paperwork stymied local officials, and ordinary citizens were confused by the array of agencies involved in the relief effort.

Citizen outrage at the slow pace of recovery astounded some public servants, who recalled that direct federal assistance to disaster victims was still relatively new in 1972, having only gradually developed from legislation first enacted in 1950. However, people's disenchantment with the disaster assistance was part of a broader trend of dissatisfaction with, and mistrust of, the government. People in the United States were unhappy with the larger but seemingly unresponsive federal government, the long and divisive Vietnam War, and the slowing economy.

Flood survivors from Wilkes-Barre confronted George Romney, the HUD secretary, with their grievances. The incident made the front page of newspapers and dominated news broadcasts across the nation, and Romney became the lightning rod for all that was wrong with the implementation of federal policy. President Nixon fired Romney and then burnished his image as a compassionate leader by sending Frank Carlucci to Wilkes-Barre as his flood czar. Carlucci, with the full force of the chief executive behind him, sped up the delivery of needed federal assistance and fast-tracked requests for housing and loans.

Victims of Hurricane Agnes looked to the media to advocate for them, but elected leaders found it intrusive and often ignorant of the nature of intergovernmental relations. The media was quick to blame and slow to explain. Some politicians, including Nixon, believed the press was out to get them. Press coverage of Hurricane Agnes seemed more prevalent than the coverage of earlier hurricane disasters, perhaps because Wilkes-Barre and Corning were geographically closer to the national news networks in New York City. Competition in the news industry was also fostering a pack mentality among reporters, which meant that if one network covered a story about Hurricane Agnes, the others were quick to follow. Media coverage of Hurricane Agnes showed how reporters were moving away from lapdog journalism and embracing a role as a watchdog of the presidency. During the Nixon era, journalists took an adversarial approach to covering the White House. Although press coverage of Hurricane Agnes was far more circumspect than that of the coverage of later disasters such as Hurricane Katrina and Hurricane Sandy, President Nixon found the press scrutiny unbearable, and storm victims and their advocates found the national media a boon for amplifying their grievances.

Hurricane Agnes struck communities in Pennsylvania and New York that were experiencing the early stages of deindustrialization. In 1972, the economies of the Southern Tier of New York and Northern Tier of Pennsylvania were teetering on the edge of decline. Hurricane Agnes exacerbated the dire economic situation. Some companies went into bankruptcy, including the Erie Lackawanna Railway, the Lehigh Valley Railroad, and Piper Air. Other industries took months to return to regular production schedules. Unemployment skyrocketed, and economic recovery in this region took over a year. Nudged or pushed by the flood, key industries such as American LaFrance and Remington Rand Corporation in Elmira, New York, closed. Many smaller businesses did not survive the flood, and others relocated from their downtown locations to the suburbs. Elected leaders and the business community saw an opportunity in the Agnes Recovery Act of 1972 and the possibility of urban renewal funding to rebuild their cities and staunch the flow of economic decline. Their redevelopment in the aftermath of disaster demonstrates the importance of the business community in shaping local government policy. Sadly for residents of the Twin Tiers, the funds merely delayed the inevitable decline of this region, which was part of a national trend that was turning the Northeast into the Rust Belt.

Local leaders played a crucial role in responding to the crisis in their communities and in flood recovery operations and rebuilding. Often neglected in studies of natural disaster policy is the way in which local leadership from government and the private sector interacted with representatives of the federal government to restore order and implement change. Especially notable in this story are Elmira city manager Joseph Sartori, Corning mayor Joseph Nasser, and emergent leaders such as Amory Houghton, Jr., who headed CGW.

Joe Sartori risked his career in the late evening of June 22 by ordering evacuations in Elmira, even though the NWS reported that the river would remain below the top of the dikes. Because of Sartori's actions, no one in Elmira died from the flood. Meanwhile, reassured by the NWS that the river would not overtop the dikes, Joseph Nasser delayed evacuation until it was nearly too late. Eighteen people died in Corning due to the lack of warning, but the death toll would have been much higher had Nasser not begun evacuations in the wee hours of June 23, 1972. Sartori and Nasser were fundamental in reestablishing order and rebuilding their cities from the disaster. To complete the latter task, they endured seemingly endless paperwork and regulations from a host of state and federal agencies that at times seem to contradict common sense. Ultimately, they mastered the cumbersome and impractical regulations and restored their cities.

Behind the scenes were influential members of the business community. In Corning, it was Amory Houghton, Jr. Houghton led the family-owned CGW, which was the largest employer in the region. After the flood crippled the glass works, some suggested that Houghton should relocate the company outside Corning and move closer to the major transportation hubs. Houghton rejected calls to relocate and not only kept the business in Corning but expanded the existing factory, which provided a significant boost in morale to area citizens. Houghton lent top managers from CGW to local government to assist with flood recovery operations and used his considerable influence and wealth to persuade Governor Nelson Rockefeller, President Nixon, and a host of federal officials to give his company special attention. Years later he could rightly be hailed as the man who saved Corning.

Municipal leaders in Wilkes-Barre similarly turned to the private sector for assistance after Hurricane Agnes. Leaders in government deferred to the business community, which called on federal court judge Max Rosenn to lead a newly formed group called the Flood Recovery Task Force. Rosenn's influence proved invaluable in his ability to pressure members of Congress and the Pennsylvania State Legislature for more funding for Wilkes-Barre. Citizens from Wilkes-Barre's working-class community feared they would be left out of the decision making and called on Min Matheson to represent their interests before the government. A former organizer for the International Ladies' Garment Workers' Association, Matheson had only just retired to Wilkes-Barre when the flood destroyed her home and that of her daughter and grandchildren.

Furious at the slow pace of recovery, Matheson organized and led the Flood Victims Action Council, which used labor tactics such as protests and rallies to bring national attention to the plight of flood victims and shame to President Nixon. Her efforts made the front page and the lead stories on national newscasts when she confronted Romney for failing to help families whose houses had been destroyed, many of whom remained homeless for months after the disaster. The combined tactics of closed-door lobbying and in-your-face confrontation ensured that Wilkes-Barre received assistance. It was Matheson who, by her actions, led President Nixon to send Carlucci to Wilkes-Barre to oversee recovery operations in that city and then to make a special presidential visit there himself to show his support for the flood victims.

The American system of federalism was created in part to ensure that government is local and close to home. Hence, Bill Smith, the New York state senator representing the Corning and Elmira area, played a significant role in the lives of his constituents and neighbors. Smith himself was part of the Agnes story.

The flood destroyed his family farm in Big Flats, New York, and Bill and his wife took refuge in their attic, from which they were later rescued by boat. Smith's passion to protect his constituents and neighbors from another disaster like Hurricane Agnes was as much personal as it was political. Smith did more for flood victims than any other elected official in New York state government. He championed their cause to federal officials, wrote letters to the president, and led a special state senate investigation into the failures of disaster policy that had exacerbated the tragedy of the flooding. His desire for policy reform at the state level met with resistance from Republican Party leaders in Albany who, under the leadership of Governor Rockefeller, preferred the status quo to significant change.

Smith's special state senate investigation uncovered a host of problems in local, state, and federal disaster management. His report showed that the lack of preparation by the government and misinformation among the populace had added significantly to the loss of life and property. For example, forecasters for the NWS had employed sophisticated computer models and satellite imagery to plot the course of Hurricane Agnes as it made its way toward the United States. The NWS used this information to issue flood warnings from Florida to New York, which led the forerunner of the Federal Office of Emergency Management (FEMA), the Office of Emergency Preparedness (OEP), to disseminate warnings and prepare for widespread flooding. However, even before the flooding occurred, communication between the NWS, the OEP, elected officials, and ordinary citizens in the flood zones broke down. Some officials did not receive the warnings about the potential for flooding, while others did not understand or heed them. The agencies tasked with issuing the warnings, however, had no responsibility for ensuring that people received and understood these alerts.

In the era before the professionalization of emergency management, state and local authorities relied on civil defense organizations to handle local crises. The Senate hearings revealed that many civil defense directors were political appointees who were often ill-trained and unprofessional. The confusion and ineptitude displayed by some civil defense agencies hindered attempts to evacuate and rescue citizens during the flooding. Even when there was a professional in charge of civil defense, such as Frank Townend in Luzerne County, Pennsylvania, there was no system for communication and coordination between governmental units. This insularity led to tragedy when Townend misread the flood warnings from the NWS and decided to sandbag along the river near Wilkes-Barre rather than evacuate. People were caught unawares when the river surged and unexpectedly spilled over the dikes and into the city.

Incapable of recovering on their own and exasperated by the delayed aid, residents of the flood-wracked cities turned to their elected representatives in Congress in hopes of speeding up recovery operations. Dozens of members of the House and Senate worked assiduously on behalf of their constituents to encourage their legislative peers to pass the necessary legislation, fast-track existing legislation, and intervene with the bureaucracy on behalf of the survivors. Of those who performed these tasks in 1972, perhaps none was more powerful than congressional representative Daniel J. Flood of Wilkes-Barre.

Flood was at the peak of his power and influence in the House when the rains spawned by Hurricane Agnes flooded his hometown. Flood was an influential member of the House Appropriations Committee. He used his clout to add an array of generous benefits to the Agnes Recovery Act of 1972, and then persuaded fellow members of Congress to move it out of committee and to a vote of the House in late July and early August 1972. Flood persuaded the representatives of federal agencies working on flood recovery in Wilkes-Barre to do his bidding. The flood recovery legislation he sponsored and the effort he expended in assisting the people of the Wyoming Valley region, which included Wilkes-Barre, Hazleton, Pittston, and Naticoke, was his most significant moment in Congress, and indeed his most lasting achievement.

The congressional representatives from Corning and Elmira, James Hastings and Howard Robison, also proved helpful to the storm victims. Hastings was in the Corning area for weeks after the disaster to represent the citizens and facilitate intergovernmental cooperation. Robison was the dean of the Republican delegation from New York and had a plum seat on the House Appropriations Committee. He used his power to influence Tom Casey, who oversaw flood recovery operations for the OEP, to bend government rules in order to help Robison's most vulnerable constituents. Robison also used his role on the Environment and Public Works Subcommittee of the House Appropriations Committee to expedite construction of a dam that many claimed would have prevented the flooding in Corning.

At the state level, the governors of Pennsylvania and New York had the responsibility of overseeing disaster recovery in their states, and they shaped the contours of federal action there. Pennsylvania governor Shapp and New York governor Rockefeller were a study in contrasts. Their personalities, party affiliations, and personal experience with the flooding in their state shaped their approaches to the disaster. Having been evacuated by rowboat from the Governor's Mansion in Harrisburg, Milton Shapp had firsthand experience with the flood. In the aftermath of the Hurricane Agnes disaster, Shapp convened a special session of the Pennsylvania legislature to send immediate aid to the storm victims. He then became a peripatetic advocate for Pennsylvanians, on whose behalf he mounted a quixotic effort to secure full compensation for their damaged houses. Shapp frequently testified before Congress on behalf of the storm victims and effectively marshaled the press to his cause. Without him, victims across the nation would have received far less federal assistance after Hurricane Agnes than they did. In contrast, Rockefeller feared that state intervention on behalf of the victims of Agnes would endanger their receipt of federal assistance and resisted attempts to reform state policy. The governor refused bipartisan calls for a special legislative session to enact flood relief and then vetoed reform proposals that came to his desk in January 1973.

President Nixon called Hurricane Agnes the "the worst natural disaster in the whole of America's history."[7] To victims, the disaster was local and personal; for the president, it was a national disaster responsible for death and damage from Florida to New York. President Nixon issued federal disaster declarations for seven states and, just weeks after the storm, enacted a generous relief bill to help disaster victims. Managing a disaster of this magnitude was beyond the institutional and constitutional powers of the president, and Nixon found controlling and overseeing the multiple cabinet departments and bureaucracies involved in disaster relief and recovery a logistical nightmare, which caused relief efforts to drag on for months. Although not personally involved in the daily work of disaster assistance, the president had ultimate responsibility for the appointees who did, including George Lincoln, as well as Romney and Carlucci.

George Lincoln was a former brigadier general and logistics expert and was head of the OEP, Romney, a former automotive CEO, a onetime Michigan governor, and a failed aspirant for the White House, was secretary of housing and urban development, and it was up to him to house the tens of thousands of people left homeless by the Hurricane Agnes flooding. Carlucci was deputy director for the Office of Management and Budget (OMB), and it was his job to prepare the Agnes Recovery Act, which granted billions in storm aid to New York, Pennsylvania, and the other states involved in recovering from the disaster. Under Nixon, the OMB served as the president's manager of other agencies, which inspired the president to appoint Carlucci to be the temporary flood czar in the Wyoming Valley of Pennsylvania, where he oversaw recovery efforts and cut through the red tape.

Despite their initiative and ability, these men found that timely delivery of disaster aid to victims of Hurricane Agnes was nearly impossible due to the tangle of intergovernmental red tape and the intransigence of some members of the bureaucracy, with the result that some people remained homeless for months after the destruction and others awaited promised government assistance that never came.

The tragedy caused by Hurricane Agnes led to a clash of opinions on how to create a more effective government response to such disasters. Months after the hurricane hit, Nixon reorganized the government to move disaster assistance agencies under the umbrella of the HUD, and in 1973, he enacted changes to the National Flood Insurance Program. Finally, the president sent Congress a reform bill that he was convinced would better protect people against future disasters such as Agnes, but the proposal stalled in Congress until 1974.

As president of the United States, Nixon had vast powers on paper, but these were useless in a battle with an opposition Congress that had grown institutionally resistant to the presidential management of the government. Congress stalled the president's disaster relief program, partially due to the belief that it would weaken existing programs rather than strengthen them. It favored more generous disaster assistance, while the president did not. Nixon's New Federalist philosophy was to encourage states, localities, and individuals to better prepare for disaster.

Disaster experts working for Nixon created the Disaster Relief Act of 1974, which laid the foundation for the training of emergency personnel and imposed new requirements for mitigation and planning on state and local government. This, in turn, fostered the birth of professionalization in emergency preparedness and management. The experts also wrote the Flood Protection Act of 1973, which was meant to enhance the National Flood Insurance Program by discouraging people from rebuilding on a floodplain and discouraging municipalities from issuing permits for new building in flood-prone areas.

Due to political considerations, the national flood insurance reforms have been far less successful than the ideals enshrined in the Disaster Relief Act of 1974. The federal government bowed to public pressure for higher dikes and levees in the Susquehanna River Basin and accelerated the building of new dams to protect Corning and Elmira. Although residents lauded the new flood control systems for making them safer, their point of view is in sharp contrast to that of experts, who believe people have been lulled into a false sense of security. Only after Tropical Storm Lee in 2011 have the people living close to the river begun to recognize what experts had been saying all along: structural barriers are imperfect safety measures against flooding, and better land management of the floodplain is the best tool for protecting lives and property.

This book, which is aimed at a general audience, uses the following terms: *natural hazard*, *natural disaster*, and *hurricane*. A natural hazard is any naturally occurring phenomenon, such as blizzards, earthquakes, floods, hurricanes, ice storms, landslides, tornadoes, tsunamis, or wildfires, that poses a potential threat to humans. These potential threats become natural disasters when they affect human society to the extent that they cause challenges in social and economic activity that are beyond the ability of individuals or entire communities to overcome. Disasters include extensive property damage, deaths, and/or multiple injuries. Hurricanes are storms that originate over the North Atlantic Ocean. (Similar storms in other parts of the globe are called typhoons or cyclones.) Hurricanes have a warm core of low barometric pressure, around which winds of seventy-four miles per hour or higher circulate in a counterclockwise direction. Hurricanes create a storm surge with waves several feet high that pound coastal areas before the storm hits. Once they make landfall, hurricanes often spawn tornadoes and torrential rainfall.

The Atlantic hurricane season lasts from May until November. To distinguish between storms that occur in a single season, the NWS adopted an alphabetical system for naming them, with the name for the first hurricane of the season beginning with the letter A and each subsequent storm receiving the next letter. Because hurricanes have different wind velocities and destructive power, the NWS rates the power of hurricanes through a system known as the Saffir-Simpson hurricane wind scale. The weakest storms, with winds between 74 and 95 miles per hour, are ranked as category one. The strongest storms have winds more than 157 miles per hour and are ranked as category five.[8] *Tropical storms* are cyclones with winds over 39 miles per hour but below hurricane strength. If given enough energy, tropical storms will turn into hurricanes; if a hurricane loses energy, it may become a tropical storm. When heavy rain from a tropical storm falls over land, it can overwhelm the capacity of a river or stream to hold the extra water, which then spreads out into the *floodplain*, the flat area surrounding riverine systems that have resulted from generations of flooding. It is here, when the water moving over the floodplain invades spaces now occupied by people who were enticed there by the building of levees and dams meant to keep cities dry, that disasters occur. If dams or levees fail to hold back the water, flooding occurs, which is what happened in the Twin Tiers in June 1972.

AMERICAN DISASTER POLICY THROUGH 1972

Growing Benefits and Expanding
Federal Authority

"Dear Mr. President," began a letter addressed to President Richard Nixon and dated September 10, 1972. "My mind is full of problems; my heart is full of disgust and disappointment," wrote the author, a "victim of Tropical Storm Agnes." The writer told the president, "I lost everything. . . . I am broke, disquieted, heart-broken, and on the verge of mental and physical collapse." Despite pledges of support for disaster victims, after three months this writer and his or her spouse still had not received the food stamps, housing, or loans to rebuild that had been promised to them. After twelve years of marriage, they were destitute and forced "to live with my in-laws."[1] The writer was one of the thousands of people displaced by Hurricane Agnes in late June 1972, and one of the hundreds who wrote the president asking for help. For most of American history, few citizens would have asked the federal government for assistance after a natural disaster, but by the end of the twentieth century, federal disaster aid had become an expectation. Behind this dramatic change was the Disaster Relief Act of 1950.[2]

Under the Disaster Relief Act of 1950, the federal government assumed a permanent role and new responsibility for assisting local communities and state governments after a disaster. The law was an extension of the New Deal, which emphasized protecting vulnerable groups in society such as the aged, the im-poverished, and those victimized by racial and ethnic prejudice. To this were now added victims of disaster. Between the 1950 legislation and the election of Richard Nixon in 1968, Congress allocated an ever-increasing amount of money toward disaster relief and added new benefits for disaster victims. As a consequence, the number of executive agencies and civil servants involved in dealing with disaster recovery multiplied. Disaster assistance, which was once aimed exclusively at state and local governments, now included direct payments to private citizens affected by natural disaster. This pattern of adding new benefits to disaster legislation culminated in the Disaster Relief Act of 1970, which made permanent all the benefits and programs found in previous acts, making these programs tantamount to a new entitlement.[3] President Nixon was not pleased with the existing entitlement programs and tried to reduce the role of the federal government by empowering the states to prepare for, and deal with, a disaster on their own.

Expanding Disaster Relief

In the nineteenth century, federal disaster relief consisted of an occasional bill passed in Congress to provide limited assistance to a specific community beset by disaster. Congress issued its first law covering disaster in 1803, and by 1950 it had passed approximately 150 such acts. Since this process was ad hoc rather than routine, the general public did not expect federal assistance. For example, it was not considered unusual when President Grover Cleveland vetoed an appropriation bill in 1887 that included $10,000 for Texans suffering from a severe drought. In his veto message, President Cleveland noted that there was nothing in the Constitution allowing the government to assist. Cleveland explained his belief that the people should "support the government; the government should not support the people."[4] In the absence of government programs, victims of disaster turned to private charitable and philanthropic organizations such as the Salvation Army and the American Red Cross.

Charitable organizations, however, were as cautious as President Cleveland about encouraging dependency and provided only what was immediately necessary after a disaster. Clara Barton, who founded the American Red Cross in 1881, wrote the bylaws to ensure that the U.S. version of this international organization assisted not only during wartime but also after a natural disaster. The first instance of the American Red Cross aiding in disaster occurred following a forest fire in northern Michigan that burned down entire communities. The Red Cross solicited donations and provided financial aid to the fire victims. The relatively unknown organization gained national prominence when Clara Barton rushed to Johnstown, Pennsylvania, following the 1889 flood, which killed over two thousand people. In 1893, the American Red Cross came to the aid of the African American inhabitants of the Sea Islands, off the coast of South Carolina, after a hurricane in 1893. However, the organization left the islands once recovery operations began, lest residents become dependent on charity and unable to fend for themselves.[5]

Despite the reticence of Cleveland and Barton, other factors at work in the nineteenth century combined to make governments more responsive to the needs of disaster victims. After the Civil War, state institutions assumed greater responsibility in caring for the poor, the disabled, and the mentally ill.[6] During the Reconstruction period (1865–1877), the Freedmen's Bureau provided direct assistance to African Americans suffering from a series of natural disasters in the South, and although this was limited in scope, it set a precedent for more federal intervention.[7] Meanwhile, the rise of the national press, which developed only after the Civil War, brought attention to the plight of those afflicted by natural disaster. By the end of the nineteenth century, disasters from across the globe became headline news. As a result, people became more sympathetic to the victims' plight and demanded that their government provide assistance.[8]

By the twentieth century, the federal government had the capacity, past precedent, and public sentiment supporting increased federal intervention following a disaster.[9] Federal intervention occurred when a significant amount of public attention became focused on disaster. Each intervention brought with it the precedent to respond in future disasters.[10] For example, after the San Francisco earthquake and fire of 1906, President Theodore Roosevelt tasked the Red Cross with distributing the donations of food, clothing, and medicine but also sent financial assistance and military personnel to the city to help with disaster relief and recovery.[11] When cataclysmic flooding on the Mississippi River struck several states in 1927, killing a thousand people and displacing six hundred thousand more, President Calvin Coolidge took the unprecedented step of organizing and directing federal disaster relief to the stricken area. Coolidge reasoned that federal intervention was necessary and proper due to the interstate nature of the disaster and the economic devastation wrought by the flooding. The president appointed his secretary of commerce, Herbert Hoover, to take charge of the disaster zone, in effect designating him a flood czar mandated to oversee relief operations.[12]

Modern historians looking back at Hoover's actions criticize him for his heavy-handed and overtly racist delivery of disaster relief. For example, Hoover segregated the refugee camps that were created to house the hundreds of thousands of people made homeless by the flooding. He placed African Americans in substandard housing and forced them, under military guard, to assist in cleanup efforts. Hoover placed white flood victims in comfortable housing and did not require them to help in the cleanup. He allocated more relief to whites than blacks and set a precedent that is all too familiar in the history of disaster assistance.[13] People of that time, however, were impressed with Hoover's successful federal intervention to relieve the afflicted population, restore order, and provide timely assistance.[14] Hoover's disaster relief effort was lauded by the press, and the efforts

FIGURE 1.   Commerce Secretary Herbert Hoover, the central figure shown here, with other officials involved in the federal flood relief operations of 1927. Courtesy of National Oceanic and Atmospheric Administration/Department of Commerce.

of "the Great Engineer" in Mississippi won him the White House in 1928. From then on, federal response to a major disaster was expected.

President Franklin Roosevelt passed significant pieces of legislation as part of his New Deal, but he also overhauled the presidency by creating the Executive Office of the President (EOP). The reorganization provided the president with an executive staff within the White House and gave the chief executive direct oversight of many executive agencies once controlled by Congress. Following the government reorganization, American presidents became more influential and the federal bureaucracy more independent from Congress. On paper, at least, the president could oversee and deliver disaster assistance.[15]

President Franklin Roosevelt routinely assigned responsibility for disaster relief to federal agencies. Roosevelt directed disaster aid to states and localities through the Federal Civilian Works Administration, Federal Emergency Relief Administration, Works Progress Administration, Public Works Administration, Civilian Conservation Corps, and Bureau of Public Works.[16] Additionally, he asked Congress to authorize the Reconstruction Finance Corporation (RFC) to make loans to state and local governments to fix or replace public facilities destroyed by a natural disaster through the Disaster Loan Corporation, which foreshadowed the use of the Small Business Administration (SBA) two decades later.[17]

President Harry Truman followed Roosevelt's example by authorizing the Federal Works Administration to donate surplus war material to local and state governments following disasters. The Surplus Property Law of 1947 allowed Truman to initiate federal disaster relief without specific funding or approval from Congress. The law proved to be a stopgap measure, as the war surplus soon ran out. However, with these New Deal precedents in mind, Congress passed the Disaster Relief Act of 1950. This legislation transferred congressional authority to provide disaster assistance to the president. The president or a designate now had broad power to declare a "major disaster" and to allocate funds to state and local governments to rebuild roads, sewers, bridges, and public buildings.[18]

Marking a turning point in the history of disaster policy, the Disaster Relief Act of 1950 created a permanent role for the federal government in disaster management and became the template for all subsequent disaster legislation.[19] The legislation made clear that federal intervention did not replace, but only supplemented, state and local responsibility to respond to and assist in disaster recovery. Federal assistance came after the governor of a state requested it, but even then federal officials had to determine whether the disaster exceeded the ability of the state and local governments to respond.

After passage of the 1950 legislation, the president took the lead in disaster relief and recovery operations but remained dependent on Congress for allocating funding and supplying the bureaucracy for implementing relief. President Truman delegated his executive power to respond to the Housing and Home Finance Agency. The fiscally conservative president Dwight Eisenhower sought to limit expectations of federal largess and used his revolving disaster funds sparingly after Hurricane Hazel in 1954, Hurricane Diane in 1955, and Hurricane Audrey in 1957. Conversely, presidents John F. Kennedy and Lyndon B. Johnson (LBJ) sought to make disaster assistance more generous and the federal presence more visible.[20]

President Kennedy used an executive order to delegate his power to supervise federal assistance for major natural disasters to the director of the Office of Emergency Planning (OEP), which he located in the Office of the President.[21] Sworn in as president on November 22, 1963, following the assassination of President Kennedy, Lyndon Johnson faced his first significant disaster just four months later, when a magnitude 8.4 earthquake struck Alaska on Good Friday, March 27, 1964. The earthquake killed 116 people, many from a tsunami that swept Aleut coastal villages along Prince William Sound and Kodiak Island. The quake also heavily damaged Anchorage, a city with a population of 100,000. The quake destroyed thousands of homes and left residents without power, water, gas, or telephone service. The city lacked any emergency response, and the one and only employee in civil defense, the director, had resigned two weeks before the earthquake. In the absence of local disaster officials, President Johnson ordered the military to restore order and urged Congress to pass a generous relief package. The bill increased financial support for the fledgling state and created the Federal Reconstruction and Development Planning Commission to oversee the rebuilding of Anchorage.[22]

On September 9, 1965, Hurricane Betsy swept over the Gulf of Mexico and into Louisiana, killing eighty-one people and causing nearly $2.4 billion in damage. The hurricane destroyed the levees protecting New Orleans and caused dramatic flooding and extensive property damage in the city and outlying parishes. U.S. senator Russell Long (D-LA) called on President Johnson to visit the city and survey the damage. Long was motivated more by politics than policy, however. Johnson had lost the Deep South, including Louisiana, to Barry Goldwater in the 1964 presidential election, and Senator Long thought that a presidential visit in 1965 would be just the thing to ensure a Democratic victory there when Johnson ran for reelection in 1968. "You lost that state last year. You could pick it up just [by] looking at it right now, by going down there as the president," he explained. Long suggested that the president remind the public that the levees "that Hale Boggs and Russell Long built are the only thing that saved 5,000 lives."[23] As a bonus, Senator Long suggested LBJ's presence would assist the reelection of a staunch Johnson supporter, local congressional representative Ed Willis, in 1966.[24]

Johnson accepted Long's invitation and made a personal visit to the area. He later signed into law the Southeastern Hurricane Relief Act, which brought disaster assistance to an entirely new level by providing direct assistance to individuals in addition to state and local governments.[25] The legislature provided loans at below-market interest rates and even forgave part of the loan. It also made unemployment benefits available to individuals who were dislocated by a disaster. President Johnson understood that by the mid-1960s, disaster costs were rising, not just for local and state governments, but also for middle-income individuals, whose property losses threatened their economic security. Johnson also understood that by implication, he was making disaster relief an entitlement on par with Medicaid, Medicare, and other Great Society programs. He also set a precedent for future occupants of the White House. One historian suggested that President Johnson created the role of "responder in chief" when disaster struck.[26]

Before he left office, Johnson enacted legislation to provide insurance for individuals and businesses that were at risk for flooding. In 1968 Congress passed the National Flood Insurance Act (NFIA), which created the National Flood Insurance Program (NFIP).[27] Before passage of this legislation, flood insurance

FIGURE 2. President Johnson understood the political implications of disaster and visited New Orleans after Hurricane Betsy in 1965. Senator Long is to Johnson's right. Courtesy of Lyndon Baines Presidential Library/Photo by Yoichi Okamoto (A1273-16).

was not available. Private insurance companies refused to issue such policies because they correctly assumed that only those who needed flood insurance would buy it. The entire philosophy behind insurance is the idea of spreading the cost and protecting the insurers against risk, which works if only a subset of those insured uses the insurance. However, if everyone who bought insurance needed to use it, either the insurance industry would go bankrupt or the premiums for such policies would have to be high enough to cover the payouts, ensuring that few people could purchase policies.[28]

More than generosity motivated Congress to enact flood insurance; a key factor was the growing cost of disasters to the federal government itself. Johnson's response to the Alaskan earthquake, Hurricane Betsy, and other disasters was generous and expensive and came at the same time that the Vietnam War was adding to the growing deficit. The late 1960s witnessed the decline in the postwar economy and the rise of inflation and slower economic growth that plagued much of the 1970s. Flood insurance was intended to save the federal government money through cutting the cost of disaster assistance by giving people the ability to receive insurance payouts for lost property. The insurance was to be funded by premiums collected from businesses and individuals located in flood-prone areas.[29]

Nixon and Hurricane Camille

President Johnson had a vision for an expansive government that protected civil rights and provided access to health care and better education and housing for the poor. Driven from office by the unrest created by the Vietnam War, he was succeeded by Richard Nixon in 1969, who vowed to reverse the tide of federal largess and liberalism. President Nixon called for returning power to local and state governments by initiating a "New Federalism." His most successful schemes included revenue sharing and block grants. Less successfully, Nixon also tried to circumvent Congress by impounding billions of dollars earmarked for environmental concerns. Nixon claimed that "a third of a century of social experimentation" had created "bureaucratic monstrosities, cumbersome, unresponsive, and ineffective."[30] Nixon wanted to eliminate, consolidate, or cut the budgets of federal agencies because he believed that they caused more problems than they solved.[31] Although he failed in his quest for bureaucratic reform, Nixon set into motion a slow but steady reversal of New Deal liberalism, which accelerated in the 1980s under Ronald Reagan. Nixon became president just at a time when the American electorate was expecting a no-extra-cost, do-everything presidency, which made the job of president challenging and implementing New Federalism nearly impossible.[32]

To helm his federal disaster agency, Richard Nixon selected retired brigadier general George Lincoln. Lincoln, known to his friends as "Abe," was the first military man to lead the OEP. Lincoln was a West Point graduate and a Rhodes Scholar, who had served with distinction as a logistics officer in World War II. He held several high-level government positions after the war and published three books reflecting his expertise and experience.[33] As head of the OEP, Lincoln was charged with conducting postdisaster damage assessments to determine if states and localities were eligible for disaster assistance. If the president issued a formal disaster declaration, it was up to Lincoln to coordinate the work of dozens of federal agencies responsible for relief and recovery measures. Richard Nixon also assigned his OEP director to work on issues unrelated to natural disasters. For example, Lincoln was on a cabinet task force on oil import controls and oversaw the implementation of wage and price controls, and he also served on the National Security Council.[34]

Lincoln and his staff faced an early challenge from the catastrophe known as Hurricane Camille.[35] Camille was the most powerful storm to hit the United States in modern history and had wind speeds near two hundred miles an hour and a storm surge of almost thirty feet. The hurricane raged into the Gulf Coast on August 17, 1969, killing 146 people and injuring thousands more. The storm obliterated towns and destroyed coastal cities in Louisiana, Mississippi, and parts of Alabama. The weather system moved north and east, spawning torrential rains. On August 20, more than thirty inches of rain fell on Nelson County, Virginia, and caused devastating mudslides. Widespread flooding in Virginia and West Virginia killed another 119 people and injured thousands more. Total property damage came to $1.4 billion.[36]

President Nixon issued a disaster declaration for Mississippi on August 18, Louisiana on August 19, and Virginia on September 23. George Lincoln attempted to direct the twenty federal agencies and forty government programs involved in disaster relief but found a lack of coordination and communication at all levels of government.[37] Tom Casey, a member of the OEP disaster team, wrote at the time that there were "serious gaps in federal and state coordination. No one truly knows who is in charge here and it may be impossible to correct this defect."[38] Lincoln's efforts in the Camille crisis inspired him to attempt new methods of delivering disaster assistance when Hurricane Agnes struck three years later. These innovations included one-stop government assistance centers so disaster victims could obtain all the necessary paperwork from the many agencies involved in disaster relief in one place. Along with the Army Corps of Engineers, Lincoln implemented the small repair program that assisted people to more quickly return to their ruined homes.[39]

While George Lincoln struggled to cope with the catastrophe, President Nixon saw a political opportunity in this disaster to further his "Southern Strategy," his idea to encourage disaffected southern Democrats to vote for him in 1972."[40] Nixon initiated this strategy in 1968 by asking Spiro Agnew to be his running mate. At the time, "Ted" Agnew, as his friends called him, was the conservative governor of Maryland, whose southern roots made him more palatable to fellow southerners. After Camille, Nixon sent Agnew to inspect the areas damaged by the hurricane.[41] Much like Johnson's visit to Louisiana in 1965, Agnew's tour of the South paid political dividends when Mississippi Democrats hosted a fundraiser for Nixon, a Republican.[42] Nixon and his wife, Pat, flew into Gulfport, Mississippi, on September 8, 1969, and were met with a "frenzy of affection" by residents. One reporter concluded that this effort was surely part of the president's Southern Strategy.[43] As he left, Nixon predicted that the area "will not only rebuild but build a new area with new ideas."[44]

Some of Nixon's new ideas included playing racial politics, much as Herbert Hoover had done in 1927. Nixon rejected the advice of aides who wanted to tie rebuilding efforts with a mandate that the schools there integrate. Nixon told Agnew that "desegregation would be attended to later."[45] Racial discrimination also played a role in the president's strategy. While the SBA was generous in granting loans to white storm victims, it was far more stringent when approving loans to African American hurricane victims.[46] The Nixon White House gave governor John Bell Williams $500,000 to create an emergency council to operate relief and recovery for his state. Governor Williams appointed an all-white council to distribute the nearly $100 million in aid, most of which went to middle-class white storm victims. The council ordered segregated housing for storm victims, with whites given shelter at the prestigious Robert E. Lee Hotel, and African Americans placed on an army base with few amenities.[47]

Rebuilding after Hurricane Camille was funded through the Disaster Relief Act of 1969. Debates over this legislation encapsulated the debate between the president and Congress over disaster policy.[48] During hearings on the bill, Nixon sent representatives from the SBA and OEP to speak against expanding the already generous terms of disaster relief. Nixon's effort to curtail federal benefits was stopped by U.S. senator Birch Bayh (D-IN), who chaired the Special Subcommittee on Disaster Relief of the Senate Public Works Committee. Bayh was the dominant figure in disaster legislation from 1966 until 1970.[49] He sponsored the Natural Disaster Act of 1966, which was the first legislation to provide government benefits directly to individuals as well as to local and state governments. The legislation was, in the words of one scholar, a natural disaster "safety net," and had much in common with Johnson's Great Society.[50]

Bayh made sure that the Disaster Relief Act of 1969 followed a similar track. This legislation allowed for the first $1,800 borrowed from the SBA to be forgiven, turning this portion of the loan into an outright grant. The bill required that the federal government assist individuals with removing debris from their property and provided unemployment and emergency food stamp benefits to disaster victims. The bill authorized the government to provide free temporary housing for up to a year after a disaster. In addition to the benefits provided for the disaster victims, the bill required the president to appoint a federal coordination officer to assist in recovery efforts, thereby signifying an expanded and active role for the federal government in disaster relief and recovery.[51] Benefits under the law expired on December 31, 1970, but the legislation directed Congress to hold hearings and "act as expeditiously as possible" to pass permanent legislation.[52]

Senator Bayh led the investigation into the federal response to Hurricane Camille and used the hearings to put a spotlight on disaster policy. His Senate colleague, Edmund Muskie (D-ME), wanted the hearings televised, perhaps to gain public exposure in anticipation of a run for the White House. Muskie had been the running mate of defeated Democratic presidential candidate Hubert Humphrey in 1968 and ran for president in 1972.[53] He might also have surmised that televising the hearings could pressure Congress into passing a bill that granted more benefits to disaster victims. Studies have shown that there is a correlation between televised coverage of disasters and the amount of money allocated by Congress for disaster relief.[54]

The televised hearings were dramatic. Public officials sparred over the propriety and constitutionality of legislation that provided disaster relief to individuals. Other officials argued over whether the disaster aid was racially biased.[55] The hearings featured complaints from state and local officials about the volume of paperwork necessary to apply for aid, the duplication and overlap of services provided by the numerous agencies involved in disaster relief, and the length of time it took federal officials to respond to applications for assistance.[56] The committee's final report cited a lack of coordination and communication among the federal agencies that came to assist after Camille, a lack of communication and coordination between the federal government and the state disaster agencies, an overall lethargy in responding to victims' needs, and racial and class discrimination by officials and the Red Cross.[57]

In preparing officials for the hearing, the Nixon administration told then to give favorable testimony, "admit that some mistakes were made unintentionally, and stress that based on experience, procedures are being developed to ensure that this will not happen in the future."[58] One unidentified spokesman for OEP conceded that there were "glaring loopholes and weaknesses in current existing federal statutes," but also expressed optimism that these problems would be resolved "before another disaster hits."[59] Although OEP officials had shown deference to their senatorial critics during the hearings, in private they sought ways to deflect blame away from Nixon. Nixon aides gave George Lincoln a set of scripted responses to use with the media and the Senate: Camille had caused the disaster, not the federal government; Camille was responsible for the postdisaster confusion, not federal officials; under the Constitution, states had the responsibility for recovering from Camille, not the federal government; and hurricanes discriminated against the poor, not the federal government.[60] The overall message of the Nixon administration was that Hurricane Camille was an "act of God" and was beyond the control of the government.[61]

For Birch Bayh, the post-Camille disaster hearings provided a platform from which to crusade for increased disaster aid and expanded eligibility of disaster survivors for new government benefits. In March 1970, after finding twenty-six cosponsors, Bayh proposed the "Omnibus Disaster Assistance Act." The bill contained three critical ideas. One was to enhance the mechanism of disaster relief by creating an Office of Disaster Assistance within the Executive Office of the President. The Office of Disaster Assistance would subsume the duties of the OEP and the Department of Defense through the Civil Defense Agency.[62] A second idea was the creation of the "Major Disaster Insurance Program," a program that would allow citizens to purchase insurance to protect their residential, business, and agricultural interests. This insurance would limit compensation to no more than $30,000. Finally, the bill mandated a nondiscrimination clause guaranteeing equal treatment for disaster victims.[63]

President Nixon rejected the Omnibus Disaster Assistance Act and countered with legislation of his own, the Disaster Relief Act of 1970, which he sent to Congress in April. This bill called for expanding existing benefits but declined to create a new disaster agency. Nixon claimed that "the present system makes maximum use of existing agencies, centrally coordinated by the Office of Emergency Preparedness."[64] Nixon also promised to create a National Council on Federal Disaster Assistance to study the possibility of a new insurance program and added a call to expand the NFIP. His proposal asked for better planning and preparation for natural hazards at the state and local levels.[65] The House version ended up as a series of "cut and bite amendments" that expanded existing law.[66] The House rejected the main provisions of the Senate bill, such as consolidating Civil Defense and OEP into one agency, and ignored the call for a new insurance program. One longtime Senate aide, Stewart McClure, suggested that members of the House Appropriations Committee killed the idea of disaster insurance in 1970, not because they feared the cost but because such a program would end the system of quid pro quo within the House, whereby members traded votes with colleagues in the process called logrolling.[67]

The final version of the bill was a compromise between the expansive vision of Birch Bayh and the limiting views of Richard Nixon. The Disaster Relief Act of 1970 replaced the 1950 statute but marked a significant turn for disaster policy going forward by making permanent a role for federal assistance for private property and individuals following a disaster. It expanded federal disaster assistance by making permanent those benefits that had accrued during the 1960s, such as providing assistance to institutions of higher education, paying for debris removal from private property, and providing temporary housing, legal services, unemployment insurance, food stamps, and expanded eligibility for Small Business and Farm and Home Loans.[68] The new legislation increased the federal cost of repairing public infrastructure to 100 percent. Although the act did not include a national catastrophic insurance program, as Bayh had suggested, the federal government was now providing an implicit public insurance policy against natural disaster losses through the array of permanent benefits.[69]

Neither Nixon nor Bayh was happy with the outcome. Nixon sought political cover by issuing a signing statement, which read in part, "the bill demonstrates that the Federal Government, in cooperation with State and local authorities, is capable of providing compassionate assistance to the innocent victims of natural disasters."[70] Birch Bayh was so displeased with the outcome that he tried (but failed) to amend it on the floor of the Senate.[71] The battle between Nixon and Congress over disaster policy did not end here; two years later Hurricane Agnes set the stage for another battle between these two branches over the direction and scope of federal disaster assistance.

AGNES MAKES LANDFALL

Death and Destruction in New York
and Pennsylvania, 1972

William Smith anxiously watched the water rising on the Chemung River. A farmer and a state senator, Bill Smith had a private number to call to learn if the river would flood. When he called on the morning of June 22, 1972, the man on the other end said he thought the water might reach as high as Smith's shrubs. As he held the phone, Smith looked outside at his farm in Big Flats, New York, and could not see his bushes for the water that covered them.[1] Smith watched helplessly as the water continued to rise over the next ten hours until it was fifteen and a half feet deep over the farmstead. Bill and his wife, Dorothy, took their family dog and escaped to their attic.[2] Boats rescued Dorothy and Bill Smith, but their livestock had no means of escape. The flood drowned many of Smith's 150 head of Holstein and Friesen cattle and 20,000 hens. It also damaged his restaurant, which was adjacent to the farmhouse.[3] Throughout the region, unexpected flooding caused farmers to scramble to safety, as some were forced to watch their cattle drown.[4] The flooding experienced by Bill Smith and his neighbors was caused by Hurricane Agnes, which struck the United States in June 1972 and affected the lives of tens of thousands of people from Florida to New York.

The First Hurricane of the Season

Hurricane Agnes was the first named storm of the 1972 hurricane season. It made landfall on June 18 in Florida before moving up the East Coast, where it met a secondary weather system moving east, out of the Ohio Valley. The two storms merged and produced torrential rains over New York and Pennsylvania, which caused unprecedented flooding. When the weather system finally dissipated on June 26, it had killed 130 people and caused billions of dollars in property damage, making it the costliest hurricane in U.S. history to that time.

The storm began as a tropical depression in the Atlantic Ocean. Once the disturbance became a fully formed hurricane, the National Hurricane Center (NHC) sent air force and naval military aircraft directly into the storm, where they deployed specialized equipment to measure wind speeds, barometric pressure, temperature, and humidity within the cyclone. Airmen made twenty-six sorties into the hurricane and relayed information back to ground stations in Jacksonville, Florida, and Charlotte, North Carolina, which was then forwarded to the NHC in Miami. When the storm was within 150 miles of the United States, ground radar in Key West began minute-by-minute storm tracking. Meteorologists used the information they gathered to plot the course of the storm and to issue warnings to coastal residents that a hurricane was heading for Florida and would make landfall near Panama City.[5]

Although Agnes was a Category 1 hurricane, the weakest of all storms, it packed enough power to drive President Nixon from his vacation spot on the Grand Cay in the Bahamas to greater security at his Key Biscayne residence. As it made land-

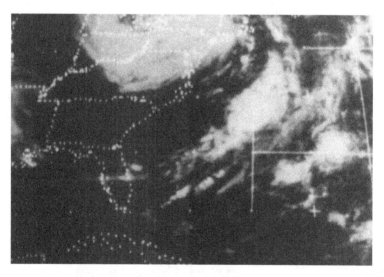

FIGURE 3. Satellite photo of Hurricane Agnes over New York and Pennsylvania on June 23, 1972. Courtesy of the National Oceanic and Atmospheric Administration/Department of Commerce.

fall in Florida, the hurricane created a storm surge of ten feet along the Florida coast and spawned eighteen tornadoes.[6] These tornadoes tore through a mobile home park in Okeechobee, Florida, and destroyed fifty trailers, killing nine people ranging in age from 1 to 104.[7]

The storm moved north through Georgia and the Carolinas, causing flooding wherever it went but also losing strength as it drifted out over the Atlantic Ocean. At this point in their life cycle, most storms dissipate and die, but in the case of Agnes, the waters off the coast of North Carolina acted like a tonic, and the storm strengthened and headed north toward Virginia. On June 21, the president's disaster agency, the Office of Emergency Preparedness (OEP), notified regional offices on the Mid-Atlantic coast to prepare for a "major disaster."[8]

Hurricane Agnes was one of a series of major disasters that occurred in the United States that year, and by late June, the OEP had already exhausted most of its resources in dealing with them. The first major disaster occurred in February when a massive mudslide killed 125 people at Buffalo Creek in West Virginia. The landslide destroyed 16 towns and left 4,000 people homeless. On the evening of June 9, 1972, a flash flood struck Rapid City, South Dakota, killing 238 people and causing $160 million in damage that left tens of thousands of people homeless. Dealing with these crises depleted the president's revolving disaster fund and exhausted the emergency personnel involved in the cleanup.[9]

The Agnes disaster, however, was not only more extensive than these other disasters but also came close to home for OEP personnel. As residents of Georgia and the Carolinas began cleaning up from Agnes, those living and working along the James and Potomac Rivers in Virginia, Washington, D.C., and Maryland experienced the storm's next wave of destruction. In Washington, D.C., both the Potomac and Rock Creek Rivers overflowed, forcing ten thousand people out of their homes in the suburbs surrounding the district. The roads into and out of Washington, D.C., became impassable, and barricades were erected around the city to keep people from driving onto flooded avenues. The National Park Service initiated special precautions to protect national monuments from the flooding.[10]

In Maryland, the Patapsco River broke over its banks into Ellicott City. It devastated that town and destroyed nearly every bridge in Howard County, turning the county into a "veritable island."[11] Many people were surprised by the flood. One woman who was attempting to evacuate with her three children became trapped in her car by the rapidly rising water. She got out of the vehicle to rescue her children from the back seat but was swept away by the fast-moving water. Grasping a tree, she watched in horror as all three of her children, ranging in ages from seven months to three years, drowned. Later that evening, two students from Antioch College returned from a date and found themselves in a flash flood. The couple climbed onto the roof of the young man's car, but the water rose over the top and pulled them into the dark waters. The man clung to a tree until rescuers arrived at dawn. Authorities recovered the body of the young woman later that day. At least half a dozen people across Maryland died in similar circumstances. Maryland's governor, Marvin Mandel, dispatched the Maryland National Guard to assist local communities in evacuation and rescue operations and sent a telegram to the White House asking for federal assistance.[12]

Richmond, Virginia, was plunged into a full-blown crisis. "When I came here," Jack Fulton, Richmond's public safety director, recalled to newspaper reporters, "everybody was talking about Hurricane Camille," the Category 5 storm that had slammed into the southeastern United States in 1969. Fulton said that Hurricane Agnes "blew that right out of the water." As a result of the torrential rains triggered by Agnes, the James River in Richmond set an all-time high when it crested at 36.5 feet and turned parts of downtown Richmond into a lake. Flooding knocked out water treatment plants and electrical power across northern Virginia and left half a million people without power or fresh drinking water. The torrent of rain downed power lines and plunged Richmond into darkness, forcing Virginia's governor, Linwood Holton, to hold a candlelight meeting with state emergency management officials.[13] An aide to Governor Holton compared the devastation to the burning of Richmond during the Civil War and dramatically exclaimed, "This is the worst thing to hit Richmond since Grant."[14] Comparing Hurricane Camille in 1969 to Hurricane Agnes in 1972, Holton echoed others and declared Agnes to be much worse.[15]

The death toll in Maryland, Virginia, and Washington, D.C., climbed to thirty-three, and the governors of Virginia and Maryland declared emergencies, closed roads, and dispatched state police and national guard units to assist local communities. The governors also waited to hear from the White House on their requests for federal assistance, which they needed to deal with the postdisaster cleanup and rebuilding. Even though these governors faced the same disaster, they worked in isolation from one another during the crisis, and after the disaster, they were pitted against one another in their bids to receive federal funding.[16]

Officials in Virginia and Maryland had their hands full with the flooding caused by overflowing rivers, streams, and creeks, but they feared a greater catastrophe would happen if the nearby dams failed. These flood control dams were constructed upstream of significant population centers and meant to control the amount of water flowing through the cities. Flood prevention dams work by taking in the water from springtime snowmelt or storms that increases the volume of water in a river to flood stage. Excessive water is diverted into the dam, where it is stored until it can be gradually released back into the river without causing a flood.[17]

Flood control dams work as long as the water in the dam does not exceed its capacity. When too much water is stored in a dam, it becomes vulnerable to failure. Officials knew all too well that collapsing dams had been the cause of horrific tragedies, including the Johnstown Flood in 1889, which killed over 2,000 people, and the Buffalo Creek disaster, which killed 118 people in less than twenty minutes.[18]

In Richmond, officials worried that a nearby dam would break and inundate the region west of the city, and they hastened to close Interstate 95 and US Route 60. In Maryland, Governor Mandel's chief concern was the safety of the Conowingo Dam, which was located just south of the Pennsylvania border. Despite having all fifty-three floodgates open, the water continued to rise to the top of the dam. Mandel hurried to the scene and remained there all night while engineers tried to keep the water flowing through the release gates. Had the dam failed, Mandel recalled, "There would have been 14 feet of water in Baltimore."[19]

Catastrophe Strikes New York

The destruction wrought along the Potomac, the James, and the lower Susquehanna seemed like only a rehearsal of the tragedy that awaited New York and Pennsylvania. Agnes left Maryland and turned out to sea, then veered back over the land and stalled over New York and Pennsylvania. A low-pressure system moving east from the Ohio Valley joined with the tropical storm, and the rain from the two storms fell on the Southern Tier of New York and northeastern Pennsylvania. Rainfall from the combined storms was equivalent to pouring out a quarter of the water from Lake Erie over the already saturated ground.[20]

In the two months before the arrival of Agnes, the Northeast had received sixteen inches of rain, which was double the average rainfall. The water filled underground spaces and reservoirs, springs, and underground rivers, and even filled abandoned mine shafts in Pennsylvania.[21] After filling the underground spaces, it then fed the streams and rivers, which spread onto the floodplain. As the swollen rivers met objects in their path, the water either moved the impediments or accumulated more water on top. All along the Susquehanna River Basin, the water acted like a snowball rolling down a hill, becoming an avalanche of water as it tumbled through and over the regular channels.

Geographically, the Southern Tier of New York and Northern Tier of Pennsylvania consist of a series of undulating hills and valleys formed by the action of ancient glaciers and rivers. Glaciers scoured the topsoil from much of the terrain and then pushed up and carved out river systems, including the most extensive river system in the eastern United States, the Susquehanna River. In New York, the Unadilla and Chenango Rivers flow into the Susquehanna to form the North Branch of this basin. In Pennsylvania, the Towanda Creek and Lackawanna River make their way into the Susquehanna as part of the upper main stem. The West Branch of the Susquehanna consists of creeks or small rivers such as the Lycoming, which flows through Williamsport, and the Juniata River, which winds its way through south-central Pennsylvania before emptying into the Susquehanna. The lower main stem of the Susquehanna flows through the heart of Pennsylvania around Harrisburg and heads for the ocean through the Chesapeake Bay.[22] Towns and cities grew up beside the river: Hornell, Painted Post, Corning, Elmira, Owego, and Binghamton in New York; Mansfield, Lock Haven, Williamsport, Wilkes-Barre, Forty Fort, and Harrisburg in Pennsylvania; and Ellicott City in Maryland.

In New York State, the Department of Environmental Conservation (DEC) had responsibility for monitoring and combating flooding along rivers and streams. On Wednesday morning, June 21, Eldred Rich sent DEC personnel to check conditions along the rivers. They made sure that the recording devices measuring the rate of water flow and the height of the river were in working order. If needed, the DEC could close roads along the levees and order sandbagging along flood-prone areas.[23] The department was empowered to alert local governments to any potential emergency, but for reasons it had to explain later, its personnel chose not to inform local officials of the imminent flooding.[24]

Flooding was rampant across New York State but was most severe along the New York–Pennsylvania border. The Tioga River broke through dikes and swept into the residential areas of Lawrenceville and Towanda, New York. Wellsville, a New York community of six thousand, was caught by surprise. Local officials, unsure as to whether the river would flood, called the NWS to see when and how high the river would crest but instead got a prerecorded message indicating that the lines were busy. Before dawn on Friday, June 23, the town flooded and residents lost power. By noon, Wellsville was surrounded by the rising river, with no way in or out.

Portville, another town on the New York–Pennsylvania border, faced disaster. The Allegheny River had swollen to twice its average size and continued to feed on the still-falling rain. Portville officials were in a desperate situation because they had only enough sandbags and equipment to protect one section of their city. They chose to sandbag along the Dodge Creek Bridge in the hope of saving the business district, but this left the dwellings south of Main Street in peril.[25]

The city of Olean also flooded. Elected leaders ordered a widespread evacuation and declared a countywide emergency. In Almond, a suburb of Olean, residents worried that their earthen dam would fail and send water into their town. The local deputy sheriff warned that if the dam broke, "It [would] wipe Almond off the map."[26] No significant dams failed during the Agnes crisis, but farmers living along the Genesee River in New York in 1972 suffered when state officials decided to relieve the pressure on the Mount Morris dam, which was nearly filled to capacity. The dam rises 230 feet from the streambed, but during the Agnes crisis, the water crept within 3 feet of the top. Officials feared that the water would overtop the dam and carry tons of debris and water toward the 300,000 residents of Rochester, New York.[27] To forestall this disaster, the Army Corps of Engineers ordered a controlled release of water from the dam, and residents along a 35-mile stretch of the river heading toward Rochester were told to evacuate.[28] The dam emptied into the farms that lay in this area, thereby creating a flood where nature had not.[29]

Despite the widespread flooding, many people remained unaware of the potential threat to their lives and property. In Corning, hundreds of people lined up along Bridge Street to watch the water rise but were oblivious to the disaster occurring in nearby Hornell.[30] By Thursday evening, June 22, Hornell was virtually isolated by the rising waters, and three residents were missing and presumed dead. Flooding severed communications and transportation into and out of that city. The rising water felled telephone poles and power lines, and Route 1, a Steuben County lifeline, was closed. A flood wall gave way, and water swept through the Erie and Lackawanna Railroad yard.[31]

For city officials, the crisis seemed to come out of nowhere. Working in isolation from one another, community leaders tried to protect their cities and towns, but their actions were mostly reactive, and they had little opportunity and even less inclination to communicate with surrounding towns and cities. Much like officials in Maryland and Virginia, elected leaders fretted about their dams and levees, knowing that if these structures failed, the disaster would move from being a few feet of water in town to a flood that might bring ten feet or more into their municipality. Incapable of dealing with the crisis, officials sought assistance from state or federal authorities.

At the gubernatorial level, neither the governor of New York nor the governor of Pennsylvania communicated with one another, but both sought assistance from Washington. The system was fragmented and discouraged the coordination of effort and communication. After receiving numerous telegrams from officials across the state, Governor Rockefeller sent New York State National Guard units into the flooded areas and requested that President Nixon declare several counties in New York State disaster areas.[32] A presidential disaster declaration meant that state and local governments would be eligible for money from the president's disaster fund to rebuild damaged roads, bridges, water mains, reservoirs, and government buildings, and to clean up any debris left from the flooding.[33]

Disaster loomed over the cities of Corning and Elmira. The city of Corning sprawls on both sides of the Chemung River, which runs east and south from Corning toward Elmira, where it enters the Susquehanna River. City residents had gone to bed the night before persuaded that their flood walls and levees provided adequate protection against a flood. The Corning *Leader* had assured residents in the lead story Thursday that the dikes would hold, and mayor Joseph Nasser had echoed this in a radio broadcast that evening, which indicated that residents had nothing to fear. Although he was reassured when he and his public works officials were told that the river would crest well below the dikes, he remained awake all night at City Hall, asking for hourly checks on the river level.

Just before dawn on Friday morning, June 23, the Chemung River overtopped the dikes around Corning. Water spilled into the city at speeds of thirty-five miles an hour, swept away five thousand homes, and killed seventeen people. Electric power systems went dark and local warning sirens shorted out. Many residents had barely enough time to grab a change of clothes before heading to higher ground on the city's south side. Around that time, a newspaper reporter from Elmira called the Corning *Leader*. "We're having a flood down here," she said. "We'd like to know the situation in Corning." The reporter did not get an answer

FIGURE 4. On the morning of June 23, 1972, flood waters covered Corning, New York, up to a depth of twenty feet. Collection of the Rakow Library, Corning Museum of Glass, Corning, New York. Original photograph loaned by Corning, Inc., Corning, New York.

because the phone system went dead. The reporter's call turned out to be the last call into the city for the next two days.[34]

In the Corning area, the first victim of the flood was Hobart Abbey, a volunteer fireman from Gang Mills, a small community on Route 15 on the Tioga River. Abbey was on duty at the Gang Mills Fire Department, going door to door warning residents to evacuate, but his truck became trapped as the river spread into the roadway. After climbing on top of his truck, Abbey was swept up in the current. The next day members of the fire department recovered his body. The Gang Mills Fire Department received his final distress call, which was answered by the dispatcher, who was his daughter Betsey.[35]

A few residents of Corning did not wait for the government to tell them to evacuate. John Fox, who ran the Corning Glass Center, the home of the Corning Museum of Glass, was worried that the Chemung might flood and had remained at the center well into the evening. As the night wore on, he made several trips back and forth between the Glass Center and his home. Finally, after 11 p.m., he led his family and a handful of neighbors over to the Glass Center, which towered nine stories above Corning and sat on higher ground.[36] From his perch atop the center, John Fox, along with sixteen other people and two dogs, witnessed the dike break in six spots, allowing the Chemung River to surge into the streets of Painted Post, Riverside, and Corning's north side. At 5 a.m. Fox watched the New York Central Railroad Bridge collapse.[37]

As the water advanced into the city, someone at the Corning Glass Works (CGW) sounded the emergency whistle to alert residents of the danger. The whistle, in turn, led the local radio station, WCLI, to begin emergency broadcasting, but the warning only lasted a few minutes before the station lost power and became unable to broadcast.[38] For those who had not already fled to higher ground, it was too late. People became trapped by the rising water and took refuge in attics or crawl spaces. At a local hotel, the Lodge on the Green, 135 people awaited rescue from upper-story porches, and another 100 people, who had been attending a graduation party, waited out the flood on the rooftop of Saint Vincent's School in Corning.[39]

One woman, who ran a local rooming house in Painted Post, had spent all day Thursday moving furniture from her basement to the upper floor in case of flooding. The woman, who was seventy-four years old, was exhausted by evening and fell into a deep sleep, only to be awakened around 4 a.m. by the sound of water rushing into her basement. She and her lone guest raced to the attic, where they found refuge and a cache of old crackers and wine, which kept their spirits up as they awaited rescue.[40] Just behind her house lay the Ingersoll Rand plant, where dozens of workers scrambled to safety on the third floor to escape the fourteen feet of water that had entered the plant.[41]

John Fox and his cohorts had a bird's-eye view of the unfolding tragedy. As they waited atop the Corning Glass Center, one in the group, an elderly woman from Corning, suffered a heart attack. Her anxiety during the crisis became heightened as she saw the flood engulf the city, and she panicked as she feared worst for sister in Painted Post and her daughter, a member of the order of the Sisters of Mercy, who lived in the convent in Elmira. After being airlifted to a nearby hospital, she made a full recovery.[42]

Not everyone was fortunate enough to escape. The Tong family was caught unaware by the flood. Kathy Tong went to a neighbor's house to escape the flood but then they decided to evacuate. As Kathy sought a flashlight the neighbor holding nine-month-old Brian Tong fell into the floodwater and struggled to hold onto the child. The force of the water proved too strong, and the infant was pulled from her arms. The infant's body was discovered the next day near the Holiday Inn in Gang Mills.[43]

Corning was a microcosm for the kind of chaos created when officials are unprepared for disaster. Individual initiative saved dozens of lives, but the lack of coordination between public officials in local and county government and lack of communication between state officials worsened the situation and caused undue grief and suffering. The local reliance on the NWS also proved problematic, as officials were unable to communicate with the agency when they needed to. Some elected officials and civil defense directors were worried about "crying wolf" and took a wait-and-see attitude toward the potential flood rather than evacuate people in the middle of the night. Mayor Nasser explained, "We did not want to panic the people, but we had to do everything we could to take precautions, but with no information available we just had to sit and wait."[44] They convinced themselves that their dike would keep them safe and feared a public backlash if they evacuated people and the flood never came.

In Elmira, a city of 40,000 people downriver from Corning, the new city manager called for evacuations despite the risk that there might be no flood and that he would look foolish. Joe Sartori had only become city manager on June 1 of that year. At age thirty-three, he had the distinction of being the youngest city manager in Elmira's history and ultimately tied for the longest-serving. He served "twelve years, which is about as much as you can take," he recalled wryly.[45] A man of short stature and a mild manner, the Syracuse native had arrived in Elmira in 1967 to join a CPA firm. He combined his skill in accounting with interest in public service by serving as Elmira's city chamberlain.

Unlike so many others in the coming crisis, Sartori felt well prepared for flooding. "Because I was the new city manager, I asked to have a briefing on our flood emergency plan. We brought together people from NYS DEC, Corps of Engineers, people that were in charge of levees, and local fire and police officials, and we briefly went over it, reviewed it."[46] On Thursday evening, the city manager called a staff meeting at 7 p.m. to discuss the potential for flooding. Before he left for the meeting, he recalled, "I told my wife I would probably be home later." As it turned out, he did not return home for two days.[47]

At the emergency meeting that night, the city manager ordered the police to measure the rising water every half hour and obtain as many reports from upstream as they could. By ten o'clock he was convinced that Elmira was going to flood. He located a flood map from 1946 to see which sections of Elmira were most likely to flood and used this information to plan evacuations. That night the neophyte city manager made a bold decision and ordered all residents in the city to prepare for evacuation. Sartori dispatched police agencies to knock on doors and warn residents to prepare for high water. "One of the people on my staff said I would be run out of town on a rail the next day. . . . It is not easy to ask people to leave their home; it was the middle of the night. This was ten o'clock, eleven o'clock and it went on to two or three in the morning, but we did get them out."[48]

Sartori was one of the few officials who sought information from surrounding cities and towns. He was also courageous in the face of uncertain data, and he saved numerous lives that night.[49] On Friday morning, water broke over the levees and flooded the now empty buildings located near the river.

Pennsylvania's Catastrophic Flooding

The situation in Pennsylvania mirrored the crisis in New York. The rain filled dams and reservoirs across the state. Along the New York border, Mansfield, Blossburg, and Tioga flooded. Pittsburgh experienced unanticipated flooding in the Point and Fort Pitt areas of the Golden Triangle. In Danville, a railroad bridge, along with a freight train, collapsed into the muddy waters. In southeastern Pennsylvania, thirty thousand people in the city of Lebanon were isolated by high water, which cut off their access to roads and bridges in all directions. Bloomsburg, Danville, Lancaster, Lock Haven, Milton, Pottstown, Sunbury, and Williamsport struggled against rampaging rivers and streams. In Lock Haven, the flood swept into residential areas and submerged mobile homes, including one with a family still trapped inside. In Williamsport and Milton, the business districts took the most massive blow. In Lewisburg, the Bull Run Creek overran its banks into residential neighborhoods, and a rescue attempt by motorboat turned tragic after the current proved too strong for a woman and the police sergeant attempting to rescue her. Both drowned in just a few feet of water as neither could swim in the swiftly moving creek. In nearby Hershey, the chocolate factory shut down after flooding disabled the water filtration plant. The nearby amusement park flooded, but fortunately, the animals from the park had already been evacuated to higher ground.[50]

The problems in Pennsylvania were compounded on Thursday when the Susquehanna River flooded the state capital of Harrisburg. The flooding stopped the publication of the Harrisburg *Patriot-News* for the first time since the Civil War, and officials in Harrisburg spent all day Thursday watching the river rise. Mayor Harold Swenson conducted three-hour sweeps of the city and remained awake for the next two days to handle the crisis. Like many public servants during the crisis created by Hurricane Agnes, Swenson was concerned that the very technology created to stave off flooding—the local dam—would turn a crisis into a catastrophe. All day Thursday the mayor kept to himself his darkest fear, that the DeHart Dam, located north and east of Harrisburg, would collapse and bring more devastation to the city. Swenson was expressed relief on Friday after hearing that the water level was retreating from the top of the dam.[51]

Meanwhile, Pennsylvania's governor, Milton Shapp, was rescued from his official residence by rowboat and became a displaced person for the next year.[52] The flooding also created havoc for the NWS, whose River Forecasting Center was flooded and lost power, making it difficult for the staff of nine to calculate how high the Susquehanna would rise and nearly impossible to communicate any such calculations to the outside world.[53]

In Luzerne County, Pennsylvania, Civil Defense director Frank Townend reassured citizens in the Wilkes-Barre metropolitan region that they were safe behind the levee. Despite Townend's optimism, however, the levee failed in nearby Plymouth. Mayor Edward Burns, along with National Guard members and local volunteers, tried to staunch the flow but could only struggle helplessly as the river poured into the city of ten thousand. By dawn on Friday, all of Plymouth was underwater.[54] Townend belatedly ordered the residents to evacuate, explaining, "The flood situation on the Susquehanna River for Wilkes-Barre and Kingston is much more serious than we had figured."[55] Still, Townend was stubbornly reluctant to order an evacuation of Wilkes-Barre, which was the largest city in the valley. He thought that if the river crested only two or even three feet above the dikes, sandbagging would avoid the need for evacuation. In a radio address broadcast across the region on the morning of Friday, June 23, Townend told listeners, "We want everyone who thinks it's worthwhile not having the river come over the dike to come out and do his share in preventing it. It is not a job for 400 men or 600 men[;] it's probably going to take at least 10,000 people."[56] Local contractors supplied the dirt and sand, and residents provided the plastic bags, pillowcases, burlap bags, and muscle to fill and stack the sandbags along the levee.[57]

Thousands of people assisted in the operation—old and young, rich and poor, black and white. Participants even included thirty to forty members of a traveling carnival, the James E. Strates Show, who were scheduled to appear at a local fair.[58] Ultimately, the sandbags could not stop the river and the sandbagging proved to be a futile gesture.[59] On Friday, June 23, just after 11:00 a.m., the Susquehanna overtopped the dike at Ross Street and Riverside Drive and within minutes destroyed the sandbag fortress that the community had spent hours assembling and placing atop the dike. People in the vicinity ran for their lives as an eight-foot wall of water came rolling through the city.

At 11:16 a.m., emergency sirens sounded to warn those who were not already fleeing to higher ground. The warning was too late for William Shock, one of the sandbaggers. Unable to escape the flood, he drowned in the muddy water. By 11:30 a.m., a total evacuation was underway, and eighty thousand people fled to higher ground, urged on by a radio broadcast pleading with residents to "Get out, and get out now. . . . If you have not evacuated Wilkes-Barre get out now."[60]

The flood covered Public Square in nine feet of water and destroyed the central business district. Now the city was isolated from the rest of the world. The North Street Bridge, the main link between Wilkes-Barre and Kingston, was washed away, and the Market Street Bridge seemed on the verge of collapse. Wilkes-Barre lost all telephone connections, isolating the community, which now could only be reached by helicopter or boat. By evening the Wyoming Valley was a large and filthy lake. A fire broke out amid the flooding, leaving fire crews unable to respond as an entire block of Northampton Street burned.[61]

Many people were caught unprepared for the rushing water. One block from the river, Jim Jiunta was in his basement moving his belongings upstairs when he heard a noise that "sounded like Niagara Falls." The noise made the hair on his head and arms "stand straight up," he remembered. Nearby, a sixty-five-year-old bachelor, Elwood Disque, was moving his furniture to the second floor when he saw a wall of water racing down the street toward his house. "By the time I got to the dining room, I was up to my knees in water. I took a loaf of bread, peanut butter, a knife, a can opener, and a package of meatloaf and went to the second floor. The water continued to rise." He made his way to the attic and slept until Saturday.[62]

The crisis turned ghastly when the flood churned up the remains of the dead. After the dike gave way at Forty Fort, floodwater surged into the Riverside Cemetery, where the already saturated earth gave up two thousand caskets. The caskets and their contents made a gruesome flotilla into the valley. After the waters receded, "there were body parts deposited in back porches, in basements, on roofs," recalled Luzerne County coroner George Hudock, Jr.

Tea and Sympathy

The thirty-two trillion gallons of water that fell on New York and Pennsylvania caused devastation that left buildings and homes in ruins and property damage estimated to be in the billions of dollars. The flood left tens of thousands of people homeless and hundreds of thousands of people without electrical power, telephones, fresh drinking water, or sewers. Many were isolated from the outside world as roads and bridges collapsed or buckled due to flooding.[63] Entering the area on the Saturday after the flood, reporters reached for metaphors to describe the scene. With the Vietnam War in its ninth year, it may not be surprising that many drew upon images of war to explain what they saw. "Like a War Zone," said the headline of the Rochester *Times-Union*, describing the situation in the Southern Tier. The streets were desolate and patrolled by National Guard units whose fixed bayonets were a warning to would-be looters. Telephone and electrical lines lay in hopeless tangles or had been carried away by floodwater, leaving survivors to hunker down with no heat, no light, and no cooking facilities. Automobiles caught in the fury of water were disabled, but even working cars were useless because most streets were crumpled or buckled by the flood and mud. Meanwhile, the homeless were crowded, much like war refugees, in shelters awaiting the all clear.[64]

By Saturday morning, June 24, the world had heard about the flooding, which was described by Robert White, head of the National Oceanic and Atmospheric Administration, as the most massive flood on record in the United States. President Richard Nixon called it the worst natural disaster in American history.[65] The event was international news. World leaders, from the oppressive ruler of Romania, Nicolae Ceaușescu, to general secretary of the United Nations Kurt Waldheim, sent telegrams of support and encouragement to Nelson Rockefeller and Richard Nixon. The leader of Sri Lanka sent a note of sympathy attached to a thousand pounds of Ceylon tea for the flood victims.[66]

Victims of the disaster and their elected representatives wanted more than tea and sympathy. After midnight on the night that the Susquehanna flooded the Wyoming Valley, congressman Daniel J. Flood (D-Wilkes-Barre) was working in his one-bedroom apartment adjacent to the U.S. Capitol building, just a few steps from his office. The apartment itself was an indication of Flood's seniority and power in the House. He was one of a handful of members of Congress allowed to keep their quarters after the apartment building was converted to office space in the 1960s. Flood was also powerful enough that Tom Wahl of the U.S Weather Service called him personally to alert him to the calamity in the Wyoming Valley. At 3 a.m. Flood called and woke up secretary of defense Melvin Laird to ask him for the use of his helicopter so that Flood might travel immediately to the disaster area. "The situation is bad, Mel," he said. "The dikes are gone in Wilkes-Barre."

He needed to leave at once. "Stand by!" he shouted into the phone after wringing a promise from Laird that he would do all he could to aid the Wyoming Valley. Wilkes-Barre had been Flood's hometown for thirty years, and when he arrived at dawn to take command, he was in a foul mood. "This is one Flood against another," he growled as he looked down at what seemed to be a new lake over what was once Wilkes-Barre.[67]

Flood was one of the most flamboyant representatives of his generation, with a penchant for wearing a cape and giving alliterative and staccato orations on the floor of the House. His face has been described as a cross between Salvador Dali and Snidely Whiplash of the "Dudley Do-Right" cartoon.[68] Born in 1903 in Hazleton, Pennsylvania, Flood went to live with his maternal grandparents after his mother died. He later went to military school and graduated from Syracuse University in 1925. After college, Flood was both a boxer and a Shakespearean actor who appeared in over fifty plays. He married one of his leading ladies, Catherine Swank, who hailed from Wilkes-Barre. Flood settled down in that city and served in local and state politics before his election to the House in 1944. For the next several election cycles, Flood was in and out of Congress until 1952, where for the next thirty years he was elected continuously to his seat. He worked tirelessly to support a district whose economic mainstay, coal mining, was past its prime.[69]

Stationing himself in Avoca, Flood phoned the Pentagon and demanded army helicopters to assist in search and rescue. "I want those helicopters, and I want them this afternoon, not tonight or tomorrow. You know, there are an awful lot of people running around the Pentagon looking for stars, but if I don't get any help, the only stars they'll see will be the ones in their eyes," he declared. In response, forty choppers arrived that day and rescued hundreds of stranded residents. Naval Reserve lieutenant Howard Glad, who was on the scene, suggested that the timely intervention of the helicopters saved hundreds of lives.[70]

Flood had no qualms about issuing orders to state officials or ignoring local ones. He thought Luzerne County Civil Defense director Frank Townend was incompetent and criticized him for refusing assistance from the governor in the early stages of the crisis and then ordering a fruitless sandbagging operation.[71] He routinely telephoned Pennsylvania governor Milton Shapp to request assistance, which he always received. Flood also summoned federal officials to meet him in Avoca, where they meekly awaited their turn to see him.[72]

The congressional representatives for Elmira and Corning responded as well. James F. Hastings (R-Olean), who represented Corning, returned to the Southern Tier when he heard about the flood. Hastings and his administrative assistant, Spencer Johnson, drove to Olean from Washington and crossed the 5th Street Bridge over the Potomac just moments before flooding in the D.C. area closed the bridge to traffic.[73] Once back in the Southern Tier, he contacted local officials to offer his services.

When news that Elmira had flooded reached the ears of Howard J. Robison (R-Owego), the congressman immediately returned to his home district. A balding, stoop-shouldered man, Robison was the dean of New York State Republicans in the House, but unlike his colleague Daniel Flood, Robison had no desire for drama and preferred to work behind the scenes. However, his anonymity backfired when Robison drove himself to Elmira only to run afoul of a national guard checkpoint. "I am Congressman Robison," he told the guardsman who stopped him from entering the city. "Yeah," said the guard in disbelief, "and I am President Nixon!" Robison managed to catch the eye of a local politician who convinced the guard of the congressman's identity.[74] He spent most of the first few days of the crisis on the telephone, with a red pen, legal notepad, and his ever-present pipe nearby. Among those he spoke with were White House staff, the Washington headquarters of the Office of Emergency Preparedness (OEP), and Tom Casey, the New York coordinator for OEP. Robison also fielded calls from his constituents in the devastated areas, assuring them that help was forthcoming.[75]

Survival was the goal of the communities during the first seventy-two hours of the disaster. Political and economic recovery became the focus of civic leaders in the weeks after, but the trauma of that summer also called for psychological healing. The powerful leader of CGW, Amory Houghton, seemed to know this on an intuitive level and made several radio broadcasts to assuage fears and encourage the community to rebound from the disaster. Many ordinary citizens, who had been through the worst experience of their lives, developed posttraumatic stress, some of which they relieved through writing poems and songs about their experience. John Nickerson of Elmira wrote a song titled, "It Sprinkled, It Rained, and It Poured," which, in the weeks after the flood, became a popular local tune and sold thousands of copies. Nickerson's wife sent a copy to President Nixon with a note that read, "I want you to know what a good town Elmira is."[76]

Mired in mud and misery, bereft of property and employment, the people of New York and Pennsylvania looked to their local, state, and federal governments for help and answers. Why had their dikes and levees failed? Why had the NWS failed to warn them there was a flood coming? Who was going to help them rebuild their homes, businesses, roads, bridges, and utilities? When would they be helped? Would life ever return to normal? These questions spurred the passage of the most generous disaster aid package in U.S. history to that time, led to massive urban renewal projects in their cities, and prompted changes in disaster policy that culminated in the Disaster Relief Act of 1974, the most significant change to disaster policy since 1950.

WHO'S IN CHARGE?

Local Governments Collapse
in the Face of Disaster

After his city flooded, Joe Sartori set up a disaster command center at Elmira College, but he found the situation difficult to command. Coordinating the activities of volunteers and city and county personnel in a city so badly damaged and divided was no easy task. "No one knows what the other is doing," he told reporters. He was visibly frustrated at the lack of cooperation among officials. Jack Gridley, chairman of the Board of Supervisors, was nowhere to be found when the flood struck. When Gridley did show up, "He became more of a problem than a solver," Sartori recalled. In a radio address to the residents of Elmira, Sartori promised, "Elmira will be rebuilt from the smallest home to the largest business." At least one local reporter was not even sure that Sartori believed his own words.[1] Sartori's plight was mirrored in the dozens of small cities, where local authorities tried to deal with a situation that was beyond their human and physical capacity.

William Wilcox, director of Community Affairs for Pennsylvania, warned Governor Shapp that local governments were incapable of recovering from the Agnes disaster on their own. In a memo to the governor, Wilcox wrote, "Scores of large and small communities along the Susquehanna have local governments, administratively weak, that are unable to organize effective recovery efforts." Wilcox added that "many governments are immobilized and incapable of effectively planning organized permanent rehabilitation efforts."[2] This was undoubtedly the case in Wilkes-Barre, where Bernie Gallagher, the city engineer, inherited the duties of city manager just one week before the flood struck. New to the job, Gallagher was unable to marshal support for response and recovery.[3]

FIGURE 5. Elmira, New York, a city of 40,000 people, flooded on June 23, 1972. Thanks to a decision by City Manager Joe Sartori, no lives were lost. Courtesy of the Chemung County Historical Society.

Congressman Dan Flood recalled that the situation in Wilkes-Barre after the flood was "one of utter and complete chaos."[4]

In the 1970s, small cities and towns throughout New York and Pennsylvania were governed by part-time officials who lacked expertise in crisis management. Furthermore, their municipalities lacked the financial resources needed to rebuild the damaged public property and restore the necessary services. Elected or appointed leaders in these small cities and towns were used to working in isolation from one another and were caught off guard when the flooding began. Even when the leader of a local government had advance warning of the coming flood, it did not occur to them to share the information with officials in other cities. The deputy mayor of Painted Post received a warning at 11 p.m. on June 22 that the river would crest in Painted Post at 1 a.m. on June 23, but he failed to share this information with anyone outside of his city.[5]

It was not only a lack of communication and coordination between cities that caused problems. Political relationships within a local government itself made governing difficult. Joe Sartori, who managed the city of Elmira, recalled, "When our city manager resigned and went to Poughkeepsie, they asked me if I would become city manager. I said 'yeah' and assumed it was a temporary thing." He based his assumption on the city's reputation. Each time political power shifted between the Democrats and Republicans, the new majority fired the city manager and hired a new one. "No one wanted to be city manager," he remembered, adding, "no one would even apply here."[6]

During the crisis spawned by Hurricane Agnes, these untrained, ill-prepared, and uncommunicative local officials were forced to make decisions and take action with only the limited resources they had at their disposal, often with tragic results. Their situation was the result of federalism, a political system engineered by the Founding Fathers, which divides powers, responsibilities, and jurisdictions between the national and state governments. Under the Constitution, the responsibility for maintaining health, safety, and security belongs to state and local government. Natural disasters that threaten health and safety are ultimately the responsibility of local officials. who turned to state and federal authorities and to the private sector to assist them in reorganizing and rebuilding after the flooding from Agnes.

State governments may have the resources to cope with the disaster, but due to political considerations, most elected officials want to maximize the amount of financial support from the federal government while minimizing the cost at the state level. Scholars have termed this response to disaster "the crying poor" syndrome, in which states exaggerate the cost of a disaster to demonstrate that they are not capable of paying for recovery.[7] Furthermore, in 1972, few state governments had kept pace with the changing nature of disasters. According to George Lincoln, few states had updated their disaster policies since the 1950s, which, in the context of the Cold War, meant they had better preparation for nuclear war than for a flood.[8]

Milton Shapp, Victims' Advocate

In the days after the flood, local officials turned to their state governments for help but found that help was not always forthcoming. The governors of Pennsylvania and New York responded differently to the flooding. The vastly different appearance, personality, upbringing, and political background of the leaders of Pennsylvania and New York shaped their response. Governor Milton Shapp, the Democratic governor of Pennsylvania, was mercurial, whereas Nelson Rockefeller, the Republican governor of New York, rarely showed his emotions. Rockefeller was tall and wore impeccably tailored suits. Shapp was stoop-shouldered and of medium height, and even his tailored suits looked like they were off the rack. Rockefeller, who had dyslexia, always memorized his speeches, which he gave with an excellent delivery. Shapp, according to one historian, styled himself a "'Jewish Harry Truman,'" was a poor public speaker whose monotone style was more of a hindrance than a help in politics.[9]

Rockefeller was synonymous with the capitalist class that emerged at the end of the nineteenth century and had inherited his fortune. Shapp was a self-made multimillionaire who made a fortune in the modern era by creating and running a cable television company. Rockefeller was the epitome of the American WASP and white privilege and the poster boy for liberal eastern Republicans, so much so that journalists used the term "Rockefeller Republicans" to describe fiscally conservative and socially liberal members of the GOP.[10] Shapp was a political outsider who fought the Democratic Party machine to get into office. He was also a social outsider who fought to become accepted into a mainstream American society that still bore the mark of anti-Semitism. Born Milton Jerrold Shapiro, he shortened his name from Shapiro to Shapp to Americanize it.[11]

Nelson Rockefeller was not interested in dramatic policy change after Hurricane Agnes and instead preferred to maintain the status quo. For some flood victims, his attitude seemed cavalier. Rockefeller made only one official visit to the disaster site. On Saturday morning, June 24, Rockefeller flew into the disaster zone by helicopter, accompanied by U.S. Senators Jacob Javits and James Buckley and local congressional representative James Hastings.[12] After the helicopter set down, Rockefeller and his entourage emerged from the air-conditioned cabin to meet local officials. Bathed, groomed, and well-rested, Rockefeller met with local leaders who, lacking electric power and sleep, sported "deeply bloodshot eyes, heavy beards, and deteriorating morale." As they asked the governor for help, each request was carefully jotted down by an aide, but Rockefeller made no promises.[13]

Returning to Albany, Rockefeller established a Flood Recovery Committee to oversee recovery and rebuilding in the Southern Tier. Chairing the committee was Theodore "Ted" Parker of the State Department of Transportation.[14] Parker warned the governor that it would be "at least a year before normal conditions are restored."[15] Rockefeller accepted the assessment and then returned to his family vacation. After that, he traveled the country making speeches on behalf of Richard Nixon's reelection campaign.[16] People in the Southern Tier were unimpressed with Rockefeller. He "didn't even get his feet wet," one local official complained.[17] One woman from Elmira wrote to Rockefeller on July 11, begging for help: "Please, for God's sake, send some help to Elmira and Corning." She added, "We need money; it is true, but mostly we need able-bodied men to help thousands of poor souls clean up and rebuild." She described the scene, saying, "The entire business section is a shambles"; "homes are sitting atop one another"; and "old people are in a daze." She reminded Rockefeller that the United States helped other countries and appealed for the same help in Elmira. "We rebuilt Germany and Japan after the war and will probably rebuild Vietnam. Can't somebody do more to help Americans rebuild a beleaguered city?" The official response came, not from the governor, but Ted Parker, the chair of the governor's task force. "We are doing all we can," was his response.[18] In the weeks and months after the flood, many people in the Southern Tier felt that New York's top leadership was invisible and inactive.[19]

Milton Shapp was also a flood victim and made several highly publicized visits to the flooded areas. Whereas Governor Rockefeller was thinking about his vacation that June, Governor Shapp was in a budget battle with the state legislature. To become the first Jewish governor elected in Pennsylvania history and the first nonparty machine Democrat to win a primary and an election, Milton Shapp battled both his Republican rivals and the Democratic political machine. Elected in a landslide in 1970, Shapp still had to fight the state legislature to secure his cabinet appointments.[20] In 1972 Shapp was in a tug-of-war with Republicans over the state budget. Despite having a majority in the legislature, he was stymied by a coalition of fellow Democrats who voted with Republicans on the budget and thwarted the governor's proposals. Under the Pennsylvania Constitution, in order to spend additional money, the government was required to have a balanced budget in place by July 1.[21]

Shapp's mind was not only on the state budget but also on the 1972 presidential election. Incumbent president Richard Nixon was busy that summer putting together a strong and convincing presidential reelection bid to erase the memory that he had only won the popular vote by a narrow margin in 1968, when he beat Hubert Humphrey by less than 500,000 votes. Hamstrung by the close vote, which denied him a mandate to govern, Nixon was forced to make concessions to congressional Democrats on policy issues. Nixon believed that winning the popular vote by a wide margin in 1972 would provide him the mandate to govern and allow him to impose new domestic policy changes in keeping with his New Federalism philosophy of a smaller federal government. On the other hand, the Democrats, especially George McGovern, calculated that the close popular vote in 1968, combined with the growing antiwar sentiment and the lagging economy, was a winning recipe to take the White House away from the Republicans. Democrats blamed their 1968 loss on the third-party bid of George Wallace and the televised debacle at the 1968 Democratic Convention, which featured a police riot against antiwar demonstrators outside the convention hall and chaos inside. The Democrats might not be able to keep Wallace from running again, but they were determined to avoid another ugly confrontation between young and old, black and white, and male and female, like the one that had torn apart the party four years earlier. Senator George McGovern crafted new rules for selecting delegates to the Democratic Convention in 1972, which required the delegates to match the gender and racial composition of the party and, by extension, embrace more liberal and antiwar ideology. Senator McGovern then sought to use his own rules to gain the party's nomination in 1972.[22]

Throughout the spring, George McGovern and Hubert Humphrey had battled for the nomination, but neither had an outright majority to clinch it. On June 19, the day Agnes made landfall in Florida, Hubert Humphrey warned that if George McGovern were nominated, the middle class would defect to Nixon. McGovern, he said, would be "a tragedy for the Democratic Party."[23] McGovern responded by saying that Humphrey was "bent on self-destruction."[24] The heated rhetoric evinced the frustration of each man, neither of whom had the delegates to secure the nomination.

Milton Shapp looked forward to the Democratic National Convention, which was scheduled to meet in Miami Beach, Florida, in July, because he saw himself as a potential kingmaker. Shapp had endorsed Edmund Muskie early in the campaign, but after Muskie exited the race, the governor had the power to deliver the Pennsylvania delegation to either McGovern or Humphrey, thereby giving one of these men the edge they needed to win the nomination. Shapp hoped that whichever candidate he supported would be grateful enough to invite him on the ticket as the vice presidential running mate.[25]

The flooding from Agnes tempered Shapp's electoral ambition of becoming the first Jewish vice president.[26] After hearing a firsthand account of the disaster from state senator Martin Murray of Luzerne County, Shapp flew into the afflicted area by helicopter.[27] For the next year, the governor worked tirelessly to secure federal aid for his constituents while attacking Richard Nixon at every possible opportunity. He convened a summit of governors from the flooded states on Sunday, June 25, and urged them to show a united front in demanding more federal aid. "This is a crisis and Washington must be made aware that this is a crisis." At a news conference, the governor disparaged the $92 million of aid offered by Richard Nixon as insufficient and warned that red tape might stall aid to the disaster victims.[28] Criticism of Nixon served Shapp's political agenda, as it was a means of dampening support for the incumbent and advancing the Democratic candidate for president. It was also part of his character. Shapp's actions after the Agnes flooding reflect the governor's well-deserved reputation in Pennsylvania for admonishing, name calling, and feuding with those he opposed. Shapp was considered a gadfly in Pennsylvania for his tendency to bounce from one subject to another. The Republican House Speaker of Pennsylvania, Ken Lee, who also represented an area flooded by Agnes, compared Shapp to a fly at a picnic who "settles on a good many dishes," which he is unable to completely consume, instead contaminating "a little bit of each."[29]

On Monday, June 26, Shapp went to Washington, D.C., where he encouraged the Pennsylvania congressional delegation to craft legislation to compensate flood victims for the full cost of rebuilding their homes and businesses.[30] The idea of full restitution to flood victims for property damage became Shapp's primary goal that summer, and he took every opportunity to advance it. Milton Shapp believed that compensating victims was a question of fairness. He testified to the House Banking and Currency Committee that flood victims were similar to Europeans at the end of World War II. "If the United States can afford to have given Germany and Japan almost $100 billion in pre-inflated dollars to rebuild their nations at the end of World War II, we cannot afford not to give our hard-working citizens all the funds they need to rebuild their lives from this great disaster," Shapp argued. His statement tapped into the roots of American discontent with federal foreign aid. Lauded in later decades as the greatest generation, many of these Americans in 1972 felt more like the neglected generation.[31]

Shapp did more than advocate for the victims. Upon returning to Pennsylvania, the peripatetic governor delivered a televised address to the commonwealth and reassured Pennsylvanians that their government was taking action to restore services, stop the looting, and rebuild their cities. His address was just what many residents needed to hear. "Thank God we have a businessman as governor and not just a vote seeker," one wrote to him. Shapp's address was heard by New Yorkers in the Southern Tier, who lauded the action taken by the Keystone State's governor. Many wished that Nelson Rockefeller would be as compassionate.[32]

To assist flood victims in the immediate aftermath of the disaster, Shapp called a special session of the state legislature and demanded aid for the disaster victims. "It is clear we must invest a substantial amount of state revenue in a disaster relief fund," he advised. The General Assembly responded by ratifying a $150 million appropriation for flood victims from a revenue surplus that he intended to return to taxpayers.[33] Months later, in August, noting that the aid package proffered by Congress was still insufficient, Shapp returned to the General Assembly and asked for legislation to supplement the federal aid. He described the plight of their fellow citizens. "One hundred thousand Pennsylvanians are unemployed as a direct result of the recent flood. Over a quarter of a million of our citizens were made homeless by Hurricane Agnes, and forty thousand are still homeless." In order to provide direct payments to people in business and individuals, he urged the legislature to pass an emergency amendment to the state constitution, allowing grants of up to a $3,000 for each home or business owner.[34]

Cadillac Bill Seeks Reform

In the aftermath of the Agnes disaster, New Yorkers may have lacked a strong advocate in Nelson Rockefeller, but they did have a champion in the form of state senator Bill Smith. Smith returned to his farmstead once the Chemung River receded and began assisting his neighbors. He stored fresh water in milk cans, which he then shared with those around him. Corning Building Co., the material supply company Smith owned with his brother Jim, provided easy credit terms for those seeking building materials.[35]

In the months after Hurricane Agnes, Bill Smith also tried to help his neighbors and constituents by reshaping disaster policy. Smith's efforts at flood recovery and reform demonstrated the strengths and weaknesses of the traditional powers of a state legislator. On behalf of his constituents, Smith met with federal and state officials, including vice president Spiro Agnew, and in each case argued for more assistance for his district.[36] Smith spoke with an entourage of cabinet members and urged them to amend the 1970 Federal Disaster Relief Act, which Smith called "inadequate and inequitable." Smith even wrote to President Nixon asking for an increase in aid for Hurricane Agnes victims.[37]

Frustrated at the foot dragging by federal officials, Smith wrote to Governor Rockefeller on August 14, 1972, asking him to call a special session of the state legislature to address the needs of the Southern Tier flood victims. It took Rockefeller a month to respond to Smith's request, and then he merely suggested that Smith refer the matter to his counsel, Michael Whiteman.[38] Smith ultimately withdrew his request when it became clear that state Democrats wanted to use the flood to criticize the Republican administration.

The leader of the Senate Democrats, Stanley Steingut, had his eye on the governor's mansion. Steingut, a downstate Democrat, made a well-publicized fact-finding mission into the Southern Tier in August of 1972 and then returned to Albany, where he issued a press release listing the deplorable conditions that still existed in Corning and Elmira two months after the flood. The only method to ameliorate the situation in the Southern Tier, Steingut told reporters, would be to convene a special legislative session. Rockefeller suspected Steingut of political grandstanding and issued a point-by-point refutation of the call for a special legislative session. Without a special session, Smith's hope for immediate state action faded.[39] Instead, he gained approval to hold a series of hearings into the conditions that led to the flood.

The stated purpose of these hearings, held in October 1972, was for Smith to propose new legislation when the New York State legislature reconvened in January 1973. He sponsored many bills meant to address the deficiencies he saw in the state disaster response system, including a new civil defense organization in New York State, which was to be prepared for all disasters.[40] In order to goad the state into action, his bill would require the governor to act as soon as there was imminent danger of a disaster. Smith also wanted to grant broader powers to the Office of Natural Disaster and Civil Defense to better coordinate the state's disaster response. He offered the legislation in the state senate, and his colleague from the Southern Tier, Charles Henderson, offered it in the state assembly.[41]

Governor Rockefeller vetoed the bill. Like most governors, Rockefeller preferred to shift the financial burden of natural disaster onto the federal government.[42] One observant advocate for reform, Congressman Ogden Reid, grumbled, "The governor finds it all too easy to send a dramatic wire to the president and then lean on Uncle Sam to do it all."[43] Michael Whiteman, Rockefeller's chief legal counsel, urged a veto and reminded the governor that it was more politically expedient and less expensive for the federal government to assume responsibility for a disaster.[44] Rockefeller was aware that the public had little tolerance for expansive and expensive new state programs. He had created the statewide sales tax in 1965 to fund new social and educational programs, but his budget was already strained by 1970, and many members of the statewide Republican Party (dubbed the "Grand Old Party," or GOP) resented the governor's liberal policies.

The starkest assessment came from George Hinman, one of the most powerful Republicans in New York, who served on the Executive Committee of the state GOP and was a member of the Republican National Committee from 1959 to 1977. Within New York, Hinman's Binghamton law firm produced a cadre of Republican leaders, including state senate majority leader Warren Anderson.[45] Hinman was Rockefeller's most trusted political adviser, and when he told the governor to stop lavish spending or face electoral consequences, Rockefeller listened.[46] Limited financial support of short duration for those affected by the disaster was acceptable to the governor. He supported legislation proposed by Smith and Henderson to grant temporary property tax abatements for individuals whose property was damaged in the flood and provide tax credits to businesses that invested in designated disaster areas. Introduced in January, these bills sailed through the legislature and were signed into law by Rockefeller in February 1973.[47]

Responding to political opponents such as Steingut and political allies such as Smith, Rockefeller offered minor changes to the state's disaster program. In his State of the State Address in early 1973, the governor announced his plan to transfer the office responsible for disasters from the Department of Transportation to the Division of Military and Naval Affairs, which he believed would make it more responsive to crises. However, this minor change did little to address the problems Smith's committee had uncovered in preparing for disasters and warning the general public of a looming disaster.[48] Rockefeller's rejection of new statewide policies reflected not just politics but also a philosophical approach asserting that a federal presence was necessary to assist in a disaster. William Hennessy, who oversaw the Natural Disaster and Civil Defense Agency for New York, believed that the federal government owed more to the people of the state. He was appalled at the lack of preparation for the Agnes disaster and believed that any disaster of that magnitude required a federal response.[49]

Bill Smith agreed with Hennessey, which is somewhat astounding given that Smith was an unlikely champion for expansive government. Indeed, he was known as an advocate for small government, lower taxes, and individual initiative. He despised the entitlement mentality normalized during the Great Society, and it was his anti-entitlement disposition that had led him into politics in the first place. His career began in 1961, when he received a letter from the Department of Agriculture inviting him to participate in their crop subsidy program. Smith opposed big government programs and was irate. "My father and I have never accepted any federal programs," he fumed. He calculated that with the amount the United States Department of Agriculture (USDA) was offering, he would get "$6,000 to $8,000 for not growing corn." He related this to his friends at the local diner, who scoffed at him, saying, "Smith, we've heard your B.S. before."[50] Smith proved his point by taking one hundred acres of his least productive land out of farming. In return, the USDA sent him enough money to purchase a brand-new Cadillac. He used the money to protest farm supports by driving the Cadillac to

FIGURE 6. This photo shows how state senator William Smith earned the nickname "Cadillac Bill." Courtesy of Bonnifer Schweizer, family of William Smith.

Washington, where he had arranged to meet with national newspaper reporters and nineteen Republican U.S. senators. The media dubbed him "Cadillac Bill," and Smith used his fame to win a seat in the New York State Senate.[51]

After his election to the state senate, Cadillac Bill continued to rail against expensive government programs. In 1969, he challenged the leadership of both parties on the practice of giving committee chairs "lulus," which were lump sums instead of reimbursement for expenses.[52] In 1971, after being named social services commissioner, Smith fired forty-three of the forty-nine staff members, arguing that they were unnecessary.[53] Inefficient state agencies were apparently on his mind in January 1973, and Smith was firmly convinced that without a single state agency to coordinate the preparation, monitoring, warning, and recovery from disasters, an Agnes-like event would again catch local and state officials off guard and lead to a similar loss of life and property.

Despite his failure to gain special recognition of the plight of the people in the Southern Tier, Smith's generosity had a political advantage. In the estimation of one local historian, Smith "was reelected to office repeatedly" because of his work on their behalf after the flood of 1972. Smith remained in office for a quarter century, only retiring to take up a new cause as the first director of Mothers Against Drunk Drivers (MADD).[54] Throughout his career, Smith worked for a change in the New York State disaster policy, but the substantive change was rejected. He found that his proposals for policy reform were thwarted or altered by fellow legislators and the governor.

Smith's experience reflected a given in American natural disaster policy, which is that singular events, even events as catastrophic such as Agnes, rarely lead to significant policy changes. Public policy in this area has never developed a sustained interest group to advocate for reform on a continuous basis.[55] In 1972 many state governments saw disaster assistance as a zero-sum game, and therefore provided limited support to local municipalities after a disaster, fearful that any increase in assistance would be offset by the withdrawal of funding from the federal government.

Thus, it fell to the federal government to assist local government and individuals after the Agnes disaster. However, Congress did not pass a disaster relief bill until August, and even after that, it was a matter of weeks and even months before money was fully available to local governments and individuals. Under existing law, the Disaster Relief Act of 1970, local governments were required to pay for all repairs out of pocket and then seek reimbursement from the federal government. In the immediate aftermath of the flooding, local leaders in Corning, Elmira, and Wilkes-Barre felt isolated and overwhelmed, and in the absence of state or federal assistance, they turned to influential individuals and business groups within their communities to help in the crisis.

Emergent Leaders Take Action

As the days turned into weeks after the Agnes flooding, local officials and individuals were dismayed at the lack of resources available to them. Officials in the small cities dotting the Susquehanna River Basin hoped that the federal government would provide financial assistance and turned to the private sector to supply both the administrative support and the advocacy prowess needed to secure more resources. By privatizing their disaster response, local governments ceded power to the business community.[56] When federal money eventually became available to rebuild the cities and towns, members of the private sector influenced the preparation of urban renewal plans, while ordinary residents were often excluded from the inner workings.

Wilkes-Barre, as it had done after previous disasters, turned to the private sector for assistance. In 1972 elected officials once again looked to extragovernmental organizations to restore their community. Business leaders gathered together to create a Flood Recovery Task Force (FRTF), which they asked federal judge Max Rosenn to lead. The group, which was made of bankers, members of the business community, and leaders of civic organizations, believed that Rosenn "had the prestige" and administrative ability to handle the problem. Rosenn took a temporary leave from the federal bench and accepted the responsibility, reasoning that his political connections locally, statewide, and nationally would be beneficial to the community.[57]

Rosenn was a lifelong resident of the Wyoming Valley. He graduated from Cornell University in 1929 and the University of Pennsylvania Law School in 1932. His impressive resume included a position as an assistant district attorney in Wilkes-Barre in 1941–1944 and service in U.S. Army JAG Corps in the Philippines at the end of World War II. After the war, he returned to Luzerne County and opened the private law firm of Rosenn, Jenkins & Greenwald. He remained politically active in the 1950s and 1960s and was appointed to direct Pennsylvania's State Welfare Office, where he earned a reputation as a civil rights advocate. In 1970 Richard Nixon appointed him to the Third Circuit Court of Appeals.[58] However, Rosenn remained in Wilkes-Barre and kept an office in the federal building downtown, which was where he helmed the FRTF.[59]

Rosenn convened the first meeting of the FRTF on July 4, 1972.[60] The goals of the organization were simple. The first was to imprint on the minds of the nation that Agnes was not just an ordinary disaster, but the "nation's worst disaster." The second was to keep the pressure on the government using media, letter-writing campaigns, and personal contacts. Rosenn persuaded former Republican governor William Scranton to write a letter to major publications, including the *Nation*. "Frankly, we need help in telling this story to the public and the opinion leaders of the county."[61] The FTRF wanted to have either the federal government or insurance companies pay the entire cost of rebuilding the Wyoming Valley. It wanted all the flood victims to have their home or business rebuilt with no out-of-pocket money.[62]

Rosenn asked Hugh Scott, the U.S. Senate minority leader and Pennsylvania's senior senator, to support this idea, but Scott said it was unfeasible. Rosenn insisted that Scott should visit the valley in person. "You've got to smell the stench of mud and find your feet slipping on floors," he told him. Only then could he "know the magnitude of the disaster."[63] Scott agreed and toured the area on July 7 before meeting with fifty community leaders at the Treadway Inn. In a bit of theatrics, Scott walked over to the phone during the meeting and, by pre-arrangement, placed a call to Richard Nixon. "Mr. President," Scott began, "this disaster is the biggest natural disaster in the history of this country. We need all the help you can give us." After Scott described the scene, Nixon is reported to have told him to contact John Whitaker and to tell him to "uncork all stops." Nixon also promised special legislation. However, the political charade fooled no one. One local Democrat walked out of the meeting fuming that the citizens of Wilkes-Barre were a prop for Nixon's reelection bid.[64]

The FRTF did more than lobby for more federal aid; the group shaped local and regional politics in the valley. Rosenn proposed government consolidation to improve efficiency. To tie the scattered communities together, he lobbied for the construction of the North Cross Valley Expressway. To develop a stronger political infrastructure in Wilkes-Barre, he called for revising the existing charter to create a robust mayoral council form of government. By the nation's bicentennial, Wilkes-Barre had a new governmental structure, and federal money had paid for construction of the expressway.[65] After his work on the FRTF, Rosenn returned to the federal bench, where he mentored the next generation of judges, including future associate Supreme Court justice Stephen Breyer. As Rosenn lived until 2006, reaching the ripe old age of ninety-six, and in recognition of service to the people of Wilkes-Barre, officials named the rebuilt federal courthouse in his honor.

Although the business community supported the FRTF, other citizens of the Wyoming Valley complained that the task force was an elitist group. In response, they formed a group called the Flood Victims Action Council and asked former labor organizer Min Matheson to lead it. Matheson, along with attorney Paul Kanjorski, urged full restitution for flood victims and demanded more input on local decision making.[66]

It was not only weak governmental structures like the city of Wilkes-Barre that needed private sector assistance. Even governments with strong political leadership found themselves incapable of handling a crisis of the magnitude of Agnes. Corning had strong leadership in the form of their mayor, Joseph Nasser, a political boss whom locals compared to Chicago mayor Richard Daley. "He was a complete dictator," said former *Leader* reporter Bob Rolfe. Joseph Nasser had been part of Corning politics since the end of World War II, when he returned home from the war and began his career as a member of the Republican Committee. "I handed out leaflets and did the little jobs you had to do to rise in the party," Nasser recalled. He rose through the ranks quickly, serving as city attorney, running the bus company, and being elected mayor in 1958. Once he became mayor, Nasser personalized the office and made sure that each subsequent run for mayor was a referendum, not about Republican politics, but about Nasser himself. Nasser was not only the mayor of Corning but also head of the local Republican Party. He controlled the city council and made all key appointments, including the fire chief, police chief, public works head, and urban renewal director.[67] During the post-flood recovery, Nasser played the role of a flood czar, making all decisions regarding relief and recovery from his office.[68] Nasser saw the flood as a personal affront. "We are not going to take this lying down," he declared. "We're gonna come back."[69]

Nasser is remembered in Corning for his successful handling of the crisis, which became the hallmark of his career. After the flood, he helped organize the rebuilding, which completely remade the city with the addition of new buildings and parks. For his efforts, Nasser was continually reelected mayor until 1983, when a mere sixty votes beat him after twenty-three years in office. His longevity gives Nasser the record for being the second-longest-serving mayor in New York State history.[70] However, in the days following the flood, Nasser was publicly criticized for failing to warn citizens of the impending danger and faced a lawsuit for his perceived mishandling of the crisis.[71] Nasser himself blamed the Flood Control Office of the state Department of Environmental Conservation and the National Weather Service for not providing his office with adequate warning, and he was exonerated when Bill Smith held a series of hearings looking into the failed warnings in October 1972.[72] Perhaps it was his relative defensiveness after the crisis that provoked his rapprochement with the local business community, as personified in the head of Corning Glass Works (CGW).[73]

Although he was an influential figure in local politics, Joe Nasser's power and influence were overshadowed by the wealth and influence of the Houghton family, who lived in a mansion called the Knoll, which sat on a steep hill overlooking Corning. From the Knoll, the Houghton family could look down over the city that they and their glass factory had helped to build. The first glass factory controlled by the family had been started in Brooklyn but was moved to Corning in 1868 and renamed the Corning Glass Works. From the 1860s on, the Houghtons' wealth and business associations gave the family prominence locally and nationally and provided them with a platform for philanthropy and public service.[74]

Alanson Bigelow Houghton, 1863–1941, son of the founder, ran the CGW factory before serving two terms in the House of Representatives and then serving presidents Warren G. Harding and Calvin Coolidge as ambassador to Germany and to Great Britain.[75] Alanson's son, Amory Houghton, Sr., ran the family business from 1930 until 1971 but also found time to serve in Franklin Roosevelt's administration in World War II and as President Eisenhower's ambassador to France in 1957–1961. In Corning, Amory was formally addressed as "Ambassador Houghton."[76] Alanson's nephew, Arthur Amory Houghton, Jr., ran a subsidiary of CGW, Steuben Glass, and used his wealth to endow the Houghton Library at Harvard University. Arthur took a leave from his position as president of Steuben Glass to serve as curator of rare books at the Library of Congress and later worked with John D. Rockefeller III to create Lincoln Center. Closer to home, Arthur donated nearly three hundred acres of land to build Corning Community College in 1960.[77]

The head of the CGW in 1972 was Amory Houghton, Jr., known affectionately as Amo. At fifty-six, the tall, thin Amo was the fifth generation of Houghtons to run the business. Before heading the company, Amo followed the tried and exact family formula for success. Like his predecessors, Amo went to public schools in Corning to learn about the lives of the people who lived and worked in the town that CGW built. Amo then attended St. Paul's prep school in New Hampshire before earning his degree at Harvard. After graduation, he entered the family business and served in a variety of departments to learn the business from the inside out.[78]

Amo Houghton had a reputation for high energy and a passion for Corning. "Corning was my universe when I was a kid . . . and it will always be my home," he maintained.[79] A complex man, Amo had a mind for business and a heart for God. He worked his way up from the accounting division and was named the president of CGW in 1961 and chairman of the board in 1964. In 1972 he was guiding CGW into investing in "fiber optics." After the flood, Amo's patience and love for Corning led him to keep the glass business in his hometown and to provide economic support and encouragement to the residents of the Chemung Valley. A generation of people in Corning remembered him as the "Man Who Saved Corning."[80] In the aftermath of the flood, Amo provided leadership, inspiration, and encouragement to the citizens of Corning. He gave three important speeches after the flood. The first was a private talk given to the board of CGW, telling them that the firm would remain headquartered in Corning and would rebuild. His second speech was an encouraging radio address to the citizens of Corning that told them CGW would rebuild and remain in Corning, and that all employees were eligible for a low-cost loan to get them through the immediate crisis. Finally, he testified before Congress on the need for federal assistance for the inhabitants of the Corning area.

To the people, who were dazed by the horrors of the flood and sickened by the stench of river mud, Houghton's radio address was a sign of hope. "We are not licked. We are going to bounce back, and for many, we are going to start again," he told them. He refuted the rumor going around town that CGW was going to leave the valley. "Nothing is further from the truth. We are not only going to rebuild what we have lost, but we are going to add significantly to our manufacturing facilities in one of our plants. And that's a fact—not a rumor."[81] People heard him and believed what he promised.

Amo Houghton did more than talk; he and his family supplied the community with necessary resources and CGW took measures to assist its employees. The company provided vacation pay advances and loaned employees up to $1,000. Houghton asked the directors of the Corning Glass Works Foundation for $400,000 to create a Youth Emergency Services (YES) program to provide summer jobs for three hundred teens to assist in cleanup and restoration.[82] Houghton testified before a subcommittee of the Senate Banking Committee, where he appeared as a community advocate, asking "nothing for myself nor the company of which I am chairman," and adding, "The help I ask, rather, is for the citizens of a devastated community." He urged that the committee grant the Small Business Administra-

FIGURE 7.   Amory Houghton, Jr., recording a speech to residents after the flood to reassure them that Corning Glass Works would stay and help rebuild the city. Collection of the Rakow Library, Corning Museum of Glass, Corning, New York. Original photograph loaned by Corning, Inc., Corning, New York.

tion authority to forgive loans, to raise the limits on how much money individuals could borrow to refinance their mortgages, and to make repairs. He urged keeping the interest rate on such loans at 1 percent. "Knowing the people of the town and seeing the damage . . . I am convinced that a forgiveness clause on loaned money is a must. There are many cases in which a person for a variety of reasons—family, health, earning power—simply must be helped further along the road the present bill contemplates." He told the senators, "We have hundreds of our young people digging out cellars, caring for children displaced by the flood, helping old people." His advice to Congress was simple: "Get going." In his self-deprecating style, Houghton recalls that when he appeared before the committee, "nobody was there" because Frank Sinatra was testifying down the hall.[83]

Perhaps Houghton had less clout in Washington than Sinatra, but he and his family were on the A-list of all the federal and state officials who came to Corning. Their first task on arriving in Corning was to ask to see Houghton. George Lincoln, director of the Office of Emergency Preparedness, wrote to Nelson Rockefeller, "I repeat my pledge to ambassador Houghton of Corning: We will not forget New York." Due to his political capital, Houghton routinely corresponded with Nixon and Rockefeller, always careful to bring up the flood and to remind the politicians of their commitments and promises. He wrote Rockefeller, thanking him for his visit to the Corning area and sending his regrets for not being there to greet the governor. He enclosed with the letter a glass figurine that had miraculously survived the flood. "We won't abuse our citizenship since there is much we are doing ourselves, but I would like to feel I could call you if we need help that only you can give."[84] Nelson Rockefeller was no less friendly, and wrote back to Houghton, saying, "I'm sad about the flood, but delighted to have such a handsome survivor."[85]

Amo Houghton oversaw the rebuilding of Corning and placed CGW President Tom MacAvoy in charge of recovery operations at the glass works. The day after the flood, MacAvoy visited Nasser's command center in City Hall and recalled seeing more bedlam than bureaucratic efficiency. He reported to Houghton that Nasser was incapable of responding to the crisis. Houghton, along with other community leaders, quietly decided to guide the decision making of Nasser by "loaning" him executives such as George Douglas. Houghton made sure that "George Douglas was in the office with Nasser every hour of every day."[86] CGW contributed significant resources in the form of money, labor, and organizational ability to rebuild the city of Corning along their specifications, which included a complete renovation of Market Street. Moreover, a combination of public and private financing led to the building of a new Hilton Hotel, a new corporate headquarters for CGW, and a Glass Innovation Center.[87]

City manager Joe Sartori of Elmira also found it a struggle to rebuild after the flood, but Elmira had no one with national prominence such as Amory Houghton, Jr., or Max Rosenn to rely on. Instead, the local business community turned to the very able leadership of S. Roberts Rose, who ran one of the largest wholesale hardware firms in the nation. Rose was a model citizen, a leader of the Arctic League, involved in Junior Achievement, a member of the Rotary Club, on the Board of Trustees of Elmira College, a board member at Arnot-Ogden Hospital, founder of the Clements Center, a member of the Chemung County Chamber of Commerce, and a board member of Marine Midland Bank. He led the Citizens Advisory Council of the local Urban Development Corporation (UDC) and helped to craft the New Elmira Plan, which was the blueprint for rebuilding Elmira after the Agnes flood.[88]

In the absence of immediate assistance from the national or state government, local governments dealt with the immediate crisis by seeking assistance from the private sector within their communities. In turn, these individuals or groups left their imprint on the reconstructed cities. Meanwhile, at the federal level, President Nixon ordered aides to prepare new legislation aimed at benefiting both the devastated cities and his own political ambitions.

4

PLAYING POLITICS WITH DISASTER
Relief Efforts and the 1972 Election

Richard Nixon mixed politics and policy in his response to Hurricane Camille in 1969 and kept the political implications of disaster relief at the forefront of his actions after that. When drought threatened Texas cattle in 1971, Nixon told Office of Emergency Preparedness (OEP) director George Lincoln that the situation was "mainly a political problem—it's a political problem." However, he did concede that "it's a disaster, too."[1] In April 1972, Nixon's campaign staff circulated a memo that described how natural disasters "have a great political impact in an area."[2] To aid in winning his reelection bid in 1972, Nixon determined to play politics with disaster relief legislation, mainly as it applied to New York and Pennsylvania, two states he had lost to Hubert Humphrey in 1968.[3] In order to gain Nixon as many votes as possible from the disaster, the Nixon White House wrote, and Congress enacted, the most generous disaster aid package in American history to that time, the Agnes Recovery Act of 1972.

Before the passage of the Disaster Relief Act of 1950, presidents had little stake in disaster legislation, all of which was generated and controlled by Congress. However, once Franklin Roosevelt centralized American domestic policy within the Executive Office of the President, the president had the tools necessary to oversee major disasters. Roosevelt's successor, Harry Truman, signed into law the Disaster Relief Act of 1950, which granted the president the power to declare a major disaster and to provide direct federal aid to local governments. Subsequent legislation incrementally added benefits for disaster survivors, first to local and state governments and later to individuals. The Disaster Relief Act of 1970 provided the federal government with the power to make direct payments to individuals who lost private property in a disaster. Other benefits included low-interest loans, emergency food stamps, unemployment compensation, and health and legal services.[4]

By the late 1960s, disaster benefits had become tantamount to entitlements, but this proved to be a mixed blessing for politicians, who found themselves judged by the press and the public on how quickly, competently, and compassionately they responded to a disaster. President Johnson gained public acclaim for his response to the Alaska earthquake in 1964 and his visit to New Orleans after Hurricane Betsy in 1965. On the other hand, mayor John Lindsay of New York suffered a political setback in 1969 when he failed to meet public expectation after a blizzard paralyzed parts of New York City for several days.[5] Playing to public expectation, members of Congress enhanced their status among voters by passing generous disaster relief packages. Their political rivals, however, vilified incumbents by condemning their reaction to disaster, suggesting that the government aid was too little and, due to the massive red tape involved in disaster relief, that it came too late.[6] Thus, elected leaders walked a tightrope between public expectations for immediate assistance and the reality that assistance came through bureaucratic processes established by Congress and supervised by civil servants.

President Johnson found that his active and visible response to Hurricane Betsy brought him an electoral advantage, and Nixon followed suit by using Hurricane Camille to promote his election schemes. The relationship between disasters and elections has generated a body of research that shows a strong correlation between when and where presidents issue a disaster declaration. Disaster declarations are more frequent in highly competitive swing states during presidential election years, and presidents favor those states that may benefit them or their party in the election, as Nixon did in response to Hurricane Agnes.[7]

Nixon Responds

Initially, Nixon was slow to act during the crisis generated by Hurricane Agnes. The president flew over the devastated regions of Pennsylvania on his way to Camp David on Friday, June 23, but he resisted calls from advisers Chuck Colson and John Whitaker to touch down and meet with disaster victims.[8] Nixon seemed more eager to get to Camp David that weekend, where he planned to make his picks for baseball's All-Star Game.[9] The president regretted his decision only after the broadcast media panned his inaction. To counteract the negative press, White House staffers persuaded Nixon to make an appearance in one of the flooded cities.[10] On Saturday morning, June 24, Nixon reluctantly agreed to a two-hour tour of Harrisburg, Pennsylvania, which included a forty-five-minute stop at a flood refugee center. At the center, he met with victims and took a photo with a young African American girl who had been separated from her family. Encountering a woman and her four children who had lost their home, he gently told her, "We are very sorry . . . everybody wants to help to the extent we can."[11]

Following a pattern he set after Hurricane Camille in 1969, President Nixon sent Vice President Agnew to survey the flooded areas.[12] The Agnew tour was good publicity for the administration but did little to mollify the victims of the disaster as the trip failed to give Nixon a clear idea of what the situation was for the residents. Agnew began the tour on Wednesday, June 28, in his home state of Maryland, where he heard complaints that the government was not providing enough assistance. "The damage is appalling," Agnew told reporters, but deflected calls for more aid by saying, "It is heartening to see neighbor helping neighbor."[13] Agnew's fact-finding mission took him to Pennsylvania, where he called out Governor Shapp for being too "excitable" and for asking for billions of dollars in aid. To those living out the nightmare of post-flood catastrophe, the comments of the vice president added insult to injury, and they expressed this in letters to federal, state, and local officials. A resident of Kingston, Pennsylvania, wrote and challenged the vice president to "come here and see the real thing." Noting that there was still no place to have a hot meal, the resident then asked Agnew, "Have you ever walked into a home after a flood has been up past the second floor?"[14] In New York, the vice president spent about 90 minutes touring Elmira and Corning and then flew to New York City to attend a $125-a-plate Republican fundraiser in Nassau County.[15] The locals were displeased. One wrote to Agnew, "People are mad at you. They wanted you to walk through the mud, look in the buildings and actually see for yourself." Agnew's political aide, James Fall, wrote a note on the letter, "This man writes what everyone thinks."[16]

When Agnew reported back to President Nixon, he downplayed what flood victims had said, and added, "My observations tend to confirm the official weather service reports that this is the greatest flood in recorded history in the Eastern United States." Agnew touched briefly on the idea of loan forgiveness, suggesting the president might wish to address this option. He told Nixon that his conversations with local officials "produced repeated assurances that [the] federal agencies participating have been entirely responsive to the needs of flood victims. Cooperation between officials and volunteer agencies has been excellent."[17] Agnew confirmed that a report from the OEP "accurately reflects the extent of damage and the general situation," and praised the OEP's efforts for the way its staffers "projected a cheerful, compassionate attitude that has set well with the victims of the flood." He told Nixon, "I would recommend a special word of appreciation to the Office of Emergency Preparedness."[18] Nixon, who had only briefly visited Harrisburg, relied for information on his vice president and OEP director George

Lincoln, both of whom were eager to shield the president from the true sentiment of the victims.

The reluctance of the president's advisers to discuss the growing disenchantment of the storm victims may have been due to Richard Nixon's expressed desire to win reelection by a large margin. Nixon was especially desirous of winning the Democratic-leaning state of Pennsylvania. Months before the June flood, Nixon had been trying to woo Pennsylvania Democrats to support him. He struck gold when Frank Rizzo, the Democratic mayor of Philadelphia, endorsed him. Rather than alienate potential Democratic allies, Nixon instructed staffers to label supporters of the Democratic nominee for president, George McGovern, not Democrats, but "McGovernites."[19]

The Agnes flooding presented a new problem for Nixon's Pennsylvania strategy in the form of his harshest critic, governor Milton Shapp. Shapp styled himself as the champion of the flood victims and maintained a barrage of criticism against Nixon. Governor Shapp was unimpressed with Nixon's flyover and his short visit to Pennsylvania and took every possible opportunity to call for a more expansive federal role in the 1972 disaster while also disparaging Nixon and his administration.

Immediately after the disaster, Shapp convened a summit of governors of affected states and used the occasion to embarrass Nixon and wrest more financial

FIGURE 8. Pictured here, left to right, are Nelson Rockefeller, Spiro Agnew, unknown person, Richard Nixon, unknown person, George Romney, unknown person. Courtesy of the National Archives.

assistance from the federal government.[20] Reacting to the bad publicity that followed the summit, the White House issued a press release reiterating that President Nixon was doing all he could for the flood-ravaged states. The press release stated that he was asking Congress for an additional $100 million in disaster aid for the flood-damaged cities and towns. Shapp denigrated this sum as insufficient and called for a billion dollars. He blasted Nixon to reporters and claimed that the president would not return his calls. "I tried five times yesterday to reach Richard Nixon by telephone but never got through," he complained. Nixon, who hated confrontation, refused to meet or speak with the Pennsylvania governor and privately grumbled to one aide that talking to Shapp ought to be Agnew's job.[21]

To stifle critics like Shapp and to reach out to potential voters, Nixon pulled together a committee to write a disaster bill intended to assist his reelection bid by providing generous benefits to the victims of Hurricane Agnes in a way that would not obligate the federal government to provide the same benefits in the future. As part of this strategy, the president drew on the newly established Office of Management and Budget (OMB). Nixon wanted the OMB to have fiscal oversight over the disaster recovery and recruited the deputy director of OMB, Frank Carlucci, to serve as the liaison with the other bureaucracies involved. White House domestic policy adviser John C. Whitaker was placed on the committee, which seemed fitting since Whitaker held a Ph.D. in geology and had once been a weatherman.[22] Other committee members included George Lincoln from the OEP; Peter Peterson, the secretary of commerce, a post that oversaw the National Weather Service; and James Hodgson, the secretary of labor. Called the Agnes Disaster Working Group, the committee began drafting a disaster relief bill after the Fourth of July holiday.[23]

Nixon, Caspar Weinberger, who headed the OMB, and domestic advisers John Ehrlichman and Kenneth Cole gathered in the Oval Office on July 11 to discuss the first draft of the bill prepared by the working group. The bill contained $1.3 billion for the Small Business Administration (SBA) to provide loans to homeowners and businesses, and $1.4 million was made available to the Farm and Home Administration for agricultural loans. An additional $200 million was targeted to replenish the president's disaster fund, which was used to rebuild public facilities and to provide temporary housing, food, and unemployment benefits,[24] and $200 million went to the highway fund to rebuild broken roadways. Finally, $40 million went to the Economic Development Agency, $16 million to the Appalachian Regional Commissions and $12 million to the U.S. Army Corps of Engineers to clean up, remove debris, and make minor repairs.[25]

While Nixon was refining the outlines of the flood relief bill, John Whitaker, Frank Carlucci, and George Lincoln met with Pennsylvania governor Shapp.

Carlucci was the number two man at the OMB, but just as important, he was a native of Scranton, Pennsylvania, and served as a counterweight to the critical Shapp. Carlucci, who was in his early forties, was handsome, polished, and energetic. He was a relative newcomer to Nixon's inner circle, having come to the president's attention through Donald Rumsfeld. Before joining the Nixon White House, Carlucci served in the Foreign Service from 1956 until 1969. He earned a footnote in history when he was accused of participating in the overthrow and murder of Patrice Lumumba of the Congo. For this and other "subversive activities," Carlucci was expelled from the Congo and considered unwelcome in other developing nations, which led him to return to Washington.[26]

The meeting between Carlucci and Shapp was window dressing for the press, meant to demonstrate that the White House was open to working with the Democrat governor of Pennsylvania. Shapp's main concern was that loan provisions in existence at the time of the flood, as detailed in the 1970 relief legislation, would diminish the ability of small businesses to maintain a line of credit, and this would strangle their ability to get short-term seasonal loans to buy inventory and make payroll. Instead, the Pennsylvania governor wanted the government to establish something similar to the Reconstruction Finance Corporation (RFC), to buy the original mortgages on damaged property and issue a new, government-backed, low-interest mortgage. Besides, Shapp wanted to encourage people to move out of the floodplain, which would eliminate government costs in the future, so he suggested expanding the flood insurance program to include the purchase of property located in the floodplain. Finally, Shapp wanted to add a surcharge on homeowners' mortgage protection insurance to create a natural disaster insurance fund so that those caught in future disasters could receive full compensation for property damage.[27]

Shapp's ideas made sense to one Nixon aide, Des Barker, who liked what he heard. After the meeting, Barker urged Chuck Colson to take the ideas directly to the president. Colson was Nixon's special counsel and one of the few people besides H. R. Haldeman who had access to President Nixon any time he wanted. Colson was often the last person Nixon talked to every day, and Nixon summed up his admiration for Colson when he said, "Colson has the balls of a brass monkey."[28] Barker told Colson that Shapp's proposals were politically valid, adding, "Each of them has good mileage for the administration." In a barbed aside, he suggested that cabinet secretaries Hodgeson or Peterson should have thought of these ideas. Barker calculated that the more generous the aid package was, the greater the electoral results would be that November. Barker thought the "political impact would be positive" and encouraged Colson to take it to Nixon.[29] Despite the pitch by Barker, however, Shapp's ideas were not in the bill Nixon sent to Congress.

FIGURE 9.   Key figures from Hurricane Agnes, pictured left to right, standing behind President Gerald Ford: Thomas Kleppe, Senator Hugh Scott, Senator Richard Schweiker, Governor Milton Shapp. Courtesy of the National Archives (photo 45644217).

Rejecting calls from Governor Shapp, the Flood Relief Task Force, and members of Congress for Nixon to provide grants rather than loans to people so they could rebuild their homes, businesses, and public facilities, President Nixon offered a mix of loans and grants to the victims instead. He settled on the idea of forgiving the first five thousand dollars of any loan, and providing the rest of the amount at the low interest rate of 1 percent. Nixon imagined the political value he would gain from this generosity. "This is a sure thing in Pennsylvania, the heart of the state," he said. Nixon was willing to be generous in an election year but was equally determined to limit this largesse to the disaster victims of 1972. To promote his policy, he planned to sell it to the public in a "simple, understandable radio speech," and to pressure Congress into passing his bill, he planned a special White House summit of state, local, and community leaders. Nixon calculated that once local officials were on board with the bill, they would do the work of lobbying Congress to pass it.[30]

With the final touches of the legislation complete, Nixon made a radio address announcing his disaster relief plan from his San Clemente home, the so-called Western White House. (Nixon, who had lavished over half a million dollars of public money on refurbishing Camp David, had also used federal funds to convert his California home into a base of operations.)[31] On July 12, at 9:25 a.m. Pacific

Time, Nixon delivered a five-minute oration. He told listeners that Agnes was "the worst natural disaster in the whole of American history." This required a massive response: "Conscience commands it; humanity impels it." Comparing those suffering from the disaster to neighbors or friends in distress, Nixon announced the "largest single amount ever allocated to recovery efforts in this country," $1.7 billion in aid and loans. Loans would be made available at 1 percent interest and with $5,000 forgiven. At the end of the address, Nixon invited nearly five hundred local officials to come to Washington to meet and learn about the relief plan.[32]

Between the radio message, which was delivered July 12, and July 17, when the proposal was sent to Congress, Nixon hosted a White House summit for local and state officials to explicate the details of the Agnes Recovery Act and to build support for the proposal.[33] The meeting was informative, but like everything else that summer, it was also political. The president's staff had debated whether to host the summit in one of the areas devastated by Agnes or to bring participants to Washington, D.C., and had decided to hold it in Washington on Friday, July 14. The timing of the event was critical. If possible, they wanted to keep Pennsylvania Governor Shapp from coming, and they knew that along with other Democratic governors, he was likely to be in Miami all that week at the Democratic National Convention. The Democratic governors, Whitaker surmised, "will be tired after their Miami experience and probably won't show up." Holding the summit in Washington on a Friday would also reduce the potential for Democrats from the House or Senate coming to the event because Congress was in recess.

Furthermore, White House aides expected only the Washington bureau of newspapers in the affected states to show up, believing that "this is no longer a national story, but a regional story at this point." The summit allowed Nixon to circumvent Democratic governors, members of Congress, and the national press corps, while promoting his agenda and himself directly to local officials, local news agencies, and by extension, potential voters.[34] Even the most skeptical participants left visibly impressed with Nixon. George Bevan, who attended on behalf of the City of Corning, along with city manager Joe Sartori, Jr., from Elmira, came back enthusiastic about the proposal. This was a public relations coup for Nixon, although it was not surprising, considering that many of Nixon's top aides had had previous experience in advertising and public relations before working in the White House.[35]

On the day of the summit, Nixon held his daily meeting with John Ehrlichman, at which the two discussed Hurricane Agnes and the Watergate break-in, both of which were now tied to Nixon's reelection bid. The saga of Hurricane Agnes culminated with the Disaster Relief Act of 1974, while the Watergate scandal ended with Nixon's resignation from office in the same year. Coincidently the two events began almost simultaneously.

On June 17, 1972, as Hurricane Agnes headed toward Florida, the D.C. police arrested five burglars caught inside the headquarters of the Democratic National Committee (DNC) in the Watergate Hotel and business complex.[36] The burglars were caught replacing and checking recording devices planted in the headquarters of the DNC, and most had ties to the Committee to Re-elect the President (CREEP). There was immediate speculation in Washington as to whether this scandal came from the White House, but full details of Nixon's involvement remained undisclosed for another two years. One reporter writing on the scandal claimed that theories about what was going on "swept through D.C. like Hurricane Agnes."[37] On June 23, 1972, the same day the floods ravaged Corning, Elmira, and Wilkes-Barre, Nixon, and his aide, Haldeman, were seeking ways to get the FBI to stop investigating the Watergate break-in. The tape of their conversation, recorded in the Oval Office by a voice-activated tape recorder, became known as the "smoking gun" tape, as it proved that Nixon and Haldeman agreed to obstruct the investigation by telling the FBI that the break-in was part of a Central Intelligence Agency operation.[38]

Nixon was insistent that his aides mask the cover-up by making it appear that the White House was fully cooperating with the ongoing investigation into the break-in. Nixon instructed them to "isolate the president and White House staff" from the scandal, and to achieve this, he sought a fall guy, someone who would take the blame and end the investigation. He settled on staffer Jeb Magruder to resign and accept full responsibility for the break-in at the Watergate complex.[39] On July 14, as Frank Carlucci was extolling the Nixon disaster relief measure and the president's virtues, the president was calculating how to mitigate his political disaster.[40]

The Watergate scandal proved to be a political disaster that grew in scale and scope until it overwhelmed the presidency in August 1974, after the Supreme Court ordered Nixon to make public copies of the tape recordings made in the Oval Office. Once revealed, these recordings made clear President Nixon's attempt to obstruct justice. On August 8, 1974, Nixon became the first president ever to resign from office. The Watergate scandal overtopped the protective wall Nixon had tried to build between the scandal and his presidency.

Congress Debates Relief

Having laid the public relations groundwork for his bill, Nixon sent the Agnes Recovery Act to Congress. Nixon told John Ehrlichman that once the Agnes bill passed Congress, the administration should "spend all the money fast."[41] The more resources he could infuse into New York and Pennsylvania, the more significant the influence he could have on the fall election. As it turned out, however, the Agnes Recovery Act did not sail through Congress without going through some troubled waters. Congress had been, almost without exception, controlled by the Democratic Party since 1933.[42] Moreover, many Democrats balked at passing an election-year bill that would help the incumbent Republican president. Thus it fell to the legislators from the stricken areas to overcome skepticism from their congressional colleagues.

Congressional skepticism of Nixon's disaster relief efforts had begun with his June request for $100 million in additional funds for the OEP. Senator Joseph Montoya (D-NM), chair of the Senate subcommittee with authority over disaster relief, objected to the request. Montoya wanted to delay action on the bill until he could hold hearings. "I didn't want Uncle Sam to be taken," he said about earlier cases in which fraudulent claims had led to federal money going to individuals who were ineligible for disaster assistance. Despite Montoya's opposition in June, the bill was not held up very long in committee, largely because of the pressure exerted on the committee by both the White House and Republican senators Hugh Scott and Richard Schweiker of Pennsylvania.[43]

The June request had only asked for millions of dollars in additional aid. The Agnes Relief Act of 1972 asked for billions of dollars in new funding, easily making it the most generous relief bill in American history to that time. This bill did not sail through the House or the Senate. The House Banking and Currency Committee received Nixon's bill on Monday, July 17, and Chair Wright Patman (D-TX) scheduled hearings for July 18 and 19. "It is my intention to hold hearings on a continuous basis with all the witnesses and then move into executive session to mark up the bill," Patman declared.[44]

Patman was no friend of Nixon. From the start of the Watergate scandal, Patman believed Nixon was directly involved but found this hard to prove, even after his committee traced the money found on the Watergate burglars to a bank account in Mexico and from there to the White House.[45] Patman was well aware that the Agnes Relief Act was a dressed-up political bill created to help the president's reelection bid. Unable to get at Nixon, he vented his ire on Thomas Kleppe, administrator for the SBA, who testified in favor of the bill. Patman was perturbed that the bill did not cover all disasters, past or future. "A disaster bill should not be used as a vehicle to pick and choose favorites," Patman told Kleppe. Kleppe, a former congressman from North Dakota, was well aware of Patman's temper and parried many of the chair's verbal thrusts by expressing no opinion whatsoever.[46]

Patman was not the only person irked by the bill. The Agnes Relief Act contained many provisions that the administration had rejected in earlier disaster bills, which angered William Barrett (D-PA). "What kind of games are you playing?" he asked Carlucci, who was on the Hill to testify in favor of Nixon's bill. Wisely, Carlucci did not reply.[47]

Criticism of the bill came not only from committee members who saw through the politics of the disaster bill but also from witnesses who were displeased that the bill did not go far enough to help flood victims. Shapp insisted that the flood victims should receive grants, not loans. He drew on the Marshall Plan to criticize government policy. "If the United States can afford to have given Germany and Japan almost $100 billion in pre-inflated dollars to rebuild their nations at the end of World War II, we cannot afford not to give our own hard-working citizens all the funds they need to rebuild their lives from this great disaster." Shapp also used his testimony to take a swipe at the Vietnam War. He called for a moratorium on war spending so the government could give that money to the citizens in the flooded regions. The governor suggested that spending money now was more logical than waiting for flood victims to become indigent due to their circumstances. "If we don't make this investment in making our people productive again, let's not kid ourselves, they will end up on welfare. The choice is clear: either we invest in the victims of the flood or we will pay for long years of dependency." To pay for natural disasters, Shapp, echoing Birch Bayh a few years earlier, asked Congress to create catastrophic insurance for all Americans to cover the cost of disaster and funded by a surcharge on every property insurance policy sold in the United States.[48]

Joseph McDade, a moderate Republican who represented Pennsylvania's Northern Tier in the House, echoed Shapp's sentiments. McDade compared the devastation in Pennsylvania to that caused by the atomic bombing of Nagasaki and Hiroshima and argued for generous government assistance. Congressman Daniel Flood compared the flood to the economic hardship caused by the Great Depression and recalled New Deal government programs that helped victims during that crisis. Representative James Hastings of New York described the devastation in the Chemung Valley and called for passage of the bill. Amory Houghton, Jr., soberly and vividly described the extent of the damage to Corning. Despite the emotional and intellectual appeals, Carlucci, speaking on behalf of the Nixon administration, rejected the idea of total equity for lost and damaged property, fearing the consequences would lead to a moral hazard, and explaining, "We think this would encourage people to build on a flood plain and ruin the federal flood program." He made it clear that Nixon would veto any legislation that included full equity.[49]

Some witnesses testified against the bill because they thought it was overly generous.[50] Walter Arader, the Republican secretary of commerce for Pennsylvania, testified against raising forgiveness over the existing $2,500, saying, "No one is looking for a handout."[51] Representative Barry Goldwater, Jr., a Republican congressman from California, opposed the $5,000 forgiveness. "If you increase the forgiveness to $5,000 for every victim of a natural disaster, it might bankrupt the federal government," warned Goldwater. "We cannot expect the federal government to pick up the tab for every private loss in every disaster." Goldwater wanted a market-based solution that would shift the risk and cost back to those living in areas of natural hazard. He believed that insurance policies should be purchased by homeowners and businesses when they obtained mortgages. Goldwater noted that this could be profitable for insurance companies. He dismissed the call for a mandatory national catastrophic insurance plan administered by the government, which had been made by senator Richard Schweiker and congressman Flood. "I have heard of suggestions that the Congress should pass a law requiring all Americans to carry disaster insurance. I would oppose this since it smacks of direct governmental intervention."[52]

The Senate was no more receptive to the bill than the House. The subcommittee on Small Business of the Committee on Banking, Housing, and Urban Affairs held hearings on Tuesday, July 18, under the direction of Senator John Sparkman (D-AL). Committee members Alan Cranston (D- CA) and John McIntyre (D-NH) expressed suspicion of the bill. They questioned Kleppe, who served as the administration's spokesperson, as to why the generous terms only applied to Hurricane Agnes. Congress, they reminded Kleppe, had already created a generous and uniform disaster relief system in the Disaster Act of 1970.[53] If the administration was going to be generous, why did they exclude the flood in Rapid City, South Dakota, which happened only a few weeks before Agnes? Kleppe suggested that Agnes was unique in that it was an extreme event that led to high unemployment in the six states affected, but neither Cranston nor McIntyre believed that this was a humanitarian gesture by the Nixon administration.

Cranston, noting that Maryland, New York, Pennsylvania, New Jersey, Delaware, and Virginia were included but not tiny South Dakota, sarcastically suggested that the administration was making a distinction between small and large disasters. "A big one is large enough to affect the Electoral College," he concluded.[54] The very next day, the White House informed Sparkman that the president had agreed to amend the bill to include South Dakota. In response, Sparkman expressed concern "over the increasing political overtones of these bills."[55] In the hearings he displayed a bit of sarcasm, asking, "It would be appreciated if the subcommittee could be informed as to exactly how many disasters the president ultimately intends to include!"[56]

Members of Congress were correct in smelling an "Electoral College rat" in the Nixon plan. When he decided to include South Dakota, the home state of Democratic presidential nominee George McGovern, Nixon instructed press secretary Ronald Zeigler to announce it so that "the story gets into South Dakota before McGovern."[57] Ehrlichman suggested that if Nixon "out McGoverned McGovern" by being generous, Nixon would win more votes in November.[58] At lunch on July 19, Ehrlichman and Nixon discussed ways to pressure Cranston into voting in favor of the legislation and decided that Senator Scott and Ehrlichman would go to Cranston directly and ask for his support. They also schemed about ways to get McGovern to repudiate Cranston for blocking the disaster relief bill. To gain Cranston's support, the administration amended the bill so that its benefits were retroactive to January 1, 1971, which meant the San Fernando, California, earthquake of 1971 would be included. White House aides believed that the California Democrat would not refuse benefits for his home state and their calculation proved to be true, as Cranston took the bait and voted for the bill.[59]

Despite the rough seas in committee, the bill went on to the Senate floor, where it faced a series of amendments. Richard Schweiker tried to amend the bill to increase forgiveness from $5,000 to $15,000 for individuals and up to $100,000 for businesses.[60] When that failed, he offered a last-minute amendment to increase forgiveness to $7,500. After this too failed, Schweiker argued that "if the damage from Hurricane Agnes had not been concentrated in Pennsylvania and been more spread out," his amendments would have passed.[61] Senator Ted Stevens (R) of Alaska tried unsuccessfully to make the benefits retroactive to 1964, the year an earthquake hit his home state, and Senator Robert Taft, Jr. (R-OH), tried to tie loan forgiveness to a person's ability to pay.[62]

The bill passed the Senate on August 4 by a vote of 76-2 and contained all the provisions Nixon had requested. The bill went to a House-Senate Conference Committee, which curtailed the benefits by making them retroactive only to January 1, 1972, and extending them to July 1, 1973, thus cutting Cranston's state out of the bill. It also restricted the application process by indicating that no application for disaster assistance could be made after the initial six months of a disaster declaration. The House took a roll-call vote on August 14, and the bill passed 360-1.[63]

When Nixon signed H.R. 16254 into law on August 20, 1972, Howard Robison, the astute congressman from Elmira, thought the president had missed a public relations opportunity by not holding a public signing ceremony. One White House aide, David Parker, had suggested that the president sign the bill into law in D.C. and then fly to Wilkes-Barre to announce it. Parker noted that signing the bill in Wilkes-Barre could provide the administration with excellent "network news coverage" and show "effective presidential leadership in forging a speedy legislative response to the domestic crisis."[64] However, Nixon rejected this idea, sufficiently happy to bask in the glow of good press and an appreciative audience, two things he had found in short supply earlier that month.[65]

"I HAVE A HUD-ACHE"
Public Discontent over Disaster Aid

Jack Gridley, chair of the Chemung County Board of Supervisors, was angry. He had survived the flood and then endured weeks without basic utilities; he had met with Spiro Agnew in June and found the vice president supportive of his ideas for assisting Elmira after the flood, and he had cheered the Agnes Recovery Act; but now, two months after Hurricane Agnes, he had had enough. The federal government was neither fast enough nor flexible enough for the situation in the Southern Tier. He wrote to President Nixon to complain of the green and arrogant officials from the Office of Emergency Preparedness (OEP), and of the arbitrary "by-the-book" attitude of the Army Corps of Engineers, which was all the worse, Gridley said, because the book "was obviously written during the Civil War."[1]

Howard W. Robison was the dean of congressional Republicans from New York and a perceptive observer of American politics. He understood Gridley's frustration and that of his constituents in Elmira. Robison, like many of his colleagues in the House, was the recipient of weekly letters from constituents who were "really angry." He believed that changes made by President Johnson had made Congress "totally subservient" to LBJ and robbed it of its ability and will to shape national policy. At the same time, Robison believed, the Great Society "had raised people's expectations too much." Overpromising and underdelivering led to citizen frustration and anger at the institutions of government, which "can't accomplish what a government ought to do."[2]

Citizen frustration with the slow speed of federal and state response to Hurricane Agnes became simmering anger among those left homeless and unemployed by the 1972 floods. As members of the executive branch worked on the

FIGURE 10. Vice President Spiro Agnew touring Elmira, New York, after the flood. Ahead of him is Thomas Casey, Office of Emergency Preparedness regional director for New York, who is carrying a briefing book. Courtesy of the Chemung County Historical Society.

details of the proposed $3.1 billion in aid and Congress scrutinized the legislation, many victims of the storm found that government regulations and rules prevented them from gaining access to the promised loans, repairs, or housing assistance. Anger mounted in New York and Pennsylvania, spilling out in a singular moment in Wilkes-Barre, Pennsylvania, when storm victims angrily confronted Housing and Urban Development (HUD) secretary George Romney with accusations of government failure in the wake of Agnes. This confrontation, which was reported nationwide by print and broadcast media, encapsulates the tension between government officials and disaster victims.

The disaster struck at a critical time in U.S. politics. Moreover, it has usually been the case that victims of floods have used the country's past achievements, such as the moon landing, or the rebuilding of Europe after World War II, as arguments to ask why the government has failed to do more for American citizens by rebuilding their stricken cities. The very success of these operations made people wonder why a competent government appeared unable to meet the needs of everyday Americans. Some came to believe it was because it did not want to. Some survivors of the disaster used the expense of the ongoing Vietnam War to question government priorities. Who, they wondered, was more important to the

U.S. government, the Vietnamese people, who were thousands of miles away, or the victims of a natural disaster in their own backyard? Governor Shapp often verbalized these frustrations, but others put these questions to government officials in letters and, when they could, in person. Public antipathy was on the rise in the early 1970s, driven in part by the government's promises and a myriad of generous programs it had created. Perhaps, as scholars suggest, this was due to the rise of the administrative state, which empowered administrators by stressing science, rationality, and bureaucracy as a means of delivering on government promises, which meant there must be regulations, paperwork, and a methodical process for delivering on, and sometimes denying, people's claims.[3]

Red Tape

Examining the myriad of delays in government assistance provides insight into how unmet expectations led to frustration and then hostility toward the government. Many of these delays were unavoidable. The Agnes Recovery Act did not become law until August 16, and until then, the Disaster Relief Act of 1970 guided government action. The OEP, which Congress cited for its dismal performance after Hurricane Camille in 1969, was in charge of coordinating the relief and recovery efforts for all the states involved, stretching north from Florida to New York. On paper, the OEP was empowered to organize and coordinate the work of all federal and state agencies involved in disaster assistance, such as the Small Business Administration, the U.S. Army Corps of Engineers, the Labor Department, and all the state disaster assistance programs, whose duties overlapped with those of the federal agencies and which had jurisdiction in implementing disaster assistance. The OEP could not merely appear on the scene and begin dispensing relief; it had to assess the property damage, process the paperwork, and then, if the property owner met the criteria, begin to coordinate relief activities with other state and federal agencies. This fragmented responsibility has been, and continues to be, an issue in delivering disaster assistance. In reality, the process has been impeded by the rivalry between government agencies and by employees unwilling or unable to take orders from other agencies.

Meanwhile, miscommunication between agencies and with the public added to the misery of the disaster victims in New York and Pennsylvania.[4] A textbook example of this miscommunication is demonstrated by the problems encountered by Francis X. Tobin, who was in charge of OEP operations in the state of Pennsylvania. Tobin, who was a career administrator, found the situation in Pennsylvania overwhelming and his attempts to implement federal policies stymied by the intransigence of state and local officials. "This is the worst I've ever seen," he asserted.[5]

In addition to the typical problems found in public administration, including the tension between career civil servants and executive appointees, disasters create new problems because emergency management agencies need to hire new employees to meet the demands of disaster recovery.[6] Moreover, not all those hired or working on contract for OEP are up to the task and this slows down the processing of paperwork required to secure government benefits. After Agnes struck, the federal government hired thousands of temporary employees to work in the disaster zones to process and review paperwork, assess damage, and perform other essential tasks. Daniel Flood, the Wilkes-Barre congressman, recalled after the flood, "two men walked in and stated to me that they were there from Washington and would begin a survey of the Wyoming Valley to determine temporary housing needs. . . . I did not see them for three days, and when they returned, covered with mud from head to toe, they were in a complete state of shock! The shock, which I saw in their eyes, was as great as that of the victims themselves."[7] The result of sending in teams of inexperienced personnel was confusion about what paperwork was needed, miscommunication about what benefits were available, and a logjam of paperwork. The ill-prepared agents of the government were often perceived by flood victims as part of the problem and not part of the solution.

The bureaucratic structure of the executive branch and civil servants were also targets of complaint. New York State assemblyman James Emery cited a local official who complained that the people from the OEP were "ill-prepared, untrained, bureaucratic, and slow to react."[8] Federal employees remained the primary target of discontent when applications were rejected or stalled by snafus. "The complaints most often heard are tardiness of government process."[9] Displaced persons lambasted HUD for failing to move trailers into disaster areas fast enough, and people awaiting checks to rebuild or repair their homes were angry with the SBA for the delay in loan approvals.[10]

Secretary Peter Peterson of the Commerce Department and labor secretary James Hodgson received a hostile reception from flood victims when they convened a meeting at the Treadway Inn in Wilkes-Barre, where they became the scapegoat for the failures of government policy. As the cabinet officials tried to explain that the federal government would supply loans but not grants, one man, who could no longer contain himself, yelled with his voice aquiver, "You've given billions of dollars to foreign countries but you're not doing anything for this country!" At this, the audience erupted in loud applause.[11] Individuals expressed their frustration after Hurricane Agnes, but this was part of growing public dissatisfaction with government and a belief that the rise of the bureaucratic state had given administrators more power than elected officials.[12]

The irony of this situation was that the federal response to Hurricane Agnes was more generous and more prompt than the federal response to any previous

disaster, yet it failed to impress those in the flood-ravaged states who saw government regulations as a catch-22. For example, the law required that local or
state governments pay for repairs up front and then receive reimbursement. The
mandate frustrated local officials, who had a narrow tax base to draw from and
limited ability to borrow money. Wellsville mayor Robert Gardner was among
those distressed by this situation because he lacked the money to pay for the work
in advance. Furthermore, preparing the requisite paperwork to get the reim-
bursements overwhelmed local officials. Gary Fraser, the part-time supervisor of
the town of Almond, New York, worked over forty hours a week to prepare the
applications required by federal agencies to repair public facilities.[13] OEP officials
tried to lessen this burden by using their experience in Hurricane Camille to
implement streamlined, "one-stop" federal centers for questions, paperwork, and
assistance, but even this system was the subject of complaints.

The people in the disaster-ravaged cities became convinced that President
Nixon was out of touch with the situation and feared that once the reporters left
the area, the federal officials would forget the victims. This belief was stoked by
Nixon's political nemesis, Governor Shapp. Shapp noted that Agnes was the
first disaster since the revisions included in the Disaster Act of 1970, which did
not take into account a disaster of the magnitude of Hurricane Agnes. "I hon-
estly don't think the president, at this moment, has a clear understanding of
the enormity of the damage here in Pennsylvania," Shapp told reporters. Nixon,
he complained, "came here; he flew over it; saw it, and went back to Washington." The Democratic governor went to the press with his complaints, and
although he praised the effort of Republican senators Scott and Schweiker, he
savaged the president. "There is a lack of understanding in Washington," he
told reporters.[14]

Perhaps reacting too hastily, Nixon supporters dismissed the governor's
complaints as political pandering. Republican Pennsylvania state senator R. Budd
Dwyer told the president, "Shapp is using the plight of Pennsylvania Flood victims
as a partisan political issue." Some of the president's aides claimed that Shapp
had a personal animus against Nixon, and in this they were correct. Shapp's antipathy for Nixon was real; he had even boasted that he was "one of the all-time
Nixon-haters."[15] However, dissatisfaction with the government was not confined
to Pennsylvania or even to the Democrats. "Get Congress off their butts to give us
help," said one New York Republican when Agnew visited the Southern Tier. As
days turned into weeks and weeks turned into months, residents felt abandoned
by government, "Eight months have passed. . . . We've worked hard to recover, but
our efforts have been futile," one fifty-two-year-old woman wrote to Vice President Agnew. "From all reports, Washington feels we are well on our way back to
being normal. There isn't anything further from the truth." Sounding discour-

aged, she asked the administration to assist her and her sixty-year-old husband. However, there is no indication that Vice President Agnew wrote her back.[16]

Congress Claims Credit

Despite assurances from the Nixon White House that help was on its way, those living in the flood-ravaged cities in New York and Pennsylvania felt that the federal government did not care about them. Many felt their only means of recourse was to turn to their elected congressional representatives, who controlled the budgets and had oversight over the agencies responsible for disaster relief.[17] Of all the representatives involved in working on behalf of their flooded constituents, none was as powerful as Daniel J. Flood. Under the seniority system in place in the early 1970s, Flood sat on the House Appropriations Committee, where he was the subcommittee chair of Labor, Health, Education and Welfare, and also served as vice chair of the Defense Appropriations subcommittee. Flood boasted that his combined roles resulted in "two-thirds of the budget" going through his hands,[18] and he used that power to assist the Wyoming Valley. Although his district had been the center of the anthracite coal industry, by the 1950s anthracite coal had declined and along with it, the Wyoming Valley. In response, Flood infused the region with new economic opportunity by sponsoring the Flood-Douglas Bill, which brought hundreds of millions of dollars in social welfare and redevelopment money to the district.

To keep the failing coal industry on life support, he steered a bill through Congress requiring that the U.S. Army heat its West German barracks with anthracite coal mined in his region. Although the army would have saved millions of dollars a year by converting to heating oil, the bill passed because Flood had clout with fellow members on the appropriations committee. Flood pushed through the Coal Mine Health and Safety Act in 1969 to assist victims of black lung disease, and the government benefits that came to the retired miners and their families once again revivified the economy. In addition to these multimillion-dollar programs, Flood dotted the Wyoming Valley with memorials to himself, including the Daniel Flood Elementary School, the Daniel Flood Industrial Park, the Daniel Flood Rural Health Care Center, and the Daniel Flood Elderly Care Center, all paid for by federal tax dollars.[19]

Due to his personality, position, and seniority, Flood influenced members from both political parties. The minority leader of the House, Gerald Ford (R-MI), whose improbable ascent to the White House was still two years away, recalled that Flood was "a man of his word" and that "he stood up for us on some tough votes."[20] After the disaster, Flood joined forces with Republican congressman

FIGURE 11.   Daniel J. Flood played a significant role in advocating for disaster victims and urging policy changes after the flood of 1972. Courtesy of the Hazleton *Standard Speaker*.

Joseph McDade, whose district included Scranton and the Northern Tier of Pennsylvania. Flood allied himself with Pennsylvania senators Scott and Schweiker, both of whom were Republicans, to advance the call for more aid to flood victims.[21]

Scott was at the pinnacle of power after a career in politics that began in 1926. He had been in Congress since 1941, and the summer that Hurricane Agnew wreaked havoc in Pennsylvania, he was almost seventy-two and still four years away from retirement. He cointroduced the Agnes Recovery Act in the Senate on July 17 and then shepherded it through the committee process, ensuring its passage in August. His fellow senator from Pennsylvania was Richard "Dick" Schweiker, the product of a middle-class Roman Catholic upbringing who was inspired by John F. Kennedy to enter politics. Schweiker first ran for the House in

1960, and two years later he sought and won a term in the U.S. Senate. Many people assumed his next move would be to the White House.[22] Although a Republican, Schweiker was highly rated by the Americans for Democratic Action, a liberal advocacy group. He opposed many of Nixon's policies, voted in favor of overriding all the president's vetoes, and opposed two of his Supreme Court nominees. Schweiker had also been one of the first Republicans to criticize Nixon over U.S. involvement in the Vietnam War. In turn, Nixon showed contempt for Schweiker, whom he included on his infamous "Enemies List."[23] It suited the president to use Schweiker in 1972 to introduce the Agnes Recovery Act in the Senate, but Nixon opposed the senator's ideas to liberalize disaster relief.

In sharp contrast to the role played by Pennsylvania congressmen, the U.S. senators from New York were relatively passive after the Agnes disaster. They cosponsored legislation and made a few speeches on behalf of flood victims, but they were mostly invisible to those living in the disaster areas. The senior Senator from New York, Jacob Javits, was a lifelong resident of New York City and a liberal Republican who was closely tied to Rockefeller. Javits was out of favor with Nixon because he opposed the war in Vietnam and had called for a repeal of the Gulf of Tonkin Resolution and a complete withdrawal of U.S. troops from Vietnam.[24] The junior senator from New York was James Buckley, brother of the well-known conservative William F. Buckley and the only person ever elected to the U.S. Senate on the Conservative Party line. Buckley's election was, in part, engineered by Agnew and the Nixon White House, and the senator reflected their philosophical opposition to expanding the federal role in disasters.[25]

James. L. Hastings (R-Olean) offered one explanation for the lackadaisical performance by Senate members. The congressional representative claimed that members of the Senate were more interested in the 1972 and 1976 elections than the Agnes disaster. "14 senators are running for President, 17 more think they should be, 10 others have tried, and the rest would settle for Vice President," he argued.[26] Hastings was born in 1926 and raised in Olean, New York. He served in the U.S. Navy during World War II and then returned to Olean, where he ran for a seat on the Alleghany Town Board while also working full time selling ads for WHDL radio and the *Olean Times Herald.* In the 1960s Hastings served two terms in the New York State Assembly and three terms in the New York State Senate. He was in his second term in the House of Representatives when Corning flooded. Hastings played a minor part in the unfolding drama but nonetheless sought credit for any federal assistance given to his constituents and was active in sending out press releases. According to a grass-roots organization that graded members of Congress, Hastings "was not a publicity hound, but his publicity office, headed by former Jamestown newspaperman Charles Pokrandt, grinds out at least one press release a day."[27] Hastings strongly believed in bringing home "the bacon" and sought credit for every bill that passed and every dollar that came into his district.[28]

Howard Robison's district included Broome, Tioga, and Chemung Counties. An affable man, Robison's ability to get along with a variety of people led to his first election to the House. When the two Southern Tier Republican factions became deadlocked in 1958, they turned to him as their compromise candidate. Once in Washington, the neophyte became enamored with the political process, so much so that he explained to reporters that he preferred staying in the capital, where he could get more work done, rather than spending time in his district politicking. He spent about seventy days a year back in New York, which was half as much as his colleague James Hastings. He served on the Public Works Sub-committee of the House Appropriations Committee as well the Republican Committee on Committees, which assigned fellow Republicans to committees. In the 1972 election he had been redistricted to another part of the state and was running as a relative newcomer, which made him furious, and he had talked, briefly, about leaving Congress at the end of 1972.[29]

Robison's private papers reveal that most of his work on behalf of constituents was done behind the scenes, as when he persuaded OEP representative Tom Casey to "bend the rules" at times in order to help the elderly and impoverished. Casey was so close to Robison that he confided in the congressional representative that his head was "on the chopping block" for ordering two hundred more trailers for the Southern Tier than requested, despite his reasoning that once the cold weather hit, many people would find that they could not live in their damaged homes.[30] Robison also tried to assist his constituents, especially farmers, by directing them to postdisaster assistance programs. He had spent his early years in the House on the Public Works Committee, where he formed close ties with the U.S. Army Corps of Engineers, and his influence in Congress and with the corps enabled him to fast-track the new dam complex.[31]

George Romney, Scapegoat

The people of Pennsylvania and New York found sympathy for their plight in their elected representatives in the House and Senate but felt little support from President Nixon. Nixon's public relations problem was compounded by his political nemesis, Governor Shapp, who blamed all government delays on the president. Making matters worse for Nixon was his journalistic nemesis, the syndicated newspaper columnist Jack Anderson. In 1972, Anderson was at the height of his career. His column appeared in over a thousand newspapers, and his progressive muckraking style won him the Pulitzer Prize for reporting.

Anderson launched a full-throated investigation into disaster relief, and his reportage highlighted government incompetence and corruption. He noted that bureaucrats had to hire Boeing management consultants to help deal with the volume of disaster assistance applications. He criticized bureaucrats who put temporary housing trailers where they were not needed and neglected the many people still left homeless. Anderson depicted the free legal aid offered to disaster victims as a boon for attorneys and a bane to victims. He mocked government contractors who were so inept that they tried running sewer lines uphill, with the predictable result that the sludge ran back into the houses. Anderson concluded that there was "utter chaos throughout the government's relief programs."[32] He also reported on fraud and claimed that a "dozen FBI agents" were investigating the problem. Indeed, millions of dollars of aid were diverted into private pockets or misused, or simply disappeared. Anderson's columns proved to be a political embarrassment to public officials and a black eye for Nixon's reelection campaign.[33]

Anderson represented something new in American presidential politics. For many years journalists had acted more as lapdogs than watchdogs of the presidency. Fearing they would lose access to presidents from Franklin Roosevelt to John F. Kennedy, journalists had been reluctant to attack presidents directly and had kept many presidential peccadilloes from the public. Journalists became more skeptical of the chief executive during the Vietnam War, however, and their skepticism threatened to veer into outright hostility after the election of Nixon in 1968. Nixon, who loathed the press, responded with venom and dirty tricks.[34] Anderson was both loathed and feared by the White House. Nixon hated Anderson and tried to discredit him by spreading a rumor that he was gay, which in the year 1972 would have made the journalist persona non grata with the public.[35] Nixon also ordered the Central Intelligence Agency (CIA) to investigate Anderson and more than once expressed his desire to have someone kill the nettlesome columnist.[36]

The perception of federal mismanagement created by Anderson's articles added to Nixon's woes.[37] Obsessed with his reelection bid, Nixon fretted that lousy press would hurt him in November. The weekend of August 5 and 6 was a public relations disaster for the administration, which was panned by the press and excoriated on Sunday morning news shows. The UPI news agency claimed that flood victims had a new enemy, "their rescuers," especially the "sluggish, unresponsive and often rude HUD bureaucracy." After reading the UPI story, President Nixon told Ehrlichman to "note the HUD parts."[38] The president's concern deepened after he received a letter from Frank J. O'Connell, a Republican leader from Luzerne County, Pennsylvania. O'Connell said that while HUD was singled out for criticism in the press, the people were turning against Nixon. "There is a tremendous amount of criticism about the fact that the President has not seen fit to pay us a visit," O'Connell wrote.[39] In response to this letter, Nixon took swift action.

On the morning of August 7, Nixon invited Carlucci, the deputy director of the OMB, to his morning meeting with Ehrlichman and Haldeman. The men had a frank discussion about Hurricane Agnes and "citizen frustration."[40] The administration sought out Carlucci for two reasons. He had crafted the Agnes Recovery Act earlier that summer, and more important, he had been born and bred in Scranton and maintained close ties there and in Wilkes-Barre. Following the meeting, the White House issued a "sharply worded" memo ordering Romney to Wilkes-Barre to assess the situation. Then he was to take charge and "stop bureaucratic haggling from interfering with flood relief." Nixon demanded a written report within three days, outlining the steps Romney would take to assist flood victims.[41] The announcement was given to the press before Romney received it. The memo, which stated that the president was *ordering* Secretary Romney to the scene, underscored how little use Nixon had for his cabinet member.

The antipathy between HUD Secretary Romney and President Nixon was evident before summer of 1972.[42] Romney was a successful businessman credited with the near-miraculous turnaround of the failing American Motors Company. He used his fame and business acumen to win election to two terms as Michigan's governor. Politics ran in the family.[43] John F. Kennedy's breaking of the religious barrier opened up the possibility that a Mormon, such as Romney, could also run and win the White House.[44] In the early 1960s, Romney was considered to be a viable candidate for the White House, but Goldwater's nomination in 1964 blocked his progress. Romney's own inept words on the campaign trail in 1968 ended his chance for the nomination that year.[45]

After Romney's presidential ambitions were dashed, he accepted an invitation to serve as HUD secretary in Nixon's cabinet, where he was meant to represent the liberal Republican faction of the GOP. Once in the cabinet, the former governor was frustrated by an inability to get things done, and he irked Nixon, who was actively working to dismantle HUD by reducing its budget and impounding its funds. Romney publicly advocated for additional programs and sought to have HUD tackle issues such as housing discrimination and suburbanization.[46] He further agitated Nixon by holding meetings with other cabinet members, which Nixon saw as a "cabinet cabal."[47] In public, Romney vented to the press about the low priority the Nixon White House gave HUD, and he expressed dismay about the "palace guard" that Nixon had erected to keep cabinet officials away from the president.[48] Privately he complained to Ehrlichman that he felt frozen out.[49]

Romney was correct to sense that President Nixon did not favor him. "In Nixon's eyes Romney was moderate, an ally of Nelson Rockefeller and a loser," recalled Ehrlichman.[50] Nixon had determined to fire Romney after the election.[51]

The president had little use for Romney, who was a member of the so-called outer cabinet, in reference to cabinet officials whose positions are subject to pressure from outside interest groups, members of Congress, and career bureaucrats within their own department. This pressure can put cabinet secretaries at odds with the president who appointed them. Presidents and their staff often keep members of the outside cabinet isolated from the executive office, and such was the case with Romney.[52]

Although Nixon disdained Romney, he needed HUD to carry out disaster relief and recovery. Following a disaster, the agency was responsible for all temporary housing and the entire rebuilding effort. Whether Nixon liked it or not, Secretary Romney was at center stage in assisting Corning, Elmira, and Wilkes-Barre, where the need for temporary and permanent housing was great. People complained that the thicket of red tape and the morass of paperwork made it too difficult to obtain what the government had promised them: public housing, temporary shelter, and loans to rebuild their homes and businesses. In the Corning area, 2,100 families had signed up for temporary housing, but only 159 families were actually in assigned housing six weeks after the flood.[53] In the Wyoming Valley of Pennsylvania, 12,000 families applied for housing after the flood and the government approved 9,000 of them, but only 903 families had received their trailers by the end of July.[54] Although the river mud had turned into dust and blown away, the citizens were in a new morass created by the bureaucracy. Senator Schweiker complained that federal efforts were "bogged down in red tape and bureaucratic lethargy," and he called on Nixon to assign a flood czar to coordinate the efforts.[55]

Romney's wife, Lenore, was upset by the treatment her husband was receiving. On August 8, while Romney was in Wilkes-Barre, Lenore sent a letter to Ehrlichman expressing dismay at the lack of loyalty Nixon had shown to the Romney family. She reminded the president's top adviser that under White House prodding, she had run for the U.S. Senate in Michigan in 1970. Furthermore, she indicated that even though Nixon repeatedly denied requests for more assistance and funding for HUD, her husband remained loyal.[56] What Lenore failed to understand was that Nixon wanted to humiliate Romney. Her letter did not endear her or her husband to the inner circle. On the contrary, after receiving the letter, Nixon was more determined than ever to fire Romney, moving the timetable up from after the election to after the Republican National Convention.[57]

While Lenore Romney stewed and Nixon simmered, events in Wilkes-Barre boiled over. Angry at the government for failing to make good on their promises to care for the victims of Hurricane Agnes, a former union activist for the International Ladies Garment Workers Union (ILGWU), Min Matheson, organized the Flood Victims Action Council (FVAC). The FVAC was a more militant group than the Flood Recovery Task Force (FRTF), which was headed by Judge Rosenn.

Rosenn's group was the more pragmatic of the two and consisted of bankers and businesspeople. In stark contrast, the FVAC was driven by ideology, and its members represented the working class.[58] Having been raised in a union household, Matheson believed she was, according to one historian, "born to organize."[59]

Matheson's father, Max Lurye, was a Russian Jewish immigrant who helped form the cigar worker's union in Chicago. In 1928, at the age of nineteen, she met and married union activist Bill Matheson. She became a full-fledged union organizer in her own right in 1941 when she began working for the ILGWU. Her work took her to Wilkes-Barre from 1945 to 1963, and then to New York City until 1972, when she retired and returned to the valley to live near her daughter and grandchildren. Matheson had barely settled into her new home in Kingston when it flooded. She and her daughter were left homeless and forced to live in a motel room, awaiting housing.

At sixty-three, Matheson looked much younger than her age. Her hair, which was without even a speck of gray, was cut short, and her energy level was high. Her personality, one person suggested, was a "cross between a Madonna and a shrew."[60] In her eyes, the federal government represented the "big guy" who was pushing around the "little guy," and President Nixon personified this problem. By early August, she had already established a reputation among flood survivors and government officials. "They hated to see us coming," she said, referring to federal, state, and local officials. By the time Romney arrived in Wilkes-Barre, Matheson was spoiling for a fight.[61]

Romney arrived in Wilkes-Barre on the evening of August 7. He attended a brief reception and then retired to the Scranton Hilton Inn. When he awoke the next day, he practiced one of his daily rituals, chasing a golf ball around the room as a form of exercise.[62] He dressed in one of his stylish suits, tailored to fit his tall frame, and capped it off with a wide tie, in preparation for his all-day tour of the Wyoming Valley.

Romney planned to meet selected victims and community leaders, including members of the Wilkes-Barre Chamber of Commerce and the FRTF.[63] Afterwards, he praised local leaders for their cooperation but neglected to say how unwelcome he was that Tuesday. During his visit to Kingston, he was met by angry housewives who shouted, "Where's our trailer!" "Why don't you get out of your car and look! Look at the inside of our homes; that's where the dirt is!" Romney also encountered a local man named Charles Vivian, who also expressed his outrage. Vivian complained that the government was more interested in Vietnam than the American people. "If this disaster were handled like the war, you bet I'd have my trailer." The bitter feeling toward government policy was echoed by Mrs. Michael Zajac, who complained that the government had spent billions on foreign aid, but "now you can't take care of us."[64]

Finished with his tour on Wednesday, August 9, Romney met with officials and held a scheduled press conference. For an hour and a half, he heard from local officials who urged the government to pay the full cost of replacing the flood-damaged property. Romney rejected this request as impossible and made Governor Shapp agree not to mention this issue to the press. When the two men emerged from their meeting, however, they found themselves confronted by Matheson's group and surrounded by the press. Matheson and twenty-five supporters were waiting for Romney and holding up signs declaring, "I have a HUD-ache!" and "Agnes took everything but our mortgages!" Angry and tired of living in the dirt and the dark without adequate plumbing, these women had had enough of government delays and excessive spending on foreign wars.[65]

One of Romney's aides noticed the protestors and told them to leave or he would have them arrested.[66] As the press conference began, some women screamed, some cried, and others silently held up signs.[67] Unsettled by the protests, Romney seemed rattled when Shapp reneged on his promise not to raise the issue of full equity and, perhaps playing to the crowd, called on the government to pay complete restitution to the flood victims. The governor noted that the government rushed money to aid Germany and Japan after World War II and bailed out Lockheed in 1970 and Penn Central in 1971.[68] Romney responded by chiding Shapp for suggesting proposals that were "unrealistic and demagogic," and explained, "I do not believe the government should assume complete responsibility for people. We must recognize that people have a responsibility too. It's going to take a combination of federal, state, local and private efforts to resolve the entire situation. The principal effort is going to have to be private." He acknowledged that the government had a role to play, but only a supportive role.[69]

Matheson, whose political commitments were the polar opposite of the Romney's, angrily shoved a picture of what remained of her daughter's house to him, shrieking, "You don't give a damn whether we live or die!" In the background, others were also shouting, "Come over to my place. There are rats all over!" and "Why can't you help us?"[70] When Romney told Matheson he would meet with her after the press conference, she shouted out, "Yeah, that's great. That's after everything has already been decided." Romney, now ignoring the press, his face tightening and his adrenaline pumping, turned on her and asked, "Are you saying you don't want the government to do anything? You want the government to pull out?" "No," said Matheson bitterly, "I don't want the government to pull out. I just want them to do a good job." Romney pointed his finger directly at Matheson, shaking and sputtering in anger. He spat out the words, "Now you listen. You listen. You are wrong. You are wrong!" Matheson would not be quieted, "Why did you come and meet with officials? They haven't done anything! They ran away and never seen flood damage. Why not meet the people?"[71] Attempting to calm both himself and the situation, Romney replied in a more polite tone, "I can understand your distress," and added that the "government has done more here in six weeks than in six months in past disasters."[72]

Shapp had been standing on the sidelines with his head down and his thoughts to himself when Romney walked over and put his arm around him. "The governor has made a very political statement here when he talks about full equity for everybody. . . . I think it's deplorable for the governor to get into a political talk." If Romney had hoped that this would quiet the crowd, he was mistaken, as it had the opposite effect. The women began shouting again and chanting, "Romney go home and get Nixon!" His face red with anger and his body shaking, his voice dripping with venom, Romney shouted back, "Politicians who build up false expectations set the case of what can be done back a hundred years!" At this point, Shapp snapped back, "My philosophical belief is that when people have suffered in this way, there is no reason why the Federal Government cannot come in and do more than what has been done!"[73]

This volatile confrontation exposed the fault line of disaster policy in the United States. Many citizens failed to understand why the federal government failed to take a more active role in disaster policy. The citizens affected by the disaster rejected the orthodox interpretation of the Constitution, which placed the responsibility for public health and safety on state and local governments. Instead, storm victims looked to the federal government to take responsibility for restoring citizens and communities to their predisaster condition. By doing this, they were demonstrating a new rights consciousness.[74] This consciousness is most evident in numerous letters to the president and vice president, state governors, members of Congress, local officials, and newspapers. The letters contain a range of arguments that declared it was wrong for the U.S. government to spend American tax dollars on foreign aid, foreign wars, or a moon mission while ignoring the plight of disaster victims.[75]

After nearly an hour, the press conference wound down. Romney wished to forget the whole incident, which he believed was a frame-up by Shapp and Matheson, whom Romney called "a professional agitator." However, Romney was forced to relive the experience the next day when headlines across the United States featured accounts of the confrontation, including photographs of the tall, imposing Romney and the shorter Matheson clashing. Romney became emblematic of a bullying patriarch, and Matheson of the smaller and defenseless victim of government disregard. The situation was untenable for Nixon. The story made the front page of most major newspapers, and it was the lead story on most of the television and radio networks.[76] Howard K. Smith of ABC TV opened his story by calling the event "Hurricane Romney." Public censure of the administration increased, and dozens of people wrote to Romney in disgust about an administration that would spend hundreds of thousands of dollars bombing Vietnam but would not spend it on U.S. citizens.[77] The incident was a public relations problem for Nixon, and it was the final straw in ending Romney's political career.

Instead of quelling public discontent, Romney had fueled it. Still, his actions drew fire from the White House and placed it squarely on the shoulders of the HUD secretary. In this way, Romney played the classic role of a presidential lightning rod, someone whom the president uses to cover up ineptitude and who rescues the president from blame. These human lightning rods usually run outer cabinet departments such as HUD. Thus, Romney became the visible embodiment of the failed disaster relief program while Nixon avoided the blame.[78]

On August 10, Nixon, Ehrlichman, and Haldeman met and mapped out the agenda for a scheduled meeting with Romney. When the secretary of HUD arrived for lunch on August 11, Romney brought with him a letter of resignation. In between eating his usual lunch consisting of cottage cheese and ketchup, Nixon handed the letter of resignation to Ehrlichman and told his advisor to keep quiet until the news was "leaked" to the press. Romney argued his case. He claimed that Shapp had set him up in concert with "that garment lady" and the "UPI gal," who colluded to create false expectations and agitate the crowd.[79] It made no difference. By the time lunch was over, so was Romney's career. Romney remained in office until the end of the year, but he was only marking time.

Just before Christmas of 1972, George Romney cleared out his Washington office in preparation for leaving the administration. For the rest of his life, Romney remained active in volunteer work and service to the Church of Latter Day Saints, but he never again served in government.[80] Matheson returned to private life and died in Wilkes-Barre in 1992, where residents honored her with a bust on Public Square. Her counterpart on the FRTF, Max Rosenn, returned to the federal bench.

Nixon Triumphant

Firing Romney was done in part to make him a scapegoat for the failures illuminated by the press, but it was also one of the few actions Nixon could take in response to his sense of frustration with the situation in Wilkes-Barre. Romney was an appointed executive who owed his position to the president, whereas most of the individuals who worked for HUD were civil servants and were beyond the reach of the president or Congress. Nixon had no power over state officials or state laws that slowed the process of setting up temporary housing and trailers.

What he could do, however, was to exercise the power of rhetoric and create a new public image for his administration.[81]

Nixon and his advisers decided that the assistant director of OMB, Carlucci, would go to Wilkes-Barre and, like the disaster victims themselves, "live in a trailer."[82] Nixon told Carlucci to launch an "intensive PR program" because he needed to "give the people spirit."[83] Carlucci left the meeting and went directly to Wilkes-Barre. The press heralded his decision to live in a trailer in Kingston. Assisting Carlucci in Wilkes-Barre was George Grace, the assistant director of Disaster Programs for OEP and a veteran of the government response to Hurricane Camille. Carlucci's mission was to work closely with flood victims, combine public and private efforts, and "steer clear of politics." Carlucci promised residents he would stay for "as long as it takes to get the job done." Politically, this meant until after the election in November. Carlucci won the trust of the local people. At one meeting, he received a standing ovation.[84]

Not everyone was impressed. however. Anderson continued his attack on Nixon by focusing his venom on Nixon's man in the Wyoming Valley, Carlucci. In mocking terms, he described how Carlucci "blew in from Washington and quickly rounded up ten government press agents." Anderson said that Carlucci directed a high-powered public relations operation focused on portraying Carlucci as a modern-day Moses who had come to part the red tape.[85] Anderson accused Carlucci of creating bureaucratic havoc, of playing favorites, and of using the Wyoming Valley only as an election ploy to assist in reelecting the president.[86]

Carlucci was not the only one to make a triumphal visit to Wilkes-Barre. On August 21, while Republicans were renominating Nixon in Miami Beach, the Democratic presidential nominee, George McGovern, toured Wilkes-Barre. McGovern met with locals such as Aloysius Teufel, who bitterly recalled the "ass [Romney]" with "his tie and his shined shoes,"[87] and Vincent Goulstone who complained about the waste of American resources in Vietnam and the lack of government concern for flood victims. "We do not count," another resident bitterly complained. After his visit, McGovern, who was running on an anti–Vietnam War platform, met three hundred supporters at the Sterling Hotel, where he decried the waste of resources in Vietnam, arguing, "Instead of bombing the dikes in Haiphong, let's rebuild the dikes here." McGovern opened up storefront McGovern Disaster Relief Centers, and McGovern campaign offices across Pennsylvania, where he collected donated items for the people of the Wyoming Valley. Matching his deeds with words, McGovern issued a report on his visit and called for a strong federal presence in disaster policy, including a federal disaster insurance program to cover the losses of ordinary Americans. He called the federal response to Agnes "inadequate, inefficient, and insensitive."

McGovern challenged Nixon to explain why he could bail out the incompetent executives of Lockheed and provide disaster insurance for the mismanaged Pennsylvania Railroad, "but when the ordinary family is wiped out by a disaster for which they bear no responsibility, we tell them that they must make it on their own!"[88]

McGovern's well-publicized visit only highlighted Nixon's decision not to visit Wilkes-Barre after the flood. In the words of one adviser, they "goofed" by having the president visit Harrisburg but not Wilkes-Barre. Although there had been a discussion about a presidential visit to Wilkes-Barre in August, the inner circle was happy that it was Romney, not Nixon, who had been the target of citizen unrest. The McGovern visit rattled Nixon.[89] It was now imperative that Nixon go. On Saturday, September 9, at his Camp David retreat, Nixon scheduled a meeting with Carlucci on progress in the Wyoming Valley. Carlucci told the president how after a month, many people were now expressing pleasure with the support the government was giving them. To capitalize on these efforts, Ehrlichman and Carlucci convinced Nixon to make the trip to Wilkes-Barre. The aides laid out their carefully preplanned itinerary and reassured the president that Governor Shapp would not be around due to the Rosh Hashanah holiday. Nixon enthusiastically agreed to go.[90]

Nixon, who has been caricatured by the likes of actor Dan Aykroyd of *Saturday Night Live* and political cartoonist Pat Oliphant of the *Washington Post* as an uptight, shifty, and nervous person, was quite the opposite when playing for a crowd. He was at his best when he visited Wilkes-Barre. He brought a giant-sized check for $4 million to aid Wilkes College and ceremoniously handed the check to the college president, Francis Michelini. Nixon told him it was "from all the people of the United States."[91] Nixon visited many of the same areas as his rival, McGovern, but without an advance team and entourage, Nixon was free to roam around the Wyoming Valley. When the president saw Frank Vivian sitting outside his ramshackle house drinking a beer, Nixon stopped to chat. After shaking hands with Vivian, Nixon briefly inspected the damage and ordered the immediate delivery of a trailer to Vivian's family. As he made stop after stop, the president amazed the citizens, who had had no warning of his visit. When he learned that a community picnic aimed at boosting the morale of residents was short on refreshments, Nixon ordered his staff to supply hot dogs and sodas for the festivities. Finally, the president surprised a young couple as they emerged from their wedding ceremony in Forty Fort and made sure that a photo of that visit appeared in many newspapers the next morning. As he left, Nixon promised that Wilkes-Barre would come back, "better than ever!" Nixon was not merely feigning enthusiasm. The visit had energized him and dissipated much of the hostility that Wilkes-Barre had felt toward his administration.

FIGURE 12.   President Richard Nixon tours Wilkes-Barre on September 9, 1972. Flood czar Frank Carlucci is in the right foreground of the photo. Courtesy of the Army Corps of Engineers.

As one woman wrote to Representative Joseph McDade, "I have been a Democrat all my life, but I will forget it a while and give Mr. Nixon a vote." Before Nixon's visit, she felt lost and alone and too old to start over, but the concern expressed by the president and the fact that he "signed a bill to get me enough to rebuild" had made all the difference.[92] On hearing of the visit, Governor Shapp expressed concern that the Republicans would go on to win the state legislature on Nixon's coattails,[93] and his assessment was correct. Nixon won Pennsylvania in November, beating McGovern by nearly a million popular votes and winning every county except one. Statewide, the Republicans gained control of the Assembly and maintained the status quo in the state senate.[94] Nixon won every state but Massachusetts and the District of Columbia, including rival McGovern's home state of South Dakota.[95]

In December 1972, at his farewell press conference, Frank Carlucci, the Pennsylvania flood czar, promised, "Even though I am leaving, the federal flood recovery program will continue here."[96] However, once he was reelected, Nixon moved away from the generous relief programs he had enacted. Almost immediately he announced his conviction that the U.S. government was too generous and permissive, leading its citizens to become dependent and weak. "This country has too much on its plate in the way of huge spending programs, social programs and throwing dollars at problems," he told Garnett Horner of the *Washington Star*. Instead, he promised "a new feeling of responsibility, a new feeling of self-discipline."[97] Few of the flood victims read Nixon's statements with any sense of foreboding, but they would come to realize that the Richard Nixon who emerged victorious in the 1972 election had a markedly different attitude than the one who sought their votes before November 7, 1972.

6

"BETTER THAN EVER"?
Rebuilding amid Industrial Decline

Upon signing the Agnes Recovery Act into law on August 20, 1972, Richard Nixon declared, "With everyone working together—with the determined spirit of the people, leadership from state and local government, and effective use of federal programs now provided by the Congress—I am convinced that the hard-hit communities can be brought back better than ever."[1] "Better than ever" became the hallmark of plans to redevelop Corning, Elmira, and Wilkes-Barre. Wilkes-Barre received $127 million from the federal government and launched a rebuilding campaign with the slogan, "The Valley with a Heart, Coming Back Better Than Ever."[2] Corning received $30 million and launched two projects, Urban Renewal Plan 1 and the Market Street Restoration. Elmira's "The New Elmira Plan" used $72 million in federal money to revitalize the downtown area. Even smaller communities such as Painted Post, New York, received funding from the government, which they used to launch a "Comeback '72" urban renewal program.[3]

While political leaders touted community spirit, individuals within these cities found themselves worse off than before the flood. To rebuild their homes and businesses, people took out loans through the Small Business Administration program at 1 percent interest. Initially welcomed after the flood, these loans caused many people to fall into long-term debt on property they had already purchased.[4] Moreover, this burden lasted for decades. One resident was just three years away from paying off her mortgage until the flood forced her to take on a second mortgage, leaving her deep in debt. "We'll never live long enough to pay this off,"

FIGURE 13. Corning, New York, June 23, 1972. Corning, with the help of Corning Glass Works, shown in the center of the photo, was successfully rebuilt after the flood. Collection of the Rakow Library, the Corning Museum of Glass, Corning, New York. Original photograph loaned by Corning, Inc., Corning, New York.

she lamented in 1982.[5] Another resident, who was sixty years old at the time of the flood, pointed out that in 1972 she had owed $5,000 on her new home, but to rebuild she had added a second mortgage of $39,000. The combined mortgage of $44,000 indebted her until age ninety.[6] According to one resident of Elmira, who served in the New York State Senate, the loans saddled the inhabitants of the communities in New York and Pennsylvania with burdensome mortgages funded by outside banks, which contributed little to the local economy.[7]

An Era of Corruption

While some people struggled, others enriched themselves. The influx of federal and state money available to local governments proved too strong a temptation for corrupt officials. In the Wyoming Valley of Pennsylvania, a handful of elected officials were charged, indicted, and found guilty of taking bribes and kickbacks from local contractors in return for issuing them favorable contracts. Joseph Piazza, chairman of the Swoyersville Borough Council, was sent to prison for taking kickbacks of $67,500 from a local contractor. The former chairman of the Hanover Township Board received two years' probation after a conviction for extorting money from a contractor. In Edwardsville, four city council members pled guilty to taking kickbacks from a contractor whom they had recommended to the Luzerne County Redevelopment Authority.[8]

The Watergate era featured many investigations into public corruption, some of which ended the career of some powerful politicians. In October 1973, Vice President Agnew resigned from office after pleading "nolo contendere" to failing to pay taxes on money he received going back to his early career as a Maryland county executive and then governor. Agnew retired from politics and returned to Maryland, where he died in 1996.[9] Political corruption also ended the career of representative James F. Hastings (R-Olean), who abruptly resigned his congressional seat in December 1975, just before federal prosecutors indicted him on charges of graft and corruption. After being tried, convicted, and sentenced, Hastings served fourteen months in a federal prison before returning to the private sector and moving to Florida.[10] Hastings returned to western New York in 1998 and died there in 2014.[11]

The ability to influence the allocation of federal contracts also led Wilkes-Barre's most potent congressional representative astray. Charges of graft and corruption against Daniel Flood first surfaced in 1975. The most persuasive evidence against him came from testimony offered by his assistant, Steven Elko. Elko claimed that in exchange for bribe money, Flood gave companies favorable treatment and enhanced access to government contracts. At the height of the Agnes disaster, Elko told prosecutors, Flood extorted bribes while stationed at the makeshift emergency command post in Avoca and had allegedly promised a government contract to the prefabricated home manufacturer Sterling-Homex in exchange for cash.[12] Federal agents insisted that Flood received as much as $65,000 in bribes during his tenure in office, although they never found the money. Following these revelations, the House censured Flood and canceled all his committee assignments. Federal indictments kept him in and out of court from 1978 until 1980, when he accepted a plea deal and resigned from Congress. Flood returned to Wilkes-Barre a broken man and died there in 1994.[13]

To the people of the Wyoming Valley, Flood remains a hero, and they have honored him by naming schools, streets, and parks after him. A memorial for Flood sits on the rebuilt Public Square and lists all the ways in which he helped the community. It briefly mentions that Flood resigned from Congress amid controversy but omits the fact that the controversy stemmed from charges that he used the Agnes crisis as an opportunity to extort bribes from would-be contractors.[14]

Era of Deindustrialized

In addition to inspiring public corruption, the Agnes Recovery Act benefited the most influential members of the community at the expense of ordinary citizens. Members of the local business community oversaw redevelopment in Corning, Elmira, and Wilkes-Barre, and in nearly every case, their interests overshadowed the ideas and input of other members of the community. Ironically, outside interests benefited the most from the generous government grants and loans provided by the federal government in a classic case of what scholars call disaster capitalism. Compounding the tragedy for the residents of Susquehanna River Basin was the steady erosion of the economic foundation of their cities by the forces of deindustrialization. Despite the best efforts at full recovery promised by politicians, redevelopment efforts could not make these cities better than ever.[15]

The post-Agnes reconstruction of Corning, Elmira, and Wilkes-Barre occurred in the era of deindustrialization, a period of widespread, systemic disinvestment and decline of the manufacturing sector of the U.S. economy and the export of these industries and jobs abroad. Even before the flood, the northeastern United States had already evinced symptoms of economic decline. Economic growth in the 1960s had boasted a healthy average of over 4 percent per year, but after 1970 it grew at an anemic pace of 2.9 percent, with most growth in the earliest years of that decade. Throughout the 1970s industrial output fell, and U.S. exports declined from 25 percent of the global total of exports to only 17 percent.[16]

Many factors explain this decline. Global competition and cheaper labor costs abroad made the United States less competitive. Technological innovation and automation in plants overseas made these plants more efficient than their counterparts in the United States. American manufacturers complained that they had less ability to invest in labor-saving technology or improved manufacturing because organized labor restrained profits for unionized companies. In the face of global competition, American manufacturers began a massive wave of layoffs, especially in metals-based industries such as steel production, automobile manufacturing, automotive parts production, and mining. Some American companies closed and others relocated their production facilities to cheaper labor markets in Mexico, Taiwan, Singapore, or Korea. U.S. tax laws at that time also discouraged capital investment in manufacturing, so instead 1investors moved into the financial services sector, which spawned the rise of the highly profitable merger and acquisitions culture that dominated in the 1980s. This led to mergers of U.S. companies, which in turn often led to more layoffs.[17]

These vast economic changes formed the backdrop of efforts by local officials and members of the private sector in Corning, Elmira, and Wilkes-Barre who hoped their post-flood rebuilding efforts would stave off economic decline. Revitalization efforts included plans to retain or increase manufacturing jobs, become a center for research and development, or restructure for the tourism industry. Unlike planners at the time, scholars now see how vital the presence of a large college or university is in providing resources and human capital for economic revitalization. This was the case for Boston, Philadelphia, and other cities. In upstate New York, the decline of firms such as Eastman Kodak, Bausch and Lomb, and Xerox threatened Rochester's vitality. However, the expansion of research and development and medical facilities run by the University of Rochester eventually filled the vacuum created by these job losses. Despite the presence of a community college in Corning, a liberal arts college in Elmira, and several colleges in Wilkes-Barre, none of these cities had the capacity to become an incubator of large-scale economic transformation.[18]

Of the three cities under consideration, only Wilkes-Barre had substantive experience with economic decline and revitalization. The collapse of the anthracite coal industry after World War I devastated the region, and by 1950 Wilkes-Barre had high unemployment, urban blight, and an aging population dependent on government programs such as social security and payments from the black-lung insurance program. Responding to the crisis, elected officials and businesspeople collaborated to open the Crestwood Industrial Park in 1958. Crestwood successfully lured companies such as the Eberhard Faber pencil company to Wilkes-Barre and induced companies such as RCA to build new operations there. Before the flood, the industrial park employed over thirteen thousand people, which offset the blow caused by jobs losses in the mining industry and kept unemployment in the region to around 6 percent. Wilkes-Barre's economic turnaround came to an abrupt end, however, with the 1972 flood, which destroyed every business in the downtown area and disrupted manufacturing across the region.[19]

After Hurricane Agnes, the Wilkes-Barre Industrial Development Authority (IDA) became a key player in plans to restore the economy as it secured low-interest loans for long-term projects. Under Pennsylvania law, lenders earned tax-free interest on any IDA-approved loans, which encouraged lenders to offer competitive loan rates with longer repayment schedules. Loan recipients were pleased because they could borrow money at a lower interest rate and extend their term of repayment for decades. However, this arrangement mostly benefited out-of-state commercial lenders, who did not invest their profits in the local economy.

The IDA drew its leadership from the commercial and construction industries in the area. It showed a decided preference for funding existing businesses rather than new enterprises, and it failed to attract large-scale industries to the region.[20] One of the projects it funded attempted to replicate the success of Crestwood Park. The IDA loan program created the Hanover Industrial Park, but unlike its predecessor, the project did little to revitalize the area. The construction industry benefited when urban renewal money helped replace the twenty-seven buildings on Public Square with a new hotel and three office towers featuring retail space on the bottom floor. However, other projects that were built following the flood, such as the cross-country expressway, may have hurt the city by accelerating suburbanization, and overall, these projects did not supply long-term employment opportunities for residents. As one astute observer wrote at that time, "one cannot help but conclude that in many ways Hurricane Agnes was a businessperson's windfall."[21]

On the tenth anniversary of Agnes, people in Wilkes-Barre were pleased with how the city had rebounded. In 1982, a member of the Redevelopment Authority said that the flood had been "a blessing to the city." Larry Newman of the Greater Wilkes-Barre Chamber of Commerce and Industry said that the downtown area was "absolutely vibrant" due to "the improvements that were made after the 1972 flood, [thanks to] the millions and millions [of dollars] that were expended." In nearby Scranton, residents jokingly called for a flood of their own so that they too could receive urban renewal funds.[22] But not everyone was impressed. Anthony Mussari, a local broadcaster and author of a book on Hurricane Agnes, thought the building projects were more political than practical, explaining that "the benefits of some of these projects were so marginal that many looked upon the grants as carefully masked incentives to support the re-election of the president."[23]

The decline of Wilkes-Barre continued throughout the 1980s. Industrial decline plagued the region as Eberhard Faber moved its plant to Mexico and the RCA plant closed, after which the facility changed hands several times. Each sale led to more job losses. By 2010 the number of employees at the Crestwood Industrial Park had fallen to 2,000 and part of the facility had been bulldozed. The population of Wilkes-Barre also fell, from 58,000 to less than 42,000, and 20 percent of residents were aged sixty-five or older, double the national rate. The downtown area no longer inspired regional admiration, as visitors were met with vacant storefronts and empty office space. "You know, people were very proud of what happened here," lamented Newman. "The problem was that what happened here was a physical fix. When we crashed, we crashed 10 years later than everybody else."[24]

As the pace of decline accelerated, elected officials and business leaders tried to retool the city for tourism, which had proven to be a successful strategy for former industrial cities such as North Adams, Massachusetts, and Bethlehem, Pennsylvania. In North Adams, abandoned factories were repurposed into art museums, galleries, and studios. In Bethlehem, the old mill became a casino and also a heritage site.[25] Wilkes-Barre emulated Bethlehem and city leaders partnered with the Mohegan tribe of Connecticut, which purchased the Pocono Downs racetrack for $280 million. The tribe closed the facility for two years for remodeling and then reopened it as Pennsylvania's first casino, the Mohegan Sun at Pocono Downs.[26] The tribe invested hundreds of millions of dollars in the construction of new hotels, restaurants, and other entertainment facilities housed at the Racino, and the entertainment complex supplied needed tax revenue for local governments, although it hurt local businesses and took profits out of the region. Luo Dominick, the owner of a small family café that struggled after the casino opened, told a reporter the casino was "sucking the valley dry."[27]

Public Square, which had been hailed in the 1980s as the symbol of Wilkes-Barre's return, became an eyesore and was deemed unlikely to attract tourists. In the words of a local newspaperman, it looked "like a living room furnished with freebies from the curb."[28] Today people express regret about decisions made after the 1972 flood. Many of the buildings that were torn down in Wilkes-Barre were large and attractive Victorian-era residences and were replaced, said City Councilman Tony Brooks, by "big, boxy, unattractive office buildings."[29] The removal of the historical commercial buildings not only took away the nineteenth-century charm, but it also eliminated the raw material for downtown revitalization, said Newman.

Despite the best of intentions and millions of federal dollars, the disaster capital expended in Wilkes-Barre did not protect the city from the long-term demographic and economic change that ultimately ravaged the Wyoming Valley.[30]

Elmira Never Recovered

The economic situation in Elmira, New York, was already precarious when the city flooded in 1972. Before the flood, Elmira might have been the poster child for the high inflation and economic factors that turned the northeastern United States into the Rust Belt. Remington Rand, the largest manufacturer of typewriters in the world, closed its Elmira plant three months before the flood, whereupon the defunct corporation's seven hundred workers added to the nearly 9 percent unemployed people in the city.[31] In the aftermath of the flood, Elmira underwent a massive urban renewal funded with millions of federal dollars, which many hoped would turn the economy around.

Within weeks of the disaster, a coalition of business leaders approached elected officials with their plan to rebuild Elmira and enhance its commercial and industrial base. Elected leaders responded by asking the New York State Urban Development Corporation (UDC) to run their urban renewal efforts. The UDC, along with appointed representatives of the business community who formed the Citizens Actions Council (CAC), together guided the reconstruction of Elmira.

The city administration not only avoided public input, it actually squelched any opposition to their plans.[32] The city held just one hearing into the plan, and only thirty-two people attended it, all of whom were either businesspersons or realtors. Half of those in attendance did not even live in the city. Despite the low turnout and lack of diversity, members of the U.S. Senate were told that the plan had been "enthusiastically accepted in several public hearings."[33] Residents told a different story, however, and expressed their dismay in letters to the governor's office. One letter explained, "The small [mom-and-pop grocery] store it seems to me was most poorly treated."[34] Some residents were bitter. "You hear all sorts of plans, but you can't tell what [is] going to happen," said one stationery store owner, who proceeded to refer to the urban planners as "clowns."[35] Others were skeptical; city councilman J. William O'Brien argued that the urban renewal funding could only work if it also attracted private investment.[36]

Local UDC director Gilbert Smith and S. Roberts Rose, who chaired CAC, implemented the New Elmira Plan, which cleared away buildings located by the river to create Riverside Park. In the downtown shopping district, more buildings were removed and replaced with two concrete parking lots intended to attract suburban shoppers. Altogether the New Elmira Plan eliminated 40 percent of Elmira's commercial space. However, in their zeal to improve Elmira, community leaders erased its character from the downtown and drove out many small merchants who had occupied the demolished buildings. Once the businesses were gone, so were the shoppers, who now shopped at the Arnot Mall in Big Flats.[37]

Meanwhile, Elmira continued to lose manufacturing jobs. American La France, Ann Page Foods, American Bridge Works, and Bendix Electronics all closed, leaving behind abandoned factories and displaced workers. The loss of jobs also had a ripple effect on the secondary businesses in the area, which had provided goods and services to those employed in the factories. Moreover, the reduction in the workforce also led to a decline in charitable giving, and just when it was most needed.[38] A decade after the flood, the Southern Tier Economic Growth Committee, which was allied with government officials and leaders within the business community and backed by the editorial page of the Elmira *Star-Gazette*, mounted a campaign to have New York State build a new prison in Elmira.[39]

Elmira's bid for a prison came amid the rise of the prison industrial complex and the carceral state. Tough on crime legislation, mandatory sentencing guidelines for judges, and an array of new laws against drug use led to an increase in crimes and criminals. By the start of the new millennium, the number of imprisoned had grown from a few hundred thousand to 2 million.[40] In New York, governor Mario Cuomo sought to build two dozen prisons but could not get either the legislature or the voters to approve the necessary spending or bonds to open the new prisons. Governor Cuomo found a way around this by turning to the UDC because it could issue bonds without voter approval. Under Cuomo's urging, the UDC issued prison-building bonds, whereby it built and owned the prisons but leased them back to the state, which operated them.

Elmira seemed a logical site for a prison since it was already home to the Elmira Correctional Facility, a maximum security prison that had been in operation since 1876. After exerting maximum pressure on the legislature and the governor, the community won its bid for one of the twenty-nine proposed prisons. In 1988 the Southport Correctional Facilities opened, bringing with it hundreds of prisoners and four hundred new jobs. Together the two prisons in Elmira housed twenty-five hundred inmates.[41] At first, area residents were happy with the building boom and the new jobs. That sentiment turned to dismay, however, when Governor Cuomo used his executive authority to turn the prison from a maximum security prison to a so-called super-max facility, for the most violent offenders. It was the first prison in the state to be an entirely solitary-confinement complex. Local stupefaction led to fear and anger when prisoners staged an uprising in 1991 that threatened the lives and safety of the hundreds of workers employed there. Following the crisis, according to Chemung County historian Tom Byrne, Elmira became best known as a prison town.[42]

The prison may have been more of a burden than a boom to the local economy, however. Although it brought in new jobs, it also placed demands on local infrastructure, while the city lost property tax revenue on the land used for the prison, and the families of inmates who moved into the area to be close to their incarcerated loved ones often needed government assistance. Neither the New Elmira Plan of the 1970s nor the new prison could stem the decline of Elmira, which remains one of the poorest cities in the state.[43]

George Winner, a former state senator from Elmira, conceded that the city "lost the downtown vibrancy when they tore it all down and built parking lots."[44] Chemung County historian Byrne noted that Elmira was now cleaner than it was before the flood, but it was also "a lot lonelier."[45] Former Town of Elmira supervisor Charles Bradley traveled through the region after an absence of two decades and observed, "There is no work there. They built prisons . . . everything else is just dead there. I couldn't believe how sad it was."[46] Elmira remains a town mired in high unemployment, a rising percentage of older and poorer residents, and a shrinking population.[47]

The situation in Painted Post, a small community east of Corning, parallels that of Wilkes-Barre and Elmira. Fully 8 percent of the buildings in Painted Post were damaged by the flood, and the small village was the first in the state to contract with the UDC to direct its urban renewal plan.[48] Using federal money, the UDC acquired and then cleared away buildings along the river to build Hodgeman Park, which also serves as a buffer against future flooding. Unfortunately, however, on many days, even in summer, the park remained a lonely and desolate spot.[49] The city obtained $29 million in urban renewal funds with which it cleared a twenty-six-acre plot and built a new shopping plaza with a large parking lot.[50] The plaza, Village Square, opened to great fanfare in 1973 with the theme, "Comeback '72." Governor Malcolm Wilson cut the ribbon and pronounced a new era for Painted Post, but within only a few years, the buildings had already begun to look tired and worn and the plaza was dotted with empty storefronts.[51]

Painted Post struggled economically after the flood. The largest employer in the village, Ingersoll Rand, followed the path of other manufacturers in the era of deindustrialization. Damaged by the flood, the plant reopened a few weeks later but saw a steady decline in its workforce through the 1970s. During the era of acquisitions and mergers of the 1980s, Ingersoll Rand merged with Dresser Industries to create Dresser-Rand. To increase profits and eliminate redundancy in operations, the company cut jobs in Painted Post until there were fewer than 400 employees at the plant.[52] The town's population, which was barely 2,400 when the flood struck, declined to less than 1,800 according to a 2017 Census Bureau estimate. Not only did the population shrink, it also become older, and the declining number of school-aged children in the area led the village to consolidate its school systems with those of nearby Corning.[53]

Corning Resurgent

Deindustrialization also challenged Corning, New York, but here the largest employer in the region, the eponymously named Corning Glass Works (CGW), succeeded in revamping the local economy and staving off the most adverse aspects of decline. The 1972 flood caused $20 million in damage to CGW, but insurance covered this loss. The economic decline of the 1970s did far more damage to the company, however. Profits at CGW fell 32 percent in 1974, and the company had to restructure dramatically. In 1975 the company sold off a division and cut 500 white-collar positions as part of its goal to reduce overall employees by 40 percent and salaried employees by 10 percent. During this period, the overall unemployment rate in the Corning area hovered at 10 percent.[54]

As unemployment rose and profits fell, Corning closed five more plants and eliminated production of domestic black-and-white television tubes, Christmas ornaments, and acid-waste drain lines. By 1980 the company had shrunk its worldwide workforce of 46,000 to 29,000. Throughout the 1980s the company moved away from manufacturing and focused increasingly on research and development, and as CGW retooled, it reduced the blue-collar workforce in the

FIGURE 14. The Houghton family proved an invaluable asset as Corning was rebuilt after the flood and struggled against deindustrialization. Left to right: Ambassador Houghton, Amory Houghton, Jr., and James R. Houghton. Courtesy of the Corning Incorporated Department of Archives and Records Management, Corning, New York.

Chemung Valley. In 1982, Amory ("Amo") Houghton gave up the management of day-to-day operations to become chair of the executive committee and then left the company entirely in 1986, when he successfully ran for a seat in the House of Representatives. In 1989, Jamie Houghton, who had taken over from his brother Amo, oversaw the change of name from Corning Glass Works to Corning Inc.[55]

Despite the regional economic decline, the City of Corning had the most success in its redevelopment. At the time of the flood, the city already had an urban renewal plan on file, which became the blueprint for subsequent rebuilding. The city tied its fate to re-creating Corning from an economy based on manufacturing to one based on tourism. Using the $30 million supplied by the federal government and supplemented by funds provided by CGW through its Community Foundation, the city redeveloped Market Street. The redevelopment transformed the area from a series of taverns and shops that sold inexpensive goods to high-end boutique style shops and restaurants, all with an eye toward creating a tourist destination. The city removed the low-income dwellings, stores, and bars that had lined the east end of Market Street and put up a new civic center that encompassed the police department, city hall, glassworkers' union hall, and public library, along with an ice-skating rink and a Hilton Hotel.[56] Not all the buildings were removed. The street features boutique shops and small businesses in the original buildings, which add to the charm and a furnish an aesthetic that would have otherwise been lost. By re-creating the area with a focus on tourism, retailers avoided a head-to-head confrontation with the stores at the Arnot Mall in Big Flats.

The Houghton family played a vital role in this remodeling of the city. They guided the redevelopment and contributed to the city's redesign by revamping and enlarging the Corning Glass Center, which became a signature building in the midst of Corning's successful urban renewal. They remodeled the Corning Museum of Glass, which was completed in 1980 and became the symbol of community resilience and rebirth.[57] To further boost the tourist industry, CGW bought the flood-damaged city hall for a dollar and then converted it into the Rockwell Museum of Western Art, which opened in 1982. Corning Enterprises, a subsidiary of CGW, purchased the Watkins Glen Race Track, which they redeveloped as Watkins Glen International, a site for NASCAR races. Even after the Great Recession of 2008, when many cities felt the pinch of budget cuts, the City of Corning continued to see new economic benefits as the Corning Museum of Glass launched a $64 million expansion to its facility.

The presence of CGW and the Houghton family made a critical difference for Corning. In places such as Elmira, the departure of their plants and corporate offices meant more than just the loss of employment. It was also a drain on social capital in the form of individuals who are committed to long-range planning and community stewardship. "Patient capital aimed at building local capacity . . . seems to be a required ingredient for community revitalization" said one expert on deindustrialization.[58] The Houghton family remained tied to the Corning area and played a role in the civic life, something that is less likely to happen in communities where the businesses are owned by national corporations, which are less interested in the consequences of disinvestment in the local economy. Additionally, individuals such as Amory and Jamie Houghton were influential enough to help attract new businesses to the region and secure federal support for local projects.[59] Thus, having retooled to become a tourist-based economy, assisted by the continued presence of Corning's corporate headquarters and social capital and enhanced by the philanthropy of the Houghton family, Corning did indeed come back better than ever.[60]

WITHOUT WARNING
AND DEFENSELESS

The Weather Service and Civil Defense
before and after Hurricane Agnes

Anger and frustration with government assistance in Wilkes-Barre and other cities
had broken out in summer 1972, but the public also vented anger and frustration
at agents of government whose job it was to protect people before a natural disaster occurred. The public was incensed at having received no warnings from the
National Weather Service (NWS) and demanded to know why their local civil defense organizations had failed in the midst of the crisis. The public demanded answers and expected to hold someone responsible for the death and the destruction
of property. Assigning blame is an integral component of American democracy; in
order for change to occur, the electorate must assign responsibility when the government fails so they can pressure officials into improving public policy.[1]

At first, the reaction among residents of Corning was to question their local
leaders. Joseph Nasser, the powerful mayor of Corning, found himself on the
defense in the weeks after the city flooded. The residents wanted to know why
the mayor had failed to alert them to the possibility of flooding. This outrage
moved from the political to the personal when two families took legal action
against Nasser. Claiming negligence, they sued the mayor for $5 million.[2] In
July 1972, Nasser defended himself to the Common Council. He told his colleagues
that he was tired of being slandered. Acknowledging that he too was a victim of
the flood, he asked, "If I knew there was going to be a flood, don't you think that
I would have done something about protecting my own home?" The NWS was
to blame, he said, because it never told city officials that a flood was imminent.[3]

In addition to the NWS, Nasser also accused the New York State Department
of Environmental Conservation (DEC) of failing to do its job because it failed to

warn the local government of the impending flood.[4] On September 11, 1972, anger against the DEC burst out in an editorial published in the Elmira *Star-Gazette* that reviewed the DEC's failures and urged residents of Elmira to contact Senator Smith, who was preparing a special New York State Senate investigation of the flood warning system. Written by Elmira City Council member Leon Markson, the editorial stated that the DEC, which had responsibility for patrolling the flood wall, had failed to give warning of the rising water. Instead, the local DEC flood control agent, Wolfgang Meybaum, had disappeared before the flood and remained missing for three days after. City Manager Joe Sartori later testified that the DEC flood control office in Elmira never contacted city officials. In his own defense, Meybaum claimed that "someone" in his office had made the proper contacts, but he was unable to identify who that person was or with whom they had spoken.[5]

In response to the public outrage, elected officials conducted a series of hearings into what went wrong before and during the Hurricane Agnes disaster. Bill Smith, who was unable to get Governor Rockefeller to agree to a special legislative session, teamed up with Senate majority leader Warren Anderson to hold special hearings into government failures during the disaster. Beginning in early 1973 and running through May of that year, the U.S. Senate held hearings in situ to see what policy changes needed to be made. These investigations would show just how tattered the disaster safety net had become in the days before Hurricane Agnes.

No Warning

Nasser was not the only person to point the finger of blame at the NWS. He was joined by employees of the New York State DEC, who themselves were on the defense from charges of negligence. Meybaum wrote a memo to his superiors blaming the Binghamton office of the NWS for not giving advance warning of the flooding in the Susquehanna River Basin, even though the weather service was required to contact the DEC in the case of flooding. Eldred Rich, assistant director of flood control for the DEC, testified to Bill Smith's special Senate committee that the DEC "does not give flood warnings." Warnings, he reminded the committee, were the prime responsibility of the NWS.[6] Members of the weather service rejected responsibility for the lack of warning. Instead, they blamed state officials for not subscribing to the National Warning System (NAWAS), which at that time was a paid service.[7] Elmira City Manager Sartori was frustrated at the blame game and wanted to get at the truth of the matter, explaining, "I'm not trying to place blame, but it should be investigated. Everything should be."[8]

The government personnel who testified deflected the blame from themselves and their agencies and instead assigned it to another agency (usually one that could plausibly be held responsible). The NWS fit this profile since the general public believed it would issue warnings in advance of danger to life and property. This apparently worked in the case of Nasser. His claim of negligence against the weather service deflected criticism aimed at him and won back the trust of the community. The irascible mayor remained in office until 1983 and oversaw the rebuilding of Corning.

A study of the NWS highlights the problem of assigning blame to this agency since public policy dictates that the "many hands" of government are required to work together to forestall disaster.[9] Created by President Ulysses S. Grant in 1870, the National Weather Bureau (NWB) has been situated beneath a number of departments in its history. Initially, the weather bureau was part of the War Department. It was moved to civilian control under the Department of Agriculture in 1890, and fifty years later to the Department of Commerce, by President Franklin Roosevelt. It remains there as part of the National Oceanic Atmospheric Administration (NOAA) created by Richard Nixon in 1970 as a means to streamline the functions of three scientific branches of government: the NWS, the Coastal and Geodetic Survey, and the Bureau of Commercial Fisheries. Nixon also oversaw the name change of the NWB to the more consumer-friendly National Weather Service.[10]

Heading up the NOAA was Robert M. White, whose brother Theodore was a novelist and father of the campaign biography. White was well aware of the necessity of providing timely weather warnings. He had attended a special hurricane safety conference on May 9, 1972, and addressed state and local officials, as well as George Lincoln from the Office of Emergency Preparedness (OEP). White told the audience that the weather service had come a long way since the time of the horrific Galveston Hurricane of 1900. He conceded that there was much work to be done in terms of predicting hurricanes, in sending timely warnings to the public, and in conducting better preparation at the local level of government. "Perfect warnings can do no good if they are not available to the people who need them,"[11] he warned. Sadly, this proved a grim prophecy just one month later when the public failed to receive timely warnings about the flood caused by Hurricane Agnes.

In 1972 the National Weather Service itself was guided by George Cressman, who led the NWS from 1965 to 1979 and is credited with bringing the agency into the space age. Cressman invented the first computer program to forecast weather in the 1950s, and when he became the director, he encouraged the development of new forecasting technologies using satellites, computers, and telemetry. Cressman supported the work of Robert Simpson, an advocate for the scientific study of hurricanes and the coinventor of the Saffir-Simpson hurricane wind scale. Cressman and Simpson successfully obtained funding from Congress for the Hurricane Research Project (NHRP) and the National Hurricane Center (NHC).[12] Cressman modernized flood forecasting and oversaw a fivefold increase in the number of river forecast centers that calculated river flow to determine volume and potential flooding dangers. Forecasters relied heavily on volunteers who manually checked rivers to measure rainfall, the river's height, and volume of the river flow. River gauges were sometimes as simple as a bucket with measurements etched into the sides or yardstick-like measurements of the height of rivers located on bridges. Volunteers telephoned data to forecasters who used computers to plot flood events and issue warnings.[13] To improve the accuracy of weather forecasting, the NWS launched its first weather satellite in 1960, and a decade later it had 18

FIGURE 15.   George P. Cressman, who oversaw the National Weather Service. Throughout his career he worked to modernize the NWS. Courtesy of the National Oceanic and Atmospheric Administration/Department of Commerce.

satellites in orbit. These technological innovations improved forecasting but still failed to provide perfectly accurate predictions.[14]

Under Cressman, the NWS desired not only to predict the weather but also to control it. One such effort, which was initiated in 1961 and dubbed Operation Storm Fury, was intended to control hurricanes.[15] Based on empirical evidence, many scientists believed that seeding clouds with silver iodide could induce a convection current outside the eyewall of a hurricane, thereby expanding the eye, decreasing the overall wind strength, and reducing the damage caused by a hurricane.[16] When word reached the public about Operation Storm Fury, some citizens worried that the weather service might unleash a Frankenstein's monster on the public, making things worse rather than better. Despite assurances from the NWS, citizen groups consisting of farmers and environmentalists questioned whether cloud seeding might increase the destructive power of nature. One group claimed that cloud seeding was responsible for the torrential downpour that created a flash flood in downtown Rapid City, South Dakota, in early June 1972. Another group claimed that government experiments were responsible for the extreme rainfall from Hurricane Agnes that fell in New York. For safety reasons, the experimental conditions for Operation Storm Fury required seeding hurricanes of a particular size and at a certain distance from land. This made such experiments a challenge to conduct and the results difficult to replicate. The government shut down Operation Storm Fury in 1983 after a meta-review of all earlier studies determined that the results obtained from these studies were flawed.[17]

Beyond the issue of prediction and control, weather warnings themselves remained problematic. Indeed, the NWS faced criticism for its inadequate weather warnings going back to Hurricane Audrey in 1957. Audrey, with wind speeds of at least 140 miles per hour, hit the Gulf Coast region and made its way up the East Coast in late June 1957, killing 416 people and causing $150 million in damage. After the hurricane, a group of angry citizens filed a class action lawsuit against the NWS, claiming that inaccurate forecasts had led to the death of hundreds of people and a great deal of suffering for survivors. The lawsuit was quashed when key evidence was mysteriously destroyed before the trial.[18]

The weather bureau did not fare much better in the public eye during Hurricane Betsy in 1965. The NWS had initially predicted that Betsy would make landfall in South Carolina, but the storm veered into the Gulf and instead hit the region around New Orleans.[19] In April 1972, two months before Tropical Storm Agnes, the OEP issued a report that stressed the failures of the NWS during Hurricane Camille in 1969.[20] Before Hurricane Camille struck, the initial warnings by the NWS had been off the mark, and there had been no warning for thousands of residents along the James River in Virginia.[21] Even when the NWS correctly predicted the path of Camille, the OEP report concluded that government officials had not adequately warned the public through the existing weather service.[22] The NWS also provided insufficient warning of the danger from flash floods.[23] The OEP report cited a lack of flood control mechanisms and trained flood forecasting staff at the NWS and recommended that Congress approve new appropriations to double the number of river gauges and other technology to improve lead time for flood warnings. The report called for an expansion of the NWS warning system known as NAWAS, especially in the northeastern United States, where it was not readily available. This proved to be the case during Hurricane Agnes in 1972. Even though the NWS had issued warnings, many people remained unaware of the danger and were killed or injured in the flash floods in Virginia, Maryland, and the District of Columbia. Even when warnings were issued, many people stubbornly remained in their homes. Some ignored the warnings, while others returned to bed.[24]

NAWAS, which was created to warn of nuclear attack, was adopted by the NWS in 1970. This subscription-based service was premised on the idea that local authorities and broadcasters would pay for weather information. However, instead of paying for the service, which was an expense that many municipal officials thought unnecessary, local authorities waited for weather bulletins issued through commercial sources such as television and radio. The Susquehanna River Basin Commission found that in Pennsylvania there were few subscribers, which led to spotty coverage, and the weather wire system was not available at all in New York. In addition to the paid service, the weather service provided a telephone number that government officials could call to get free updates, but local officials found it difficult to get through to the office the entire week leading up to the June 23 flooding. For some, this meant the difference between life and death.[25]

NAWAS was not the only system that broke down in June 1972. The Flood Forecasting Center, which sent out flood warnings, was high atop the eleventh floor of the federal building in downtown Harrisburg, Pennsylvania. Here scientists computed and predicted river stages along the Susquehanna Basin. Harrisburg was one of the cities that was flooded when the Agnes rains struck, and the center was high but not dry. Flooding knocked out telephone lines and cut electricity to the center for days.[26] Even before they lost power, information coming into the river center was beyond computational settings, as the water volume was so high in the rivers across the Northeast that instead of calculating river levels, the computer began to spit out unreadable measurements resembling stars. Without power, forecasters used lanterns and slide rulers to calculate the river heights. The reduction in forecasting accuracy had deadly consequences.[27] In fact, the failure in communication was catastrophic, as city officials throughout the flood-prone area made blind decisions in the critical hours that followed.

The center lacked the personnel to keep up with the storm. "We were not staffed for 24-hour coverage," one forecaster recalled. Hydrologists at the River Forecast Center were under the direction of O. D. White, a soft-spoken man much admired by his staff for his keen predictions and courteous manner. White and his crew were doing all their calculations by hand. They manually calculated that the Susquehanna would crest in Wilkes-Barre at forty-three feet, about seven feet *above* the dikes. Unfortunately, these calculations were not completed and sent to the Wyoming Valley until 10:14 a.m. on Friday morning, just an hour before the river overtopped the sandbags and sent streams of water into downtown Wilkes-Barre.[28] Conscious of the danger to the valley, White and his colleague Myron Gwinner urged Luzerne County civil defense director Frank Townend to evacuate the area. Townend ordered the evacuation of Plymouth, Kingston, Forty Fort, and low-lying areas in Wilkes-Barre, but some people ignored the warning. Many remained in their homes, believing that Wilkes-Barre would not flood. "I didn't think it would turn out like this," said one of the many who was rescued by boat and brought to an evacuation center. Another victim, Francis Smith, claimed it was worse than in 1936. "There was just no warning that this would be as deep of a flood."[29]

Angry flood victims contacted their congressional representatives, who exercised their power of investigation to review the work of the weather service.[30] John Heinz, R-Pittsburgh, and millionaire heir to the Heinz Ketchup fortune, used his role as a member of the House Government Operations Committee to excoriate the nation's weathermen.[31] Texas congressman Jack Brooks directed the hearings and noted in his opening statement that "weather forecasts were either not made" or so long delayed that they were of "little or no value."[32] The NWS issued warnings at 2:30 a.m. on the night Pittsburgh flooded, Brooks noted, adding "When you put out a Weather Service notice at 2:30 . . . I think it is pretty obvious that most people are asleep . . . the average man has no way to find out a cotton picking thing until the next morning at 7 o'clock when he wakes up." Brooks expressed incredulity that "you were sitting there watching it [the storm] but did not say anything about it." Brooks, whose hometown of Beaumont, Texas, had its fair share of hurricanes, rebuked White by reminding him that when a hurricane comes, "you can guarantee you are going to get wet, real fast."[33]

White, speaking as head of the NOAA, confessed that his agency did not anticipate that the storm would move inland over western Pennsylvania. He blamed this on the extreme nature of the disaster. "Never before had the Weather Service been faced with the threat of simultaneous flooding over such a large area, affecting and afflicting so many populations."[34] Rather than dwell on what the NWS missed in the Agnes event, he focused on what the weather service got right. Warnings issued to the eastern regions, White said, were critical in saving lives and property in many locations along the eastern seaboard. He noted that the warnings had saved the Mount Morris Dam in upstate New York, and that this, in turn, had saved the city of Rochester from massive flooding.

Bill Smith's special task force investigated the cause of the flood warning failures.[35] To maximize the event politically and extract the most satisfaction for himself and his constituents, Smith held the hearings in the cities that had been flooded in June. On October 12, Smith's committee met in Elmira and then Corning, accompanied by state senators Warren Anderson of Binghamton and Jess J. Present of Olean.[36] Smith singled out the NWS for failing to communicate to localities the danger to lives and property. He took it as a personal affront that his farm had flooded and his family had been endangered. According to one reporter who attended the hearings, Smith "wanted the head of anybody associated with the National Weather Service."[37]

Smith put the preponderance of blame for the flood warning breakdown on the NWS. He cited evidence such as the fact that the River Forecast Center issued a flood warning for Corning at 1:45 p.m. on Friday, June 23, nine hours *after* the flood.[38] Local officials throughout the Southern Tier testified that they received

FIGURE 16. Smithome Farm on June 23, 1972. This was the home of state senator Bill Smith, who tried to reform disaster policy in New York State. Courtesy of the Big Flats Historical Society.

no warning of the flood.[39] Corning's mayor testified that without having received any information, he "did not want to panic the people" and so just sat and waited.[40] Smith vented his wrath on a critical witness, Albert Kachic, an assistant hydrologist with the NWS. Settling into his seat in the conference room at Elmira College, Kachic testified that the NWS was not responsible for the disaster. First, the NWS had no arrangements with New York State to provide weather data in cases of emergency. Second, during the crisis, the NWS had assigned New York "a lower priority" in preparing flood forecasts because it believed, based on the experience with Hurricane Camille in 1969, that Virginia was in greater danger. Finally, he admitted that the NWS data-gathering system collapsed during the crisis. The situation at Harrisburg "was so chaotic, so quick and so intense that we were falling behind in our data."[41] When Smith, speaking in a harsh tone of voice, pressed Kachic as to the lack of preparation by the NWS, Kachic replied, "It's particularly difficult to forecast a rare event."[42]

Kachic insisted that local officials and the media could have called an unlisted phone number to obtain weather data. In rebuttal, T. Robert Bolger of WNBF TV Binghamton and Robert Rolfe of the *Corning Leader* testified that they never received the unlisted number for the NWS and could not obtain it. Warren Anderson, the New York State senate majority leader, noted that many Corning area residents had gone to bed the night of June 22 thinking they were safe behind their dike. Kachic's reply offered no comfort and he undoubtedly provoked Smith even further when he said that going to bed during a flood event was "asking for trouble" and suggested that state and local leaders "should take responsibility for action" when weather service networks fail.[43]

The bad press caught the attention of the White House, and Nixon ordered secretary of commerce Pete Peterson, whose cabinet department oversaw the NWS, to explain the lack of warnings. Peterson, in turn, directed Cressman, as the head of the NWS, Cressman, to prepare an account of what happened before, during, and after the floods.[44] The NWS published these findings in October 1972 in a report that placed only slight blame on the weather service itself, citing its "excellent" work in warning Wilkes-Barre of the flood and then grudgingly admitting that its service to the Chemung Valley had been inadequate.[45]

The nation's weathermen conceded that they might have done better work in the Chemung Valley but quickly shifted attention to the organizations they believed were the real culprits ion the disaster. First, they blamed the State of New York for failing to subscribe to their paid NOAA Weather Wire Service, NAWAS.[46] Second, they blamed the local media outlets for failing to disseminate the warnings issued in and around the Corning and Elmira area after 4 p.m. on Thursday. Finally, they blamed the victims themselves by pointing to the failure of some citizens who had refused to leave their homes.[47] The NWS report painted a heroic portrait of the efforts of the NWS during the Agnes crisis. Included in the report were comments that the rivers throughout the Northeast were rising higher than at "anytime in recorded history." The report also stated that rising water knocked out a third of the river gauges, and although the forecasting center in Harrisburg experienced a power failure, the staff remained in the dark center performing manual calculations by lantern light. The report repeatedly noted the unprecedented nature of the disaster and its historical nature, subtly suggesting that Agnes was an act of God.[48] An independent investigation of the NWS exculpated it for responsibility, concluding that the performance of the National Weather Service was excellent. The panel said that the NWS was not to blame but rather that the problems were due to the fragmentation of the warning system.[49] The final report put the ultimate responsibility for the flood warning breakdown on local and state agencies who failed to subscribe to NAWAS.[50]

In the aftermath of the hurricane, Congress responded to the problems uncovered by federal and state investigations. The public may have been unable to hold someone or some agency responsible for the lack of flood warnings due to the many hands involved in generating and disseminating flood warnings, which made assigning responsibility difficult. Still, the gaps in the disaster safety net were noted, and new ideas were incorporated into the Disaster Relief Act of 1974, which required that the president ensure that "all appropriate federal agencies be prepared to issue warnings" to state and local officials. Congress provided more funding to expand the NAWAS and increased the effectiveness of the weather radio system, which now broadcasts 24 hours a day, seven days a week. Due to these changes, there are currently over 1,032 transmitters providing weather warnings to 95 percent of the U.S. mainland and outlying territories.[51] The weather service's move from institutional warnings to individual warnings began with weather radio but now also includes warnings to the public over their smartphones.[52]

Nobody's in Charge

Whereas the weather service warnings proved inadequate, the civil defense organization failed altogether to warn and evacuate residents who were at risk from rising rivers. Civilians assumed that their local civil defense office was prepared for floods and other natural hazards, but their assumption was misguided. Across the Twin Tiers, local civil defense agencies fell apart or failed to respond to the danger created by the flooding. In Tioga County, New York, the civil defense (CD) director, the chairman of the county legislature, and the county sheriff got into a brawl over who was to be in charge during the crisis. In Owego, New York, the civil defense director, Walter Robbins, refused to speak with sheriff Ron Beauter, so each man created a separate disaster center, neither of which coordinated with the other. Arthur Sykes, the civil defense director for Chemung County, New York, was a bar owner and former boxing champ whose bar served as the watering hole for local politicians. His appointment smacked of political cronyism and favoritism. If it was a political favor, it was one Sykes did not return. He went missing for three days after the flood struck Elmira, trapped, he said, on the third floor of the county building after flooding destroyed his basement command post. In the absence of Sykes, it fell to the Elmira city manager to take charge of the situation in the city and surrounding areas. Ironically, the man who appointed Sykes to the position, Jack Gridley of the Chemung County Board of Supervisors, later called Sykes's work successful.[53]

The sometimes-amateurish nature of the response to the Agnes flooding was the result of an organization that lacked funding, training, and professionalism. Civil defense was a patchwork of local, state, and federal agencies, often loosely coordinated and underfunded. This was because the civil defense organization was amorphous and had no single center of control. It was controlled neither from Washington nor from the state capitals, not even in the cities across America where its work was carried out. The problems with the civil defense system that were revealed in the aftermath of Hurricane Agnes exemplified how federalism shaped natural disaster policy in 1972. Its emphasis on military preparation undercut its ability to deal with natural disaster, an issue that persisted into the administrations of George H. W. Bush and George W. Bush.

The Civil Defense Administration was created in 1950 to prepare the United States for a military attack by the USSR.[54] Despite its defense posture against the Soviet Union, which suggests a national mandate, the congressional legislation creating the Civil Defense Administration emphasized that public safety was ultimately and constitutionally the responsibility of individuals, along with local and state governments. To ensure that civil defense remained the responsibility of state and local governments, Congress voted the agency only a token operating budget.[55]

Americans were well aware of civil defense in the early 1970s, primarily due to widespread public service campaigns such as "Duck and Cover," a campaign featuring a turtle named Bucky who found shelter when nuclear bombs threatened. In some cities, civil defense personnel dressed as Bucky the Turtle and handed out leaflets describing how to survive a nuclear attack. Also familiar was the black triangle on a yellow background marking buildings designed as fallout shelters. This symbol was a familiar sight to most Americans in the Cold War era.[56] Publicity campaigns encouraged citizens to entrust their safety to state and local civil defense organizations, but a study commissioned in 1970 by the Department of Defense

(DOD) made it clear that protection was an illusion. The study found that most local officials were unwilling to fund or even manage the civil defense operations in their cities and counties. Public officials reflected the widespread public apathy toward civil defense by the majority of Americans.[57] Community leaders wanted the civil defense organization to stop preparing for a hypothetical attack and instead provide resources and guidance on how to use civil defense when floods, fires, hurricanes, and earthquakes occurred.[58] To improve public investment in civil defense, disaster consultants hired by the DOD recommended a publicity campaign to publicize the role of civil defense in protecting lives against natural disasters. Perhaps this explains the insistence by John E. Davis, Nixon's appointee to lead civil defense, that any preparation for a nuclear attack was useful when a natural disaster struck.[59]

The National Governors Association reported that the civil defense organization's mixed mission led to "fragmentation" between federal, state, and local civil defense agencies.[60] The outcry against the emphasis on nuclear war became louder after the dismal performance of civil defense before, during, and after the flooding generated by Hurricane Agnes. "The community got caught with our pants down," said one director of civil defense, who ruefully noted that he was a director in name only, as his budget was nonexistent and his staff made up of volunteers who lacked even basic equipment.[61]

Smith's special Senate investigation uncovered ample evidence that local civil defense organizations in New York and Pennsylvania had failed to cooperate or coordinate their efforts. For example, the NWS warned Elise Jane Beck, the Cattaraugus County civil defense director, to expect "the greatest flood in the history of our country," but it never occurred to Beck to share this information with other counties or state agencies.[62] Wendell McWatters, the Steuben County civil defense director, spoke to Corning mayor Nasser only once during the crisis, and that occurred an hour before the flood. McWatters testified that he was monitoring the situation through the NWS National Warning System (NAWAS), but around 4 p.m. on Thursday, June 22, the NAWAS system went down. Smith asked McWatters who was contacted about the system failure. "Nobody," McWatters said, and then justified this answer by stating that there was nothing in the civil defense manual about what to do if the system failed. McWatters only learned about the flood when someone called his home phone early Friday morning. He returned to his office but did not take charge of the operations, deferring to the local sheriff, Jack Lisi.[63] Sheriff Lisi quipped, "The system didn't break down" because in fact there "was no system at all."[64] The lack of training and preparation of McWatters was evident. Perhaps if he had been more proactive than passive, the unexpected flooding that struck in the dawn hours might have been mitigated by evacuations.

The situation in Pennsylvania was similar. In Athens, Pennsylvania, civil defense director Donald Wheeler resigned during the crisis created by the flood. When the mayor of Athens heard this, he was surprised but not for the expected reason. The mayor asked, "Is he still CD director?" and confessed that when it came to civil defense, "I don't know much about it . . . never paid much attention to it."[65] In Wilkes-Barre, the site of the Luzerne County Civil Defense Agency, the CD director was Frank Townend, a retired general from the Pennsylvania National Guard. Townend's office was located in the basement of the Luzerne County Courthouse, which was situated beside the Susquehanna River. The location made sense when civil defense officials were concerned about nuclear war, but it proved a mismatch for a river flood. Townend's office was one of the first casualties of the rising water, and his staff had to relocate to a nearby office building. Critics of Townend claimed that he had a "go-it-alone" attitude and failed to contact or coordinate with other civil defense offices and governments during the Agnes flooding. Congressman Flood, who flew into Wilkes-Barre after the flood and established a temporary command post at the airport in Avoca, believed that Townend was incompetent. He was enraged that Townend had ordered a fruitless sandbagging operation and refused assistance from the governor in the early stages

FIGURE 17. Frank Townend, pictured here on the far left, was civil defense director of Luzerne County when the flood struck. From the Photograph Collection of the Luzerne County Historical Society.

of the crisis. This infuriated Flood, who immodestly told one reporter, "Someone had to take over, and I guess it was me," when explaining why he usurped Townend's role.[66]

Scholars of disaster policy point to two common problems during any disaster: vertical fragmentation, which involves a lack of coordination and communication between local, state, and federal representatives, and horizontal fragmentation, which involves a lack of communication within one level of government such as local police agencies and county emergency management officials.[67] The fragmentation of civil defense was both horizontal, reaching across the local and county agencies dealing with disaster, and vertical, occurring between the state and local authorities. New York's primary agency for dealing with response and recovery to disasters was the Natural Disasters and Civil Defense Agency. A year before Hurricane Agnes, Governor Rockefeller had relocated the agency within the Department of Transportation (DOT), mainly as a money-saving measure. R. J. Barburti, deputy director of the State Office of Natural Disasters and Civil Defense, expressed his concern a few weeks before the 1972 floods that in the event of a major disaster there would be an "exhaustion of personnel resources" in the agency.

At the time of the flood, DOT commissioner Theodore Parker was actively lobbying Governor Rockefeller to place the disaster agency in what he called "a logical department," such as the Division of Military and Naval Affairs. Months later, Rockefeller himself acknowledged that moving the agency into the DOT "was an unfortunate demonstration of the fact that, in the interest of economy, too deep a cut was taken in the capacity of civil defense."[68] Even if it had worked well, Arnold Grushky, the deputy director for civil defense in New York State, told Smith's committee that irrespective of what they thought, providing warnings was not the responsibility of his agency.[69] After hearing testimony in the special Senate subcommittee, it became apparent to Smith that no government agency seemed to exist to tell residents "to get the hell out of here because a flood is coming."[70]

In summarizing the findings from the post-Agnes hearings, Smith concluded, "The people of the Southern Tier received almost no warning at all that disaster was imminent—even as late as a few hours before the flood water overflowed the dikes." To ensure this did not happen again, Smith called for a more powerful state Civil Defense Commission to integrate the disaster warning systems in the state and to serve as a liaison agency with federal and local authorities.[71] He then introduced legislation to require the governor to act before a disaster, when danger was imminent. Rockefeller vetoed the bill, explaining that he felt it put too much emphasis on the governor's response to a disaster. Rockefeller also criticized the bill for emphasizing the state's role in disaster and expressed concern that this aspect of the bill might reduce the amount of expectable aid from the federal government.[72] Instead, Rockefeller merely transferred the state's agency that dealt with disasters from the Department of Transportation to the Division of Military and Naval Affairs.[73]

Smith's fear that another Agnes-like disaster could happen came true in September 1975, when Hurricane Eloise created devastating rains and flooding along the Susquehanna River in New York and Pennsylvania. The flooding destroyed hundreds of structures, drove tens of thousands of people from their homes, and killed at least seventeen people. Smith vowed to reopen the question of disaster policy again and convened another commission to study the state's ability to respond to a disaster. Understanding that neither the state nor the federal government seemed inclined to help, in 1976 Smith proposed relocating natural disaster responsibility from Albany to the counties. Once again his effort failed, however, as members of the New York State Legislature balked at the proposal and killed it in committee.[74]

William Smith worked for policy change until he retired from office in 1986, although his focus shifted from natural disasters to the scourge of drunk driving. In March 1973, when Smith was busy working on flood legislation, he suffered a personal tragedy that reshaped his personal and professional life when a drunk driver killed his daughter Judith as she left the campus of Ithaca College. Charged with driving while intoxicated (DWI) and criminal negligence, the driver received only five years' probation. Smith launched a crusade to tighten DWI laws but found it was an uphill fight. "I couldn't even get a bill out of committee," he said. Ultimately, Smith managed to reshape the drunk-driving laws in New York State and initiated the STOP-DWI Program at the county level. Smith served as a national director for Mothers Against Drunk Drivers (MADD), and Ronald Reagan appointed him to the national committee on drunk driving. After he retired, he returned to Big Flats and Smithhome Farm, where he died in 2010.[75]

8

THE RISKY BUSINESS OF FLOOD CONTROL
When Dams and Levees Put People at Risk

Frank Townend had been the civil defense director for Luzerne County, Pennsylvania, for over a decade when Hurricane Agnes struck. With his snow-white hair and dark glasses balanced on his slightly overweight frame, he was once described as a man people either loved or hated. The strong-willed former brigadier general ignored the warnings coming from the National Weather Service. He was sure that the dikes could hold back the Susquehanna River. Convinced that the levees would protect the city, he did not order an evacuation of Wilkes-Barre before flooding began on Friday, June 23. Local newspapers likewise misjudged the river's rise, and one printed a headline stating that the Susquehanna would crest at 34 feet, 3 feet below the existing levee system. The next day, however, the dikes were overtopped and then collapsed.[1]

In the hours before the Agnes-induced flooding, officials reassured the public that they would stay safe and dry behind their protective flood walls, but they soon found their themselves and their property in peril. On Thursday evening, June 22, 1972, the headline in the Corning *Leader* reassured residents that "Sturdy Dikes Save Corning Once More."[2] The very next morning, the greatest flood on record overwhelmed Corning, Elmira, and Wilkes-Barre. The tragedy is that while residents of the cities were unaware they were at risk, for many years scholars had been warning that structural barriers to flooding were not flood proof and instead encouraged risky behavior in river valleys. The floodwalls, as we have seen, lulled people into believing they could safely build residences and businesses on the river's natural floodplain.[3] Disaster scholars use the term "moral hazard" to describe government policy that increases public risk taking. Dikes and levees along the Susquehanna become a moral hazard because once they had been installed, local officials encouraged floodplain development to maximize land use and increase local tax revenues.[4]

Controlling Nature

Flood control policy began in the nineteenth century when the federal government tasked the U.S. Army Corps of Engineers with building levees along the Mississippi River.[5] The 1852 Rivers and Harbors Act required the corps to dredge harbors and maintain interstate waterways that had a clear commercial or defense value. In 1879 the War Department established the Mississippi River Commission and charged it with planning and implementing flood control on the lower Mississippi. And in the twentieth century, Congress extended the mission of the U.S. Army Corps of Engineers after a series of flood disasters.

Flood control began slowly because of the narrow reading of the Constitution that dominated the Courts until the New Deal. Since flood control was not specified in the enumerated power and not explicitly tied to the commerce power granted to U.S. Congress in the commerce clause, the body ceded to states and local governments the responsibility for dealing with floods. Members of Congress also hesitated to embrace flood control initiatives because they suspected they would become expensive pork-barrel projects and a needless waste of taxpayer dollars, which in time they did. The expansion of the U.S. Army Corps of Engineers into flood control was, like other areas of disaster policy, event-driven.

In 1913 catastrophic flooding struck both the Ohio River Valley and lower Mississippi River, killing hundreds of people and causing hundreds of millions of dollars in damage.[6] The interstate disaster prompted Congress to create a House Committee on Flood Control, which expanded the role of the U.S. Army Corps of Engineers by directing it to conduct post-flood surveys across the United States to determine if and when flood control improvements were practical. When the corps recommended flood control projects, Congress paid for the initial structure but required state and local communities to bear the cost of maintaining them.[7]

Disaster struck again in 1927 when heavy rains across the Midwest and South caused cataclysmic flooding along the Mississippi River, leading to a further expansion of the corps's role in flood control. That year the Mississippi was so swollen that water could not get through the mouth of the river and instead backed up on itself. The flood destroyed levees and sent torrents of water rushing into unsuspecting communities in Arkansas, Illinois, Kentucky, Louisiana, Mississippi, Missouri, and Oklahoma. Hundreds of people died, and nearly 750,000 were made homeless. The economic devastation was catastrophic, and the event catalyzed the

FIGURE 18.   The Great Flood of 1927 swept through the lower Mississippi, killing 500 people, displacing 700,000, and causing a billion dollars in damage. Courtesy of the National Oceanic and Atmospheric Administration/Department of Commerce.

mass exodus of African Americans from the South, which was known as the First Great Migration.[8] Congress committed the U.S. Army Corps of Engineers to flood control on the Mississippi, and the corps finally abandoned its levees-only policy and began building dams and reservoirs to contain the Mississippi and reduce flooding.[9]

The philosophical and practical limitations on federal involvement in flood control changed during the administration of President Franklin Roosevelt, who successfully established the idea that the Constitution is a living document meant to fit the needs of the times. Roosevelt's doctrine of a "living Constitution," while not new, prevailed over a long-standing belief that the Constitution limited government. After his election in 1932, Roosevelt proposed a new set of government agencies, policies, and responsibilities meant to protect American citizens in a new constitutional arrangement that is collectively known today as the New Deal.[10] Some scholars have suggested that the philosophical underpinnings of the New Deal came from ideas first articulated in disaster policy, whereby members of the Roosevelt administration depicted the Great Depression as a new kind of disaster that required government intervention. Thus, it was logical that the same ideas which inspired new economic security would lead the government to restore society after natural hazards.[11]

During Roosevelt's term of office, severe flooding in 1935 and 1936 led members of the Senate to abandon their concerns about pork-barrel politics. A torrent of rain fell between July 7 and July 9, 1935, causing widespread flooding in the Southern Tier of New York. The flooding left forty dead and hundreds of millions of dollars of damage. In response, New York governor Herbert Lehman sent the Rochester National Guard to the afflicted cities to conduct search-and-rescue missions. Governor Lehman followed them into the stricken area to personally inspect the damage. Upon his return to Albany, Lehman contacted President Franklin Roosevelt and urged him to endorse a federal flood control act.[12]

Ten upstate New York congressmen formed a bipartisan coalition and urged their colleagues to support expanding federal oversight for flood control. These congressmen invited Riley Wilson, the chair of the House Flood Control Committee, to visit the devastated communities. Wilson was already an advocate for expanding federal flood control projects and was eager to come, but he wanted to include members of his committee who were more resistant to the idea of federal intervention in flood control. Wilson arrived in the Southern Tier with members of his committee, many of whom were appalled at the destruction. When he returned to Washington, Wilson drafted flood control legislation to cover the Susquehanna River Basin. The bill passed the House but languished in the Senate, which balked at the nearly $400 million price tag.[13]

Wilson's dormant bill was resurrected the following year in the midst of more flooding. In March 1936, extensive flooding occurred from Maine to Maryland and from New York to Ohio, killing 107 people and damaging 82,000 buildings. This time Wilson had a new ally in the Senate, Royal S. Copeland of New York, who chaired the Senate committee that had oversight for flood control. Copeland, a fiscal conservative, had voted against Wilson's bill in 1935, but after two devastating floods in his home state of New York, he signaled his willingness to support legislation to transfer flood control to the federal government. After Wilson reintroduced the bill in 1936, Copeland stripped it of nearly $100 million in spending and then skillfully guided it through the Senate.[14]

Pressured by the business community, local officials, and political party leaders from the flooded regions, many senators voted for the bill, which required the U.S. Army Corps of Engineers to build dikes and dams to protect cities and towns across the United States.[15] The Copeland-Wilson Omnibus Flood Control Bill was a turning point in the history of flood control disaster policy as it initiated flood control protection on a national scale and acknowledged that "flood control is a proper activity of the federal government."[16] The legislation appropriated $310 million for 250 projects in all forty-eight states. The process remained a joint effort between the federal and state government. After the corps had built the dikes, it was up to state and local officials to maintain them.

The Flood Control Act of 1941 and its offshoot, the Flood Control Act of 1944, generated over 100 flood control projects along the Susquehanna River. Surveying the 444 miles of the Susquehanna from Cooperstown, New York, to the Chesapeake Bay in Maryland, the U.S. Army Corps of Engineers reported, "The flood of March 1936 has demonstrated that the flood problem on the Susquehanna is much more serious than was previously realized."[17] Earthen levees and concrete walls were built to protect the cities of Wilkes-Barre, Kingston, Forty Fort, Pittston, Williamsport, and York, Pennsylvania. Similar structures followed in Binghamton, Elmira, Corning, Painted Post, Addison, Bath, Avoca, Canisteo, and Hornell, New York.[18] The most massive project in the Susquehanna Basin, which drains 27,500 square miles, was a $9 million levee system built along the cities of Wilkes-Barre and Kingston, Pennsylvania.[19] These actions by Congress constitute what political scientist Raymond Burby called the "safe development" policy, whereby shortsighted government policies aimed at making certain areas safe for development instead make them targets for catastrophe.[20]

The towering walls holding back the river were tangible promises of security for the people living along the Susquehanna River and encouraged them to build more homes and businesses along the river and in its floodplain. Ordinary citizens assumed that they were in no danger of flooding. Real estate agents, local contractors, and builders had no incentive to stop development along the river because they also believed that the floodplain would remain dry. For the two decades before Hurricane Agnes, dikes and levees along the Susquehanna River Basin did indeed keep the cities dry. As each year passed, increasing numbers of citizens forgot about the floods of the mid-1930s and 1940s and enjoyed a false sense of security. In addition to ordinary citizens, officials were also lulled into believing a flood was impossible, which reduced their sense of urgency when the Agnes rains struck.

Gilbert White's Prophetic Warning

At the same time that the federal government was embarking on what Senator Arthur Vandenberg called "one of the greatest public works projects the world has ever seen,"[21] which involved the building of dikes and levees along the Susquehanna River and its tributaries, scholars had begun questioning the efficacy of relying on dams and levees to protect against river flooding. Flood control structures are built to withstand a 100-year flood, calculated to be as the highest flood on record over the last one hundred years, but any flood exceeding this can spell disaster. In the words of disaster scholar Thomas Birkland, flood control is a short-term palliative rather than a long-term solution to flooding since flooding are inevitable, and no structure is entirely flood proof.[22] Shortsighted government policy dominated flood control policy between World War II and 1972, promoting occupancy on floodplains by allowing development of homes and businesses there, in no small measure because these structures brought in higher local property tax revenue. All of this put people, animals, and property at risk.

Gilbert White was one of the first and perhaps the most widely cited among scholars to suggest that dams and levees might pose unanticipated risks. A geographer who specialized in floods and human behavior, he criticized the federal government for relying on structural barriers such as dams and levees to mitigate flooding. He suggested that these only encouraged people to live close to rivers and on floodplains that would inevitably flood. As a doctoral candidate at the University of Chicago, White wrote a thesis that challenged the notion that structural flood protection was adequate or even appropriate for mitigating disasters. His 1942 dissertation called for nonstructural adjustments to flooding, such as flood insurance, floodplain zoning laws, and the relocation of dwellings from repetitive flood zones.[23] Instead of building dams and dikes, government policy should decrease flood risk by enacting strict building codes for any structures in a flood zone. The most minimally invasive code could require buildings in the floodplain to be elevated several feet above ground to reduce the risk of flooding. More stringent zoning laws could even prohibit building anything in areas that were prone to flooding and deny building permits, which would further decrease the risk of death and damage from floods.[24]

Initially, White's arguments failed to convince elected officials to change flood protection policy, but his work inspired a generation of scholars who expanded on it.[25] After the publication of his book, *Human Adjustment to Flooding*, nearly every discussion of flood control began with the premise that "man, not nature caused flood losses."[26] These new insights, which were centered on the economic losses caused by unregulated floodplain development, prompted the Council of State Governments to issue a call for state legislatures to pass legislation to ban development on floodplains.[27] The work inspired Congress to pass the Flood Insurance Act of 1956, which was an attempt to induce private insurers to provide flood insurance, but the industry rejected this proposal and Congress allowed the legislation to lapse.[28]

In a follow-up to his dissertation, White published a review of flood control policy in 1958 entitled *Changes in Urban Occupancy of Flood Plains in the United States*. The publication found substantial evidence to support his thesis that without incentives to restrict development in flood zones, occupancy on the floodplains had increased, even in cities where populations were declining. White noted that the Disaster Relief Act of 1950 had created the belief that if severe flooding occurred, the federal government would deal with it.[29] In other words, federal policy had become a moral hazard that encouraged riskier behavior across the United States.

In the late 1960s, as disaster relief costs soared, Congress appointed White to head a task force on flood control policy. White suggested that forcing people to buy insurance would encourage better land use. He surmised that insurance premiums would rise in conjunction with the cost associated with building on a floodplain, and the higher premiums would dissuade people from constructing homes and businesses in areas prone to flooding. Presumably, flood insurance would reduce the cost of federal disaster assistance because now property damage was covered by the insurance.[30]

White's task force calculated that the federal government had spent $9 billion on engineering responses to flooding, yet these structures had only increased the amount of property loss. Levees, dams, and dikes encouraged more significant development and occupancy on floodplains, which ultimately flooded, resulting in the destruction of valuable property and sometimes death. White recommended federally subsidized flood insurance to cover flood losses. Insurance, he surmised, would mitigate future disaster and lower costs for the government. By imposing an insurance fee, some builders would be discouraged from developing on the floodplain. Those that did build would pay insurance premiums that would then be used to compensate those who suffered losses in a flood.[31] The Department of Housing and Urban Development (HUD) had initiated its own study and come to the same conclusion.[32]

Congress accepted these ideas and passed the National Flood Insurance Act of 1968, which created the National Flood Insurance Program (NFIP). The NFIP was the first nonstructural approach to flood mitigation ever taken by the federal government. The program made insurance available to property owners in regions designated by the federal government as flood zones. If a community accepted federal restrictions on further development in a flood zone, citizens of the city, town, or village were eligible to purchase insurance. For those who had already built in a flood zone, subsidized insurance was made available. Once a flood zone was mapped, new structures on the floodplain would be ineligible for subsidized insurance, and it would become prohibitively expensive and extremely risky for commercial or residential builders to attempt such developments.[33]

Although flood insurance is meant to dissuade people from living in a flood zone, Dunham warned in a 1959 study that it might encourage flood zone occupancy "if the rate charged for the insurance is not accurately calculated to reflect risk." That is, if people were not charged higher premiums for living in more hazardous areas, it would not reduce new construction in floodplains and would only serve to offset some of the cost to the government. Dunham drew an analogy with premiums for fire insurance. Brick buildings are more expensive to build than wooden ones, but they are also less liable to burn. Lowering the risk of fire leads to lower insurance premiums. Hence, insurance for brick buildings is cheaper than insurance for wooden buildings because the latter are more likely to catch fire and burn. If all fire insurance policies cost the same, irrespective of the risk of fire, these policies would likely encourage the construction of more wooden buildings and fewer of the more expensive but also more fire-resistant brick buildings.[34]

Despite Dunham's warning, the government followed a course of action that diminished the cost of flood insurance so that it increased risk. In 1969 the government offered the first subsidized flood insurance in exchange for an agreement by municipal governments to enact more stringent land use for future development in areas mapped as flood zones. Few local governments signed up for flood insurance. In the first year it was offered, only 4 of the 160,000 communities that were eligible adopted the stringent land use standards that allowed them to purchase it. Worried about the lack of interest, Congress amended the law to allow communities to sign up for flood insurance during an emergency phase after a flood had occurred and before they enacted zoning laws that kept developers from building in a flood zone. Participation increased, but only to about 1,200 communities, or 95,000 policies, by June 1972. Of those policyholders, only one was in Wilkes-Barre and only two were in Corning.[35] To encourage greater participation in the flood insurance program, the federal government increased the subsidies and lowered the cost of premiums for participants, which set into motion the unintended consequence, suggested by Dunham, of making flood insurance, not a prohibition to floodplain redevelopment, but actually an inducement. After all, the insurance covered the costs of rebuilding property damaged in a flood and thereby reduced the financial risk to developers who built there.

Following the Agnes-induced floods, some government officials questioned the wisdom of allowing communities to rebuild in areas that are prone to repetitive flooding. Senate minority leader Hugh Scott asked Thomas Kleppe of the Small Business Administration (SBA) why his agency did not merely relocate citizens from flood zones rather than encourage rebuilding there. Kleppe archly reminded committee members that the SBA did not have the constitutional power to force people to relocate but could only encourage them to do so. He also reminded Senator Scott that Congress had written the rules that governed the SBA loan program.[36] Kleppe's response to Scott's question on relocation reflects the fact that until the 1970s, Congress had been reluctant to regulate local land because nothing is more sacred in America than private property. Furthermore, there is a constitutional argument against congressional interference. The Tenth Amendment does reserve power to the states, and this includes the regulation of private property. Altogether, the political and constitutional arguments made the congressional regulation of property politically unviable.

Human Adjustments to Flooding

Because he was well aware that flood control policies had failed to protect lives and property, after his reelection, President Nixon turned his attention to flood control politics and flood insurance. In order to reduce federal costs and encourage states to mandate floodplain regulation, the White House drafted the new legislation so as to shift the cost and responsibility for flood management back onto the states. Nixon's plan moved the government away from an overreliance on dams and levees to protect the public and toward changing the human behavior that increased the risk of disaster. To this end, the president tied disaster relief assistance to a requirement that government officials should prepare plans in case of disaster and take measures to reduce the risk of flooding before disaster struck.

Nixon sent the Flood Disaster Protection Act of 1973 to Congress. The bill expanded flood insurance benefits but also mandated that communities enrolled in the NFIP must establish ordinances restricting new development in local floodplains.[37] The amendments to the NFIP were significant. Whereas the original legislation only encouraged efforts at the mitigation and prevention of flooding, Nixon's plan mandated such planning. The bill tied eligibility for flood insurance to the requirement that communities address mitigation and demonstrate that they had engaged in predisaster planning. Cities and towns had to show improvement in how they dealt with new construction in a federally mapped floodplain.[38]

Moreover, the law came with some strings attached. The legislation encouraged local officials "to adopt and to enforce adequate and appropriate land use and other control measures." Thus, for communities to be eligible for flood insurance, the local government had to promise to curtail new construction in flood-prone areas.[39] The law mandated that individuals receiving a federally backed mortgage, for property mapped as a flood zone also had to purchase flood insurance. The responsibility for mapping flood zones fell to the federal government.

An added benefit to this was that insurance meant that people who suffered losses on their property would not need to obtain a second mortgage through the SBA program and could avoid becoming burdened with new debt. On December 31, 1973, President Nixon signed into law the Flood Disaster Protection Act of 1973. The law substituted insurance benefits for the SBA loans provided in previous disasters. This also served to correct an issue in the legislation that had enacted the SBA loan program. Under laws in effect when Hurricane Agnes struck, anyone who suffered property damage could obtain an SBA disaster loan at below market cost, irrespective of the availability of other sources of funding. There was no needs test for these loans, leading Robert Schnabel, who was chief of the preparedness division for OEP, to circulate a memo to the White House plaintively asking, "Why should the US Treasury be the primary lender?"[40]

The 1973 Flood Disaster Protection Act mandated communities enrolled in the NFIP to establish ordinances restricting new development in local floodplains.[41] Nixon hoped that mandating coverage in the Flood Disaster Protection Act of 1973 would shift some of the costs and risks back to those individuals who lived on the floodplains. To provide maximum protection from property loss and reduce the cost to the government, the plan mandated that anyone obtaining a federally backed mortgage in a designated flood zone had to purchase flood insurance.

Eligibility for flood insurance was contingent on an agreement by local government to take active efforts to reduce new building in flood zones and protect existing structures from future disasters.[42] The legislation further required all federally regulated mortgage lenders to require that homeowners buy flood insurance for the purchase of property in areas designated as flood hazard zones. Thomas Dunne, in testimony to Congress in 1976, remarked that "if Congress is gutsy enough to keep the Flood Disaster Protection Act on the books for the next 15 to 20 years we will see substantial savings in dollars and lives."[43] This would end the "foolishness" of allowing people to rebuild on the floodplain, which would doubtless flood again.[44] Because of these new mandates, the number of flood insurance policies increased to around 2 million by the early 1980s.[45]

On paper, the mandates meant fewer people could build in a flood zone, thereby reducing the need for flood insurance, but the reality of politics and human behavior undercut this goal. Realtors, private individuals, and local government officials attacked the HUD flood maps, claiming that they needlessly forced people who needed mortgages to buy additional flood insurance. Developers and local officials argued that the land use restrictions mandated by the law were too burdensome and were tantamount to the federal government usurping private property. Others declared that removing federal disaster assistance from communities that failed to participate in the flood insurance program was discriminatory and punitive. The Congress, which was intimidated by the public outcry and negative media coverage, was quick to waive the most stringent requirements of the NFIP. Congressional actions took the threats out of the bill and limited the dramatic changes the law had promised to bring.[46]

Once Congress had removed the linchpin of Nixon's plan, flood insurance encouraged more people to move into hazardous flood zones. Government subsidies kept insurance premiums sufficiently low and generous insurance payouts were provided to individuals to rebuild homes that flooded, sometimes repeatedly. Individuals were pleased because they were now guaranteed government protection of their private property. Local governments were happy since the higher land values along waterfronts provided more revenue in the form of property taxes.

It may have been a win-win situation for those living in flood-prone areas, but it was a losing proposition for those in the private insurance market. Between 1974 and 1982, 130 insurance companies stopped underwriting flood insurance policies, and by 1983, the program was entirely run and financed by the federal government, which set the insurance rates, mapped the flood zone, and wrote the rules for who received benefits.[47]

A series of costly disasters in the early 1990s, including Hurricane Andrew in 1992 and flooding in the Midwest in 1993, drove the flood insurance fund into the red. Congress reacted by revisiting the ideal behind the Flood Disaster Protection Act of 1973 and passed the National Flood Insurance Reform Act of 1994. Much like its predecessor, the law made all future assistance in flood zones contingent on whether individuals had purchased flood insurance; however, when disaster victims cried foul and the media brought attention to their plight, federal officials feared public opprobrium and therefore waived the flood insurance requirement.[48]

The lack of enforcement further encouraged risky behavior by individuals who rebuilt in coastal areas, riverine valleys, and other areas prone to repetitive flooding, and the NFIP has often had to pay to restore the same property several times over.[49] Although "severe-repetitive-loss-properties," as the Federal Emergency Management Agency (FEMA) calls them, account for only 1 percent of those insured, they make up 10 percent of all payouts. One of the more egregious examples of this program is that a house in Spring, Texas, was repaired 19 times for a total cost to the NFIP of $912,732, even though its value was only $42,024.[50] A leading scholar on disaster economics believes that a failure to enforce the Nixon-era regulations effectively turned disaster assistance into an implicit form of disaster insurance. Knowing that Congress will provide disaster relief encourages the moral hazard of rebuilding because the property owner bears no risk. After experiencing flooding, individuals assume, correctly, that the federal government will provide for them.[51]

A General Accounting Office study in 2003 found that repetitive claims on flood-damaged property account for the largest share of flood insurance claims.[52] Responding to this report, Congress passed the Flood Reform Act of 2004 to end repetitive insurance claims and federal payouts.[53] The law put a limit on the number of times one property owner could receive federal disaster assistance. However, a property owner could skirt the law by selling the land to another individual, who would then be eligible to file a claim if the property flooded again.[54]

After Hurricane Katrina in 2005 and Hurricane Sandy in 2012, the NFIP ran a $25 billion deficit. Congress, determined to rein in the program once and for all, passed the Biggert-Waters Flood Insurance Reform Act of 2012, which eliminated government subsidies to flood insurance and passed on the actual cost of insuring the property to property owners. As a result, annual premiums, which had averaged $1,000 per household, rose to $10,000 or even higher. One property owner in New Orleans learned that his yearly insurance premium had skyrocketed from $900 to $28,000. The legislation purposefully made it cost prohibitive to live in flood zones, thus meeting the goal of the Flood Disaster Protection Act of 1973.[55]

Public outrage, negative press, and pressure from local and state officials, the National League of Cities, the National Association of Homebuilders, and the National Association of Realtors led Congress to reconsider the legislation.

FIGURE 19. In 2005, Hurricane Katrina caused the levees to fail in New Orleans. As a result, 1,800 people died and the region suffered $125 billion in damages. Courtesy of the National Oceanic and Atmospheric Administration/ Department of Commerce.

Cosponsor Maxine Waters went so far as to claim that she had been unaware that premiums would spike under the law.[56] In March 2014, Congress passed the Homeowners Flood Insurance Affordability Act, which repealed the drastic increases in flood insurance premiums and limited all future increases in flood insurance rates to no more than 18 percent. The law also created and funded a new position for a consumer advocate who would be paid by the government to advocate against programmatic changes that property owners felt were too harsh.[57] With the establishment of these guidelines, however, Congress has not only undercut the ideals of the Flood Protection Act of 1973; it has also increased the risk-taking behavior of property owners and governments alike by promoting redevelopment in floodplains.[58]

State lawmakers found it even more difficult to resist the reoccupation of floodplains. Local people in business resisted efforts by the government, environmentalists, and those interested in behavior adaptations to flooding to clear away all buildings from the riverfront. After Hurricane Agnes, there was a discussion about relocating building and rezoning property along the river in Wilkes-Barre, but the local chamber of commerce opposed these ideas. The chamber demanded that the government restore their community precisely the way it had existed on June 22, 1972.[59] However, one Pennsylvania state legislator thought it unwise to rebuild homes in the floodplain. "Flooding is a normalized inevitable act of nature. Flooding is not a freak event," state senator Franklin Kury declared.[60] Kury led the charge to enact a state law that would take the management of floodplains out of the hands of local officials, who usually sought redevelopment along the rivers.

In 1973 Kury proposed the Pennsylvania Flood Disaster Act, which would have extended state power over health and safety to include control of flood-prone property and required that local governments restrict new building in mapped flood zones. The act passed the state senate but was held up in committee in the state assembly. Kury introduced the bill annually for the next five years only to see it rejected. It took another flood disaster to overcome opposition. In 1977, two inches of rain fell in four hours over Johnstown, Pennsylvania, and the resultant flood killed 84 people, caused $300 million in damage, and left 150,000 people with damaged or destroyed property. This event led state legislators to pass Kury's bill, which on paper granted the State of Pennsylvania broad powers to hinder both new and remodeled structures in any floodplain. In practice, however, the law was neglected and unevenly enforced.[61]

Richard Nixon further reframed disaster policy by addressing the moral hazard of relying on structural barriers such as new dams and levees. First introduced in September 1973, Nixon's legislation eventually passed as part of the Water Resources Development Act of 1974, which required the U.S. Army Corps of

Engineers to consider nonstructural adjustments to flooding before building new dams or levees. Theoretically, this meant better floodplain management and reduced the risk of flooding across the United States.[62]

The regional and local response to the flooding caused by Hurricane Agnes shows why the federal and state efforts to stop or restrict floodplain development have failed. Most people whose property was threatened or damaged by the 1972 flooding objected to the idea of the government taking their property, and the argument that their dikes and levees had made them less safe would have been considered outrageous. Rather than focus on moving people off the floodplain, congressional representatives from Corning, Elmira, and Wilkes-Barre called for the building of more dams and raising of levees. They blamed the U.S. Army Corps of Engineers for failing to secure the levees in Corning, Elmira, and Wilkes-Barre before Hurricane Agnes struck. Howard Robison had for years been a member of the House Public Works Committee, which had oversight over the corps, and he preferred structural barriers to flooding over land use regulation.[63]

The Public Works Committee had plans to build a dam on the Tioga River that some believed would have protected Corning and Elmira from the Agnes flooding. Frank S. Davenport of the New York State Department of Environmental Conservation (DEC) claimed that if the dam had been built before the Agnes storm, it "would have made one heck of a big difference" in sparing Corning and Elmira from the flood. The corps, which was sensitive to the criticism and fearful that it might hurt their congressionally approved budgets, sent out a press release exculpating themselves by indicating that "citizen opposition blocked three dams which would have prevented" much of the damage in Corning and Elmira.[64] Although it was approved by Congress in 1958, the dam remained on the drawing board because of litigation sponsored by farmers and environmentalists who opposed it.[65] One week after the flood, Robison convened his public works subcommittee and pushed for a vote to fast-track the Tioga and Hammond Dams.[66] Robison did not remain in Congress long enough to see the Tioga Dam completed. Despondent over the stain on the Republican Party caused by the Watergate scandal, Representative Robison declined to run for reelection in 1974. Instead, he retired from office and became a lobbyist for the American Railroad Association until his death in 1987.[67]

Public opinion and interest group politics also pushed members of Congress to demand that the corps increase the height of floodwalls along the Susquehanna River. Despite efforts by Gilbert White and others to educate the public on non-structural adjustments to flooding, elected leaders and residents of Corning, Elmira, and Wilkes-Barre did not want a radical solution to flooding. Responding to Congress, the U.S. Army Corps of Engineers extended and raised the dikes and levees by three to eight feet in Corning, Elmira, and Wilkes-Barre.[68] The population of the Susquehanna River Basin returned to their homes, once again feeling secure from a flood.[69]

Ultimately, local officials purchased and removed a few properties abutting the Susquehanna River and its tributaries and replaced them with new green spaces. These communities then constructed new memories of the flood, which allowed them to lull future generations of residents into believing that their cities would remain dry. In the decades after Hurricane Agnes, public commemorations of the disaster incorporated the belief that the flood walls were the best protection against future flooding. The latent message within community celebrations is that humanity can control nature with technological ingenuity.[70] For example, in 2009 Wilkes-Barre opened a park called River Commons along the Susquehanna River and proclaimed that the newly enhanced levees had tamed the river.[71] Nearly every local newspaper in Corning, Elmira, and Wilkes-Barre has commemorated the flood with stories that celebrate the enhanced levees, dikes, and the new dams.[72] The fortieth anniversary in 2012 included newspaper stories assuring readers that flood control mechanisms had indeed made citizens safer than in 1972. The Tioga-Hammond and Cowanesque Dams, which were completed at the end of the golden age of U.S. Army Corps of Engineers dam building, are nearly always cited in newspaper accounts of the Agnes-induced flood of 1972 as engineering marvels that now protect the once vulnerable population.[73]

The corps is also responsible for sending a message that human ingenuity can end flooding. After the 1972 flood, the corps was enlisted to build the Tioga-Hammond dam complex in Pennsylvania and to build higher and longer levees surrounding the afflicted cities. The corps does more than simply construct physical barriers to flooding, however; it also constructs histories and draws lessons from the role the corps played in the disaster associated with Hurricane Agnes as part of the official histories of the various engineering districts.[74]

The public history offered by the Corps at the Pennsylvania Welcome Center, which is located just above the Cowanesque Dam, confirms this celebratory message. The Army Corps also promotes the Tioga-Hammond and Cowanesque Dams as serving to save lives and property. The U.S. Army Corps of Engineers Baltimore District created two portable museum panels for the Pennsylvania Visitor Center, which overlooks the dam. These panels relate how the dams protect the north branch of the Susquehanna River Basin by providing flood control protection, opportunities for outdoor recreation, and environmental stewardship. The panels do not explain how the project manages to achieve these incompatible goals but focus instead on images of the dams and the lakes they have formed.[75]

The corps has a similar message displayed at the Mount Morris Dam, which is located near Letchworth State Park, south of Rochester, New York. The dam has a visitor center that is also a shrine to the dam's role in protecting lives and

FIGURE 20.   Mount Morris Dam became filled to capacity on June 23, 1972. Had it failed, the river would have unleashed destruction on Rochester, New York. Courtesy of the Milne Library Special Collections, State University of New York College at Geneseo.

property. Even before reaching the visitor center proper, the public enters a "Mount Morris Commemoration Kiosk," which tells of the dam's role in preserving life by protecting Rochester in 1972. Once inside the visitor center, people can watch a video history of the dam's role in staving off disaster in Rochester during Tropical Storm Agnes.[76] To an accompaniment of dramatic music, the video informs viewers that Hurricane Agnes was a "once every 290 years" event. The video acknowledges that during the Agnes event, the corps had to release some of the water stored in the dam because it had reached capacity and had intentionally flooded farms south of the dam. The video twice indicates that this resulted only in "minimal damage from the excessive flow."[77] But perhaps this was not the view of the farmers who experienced flooding as a result of the flooding along the Genesee. The permanent exhibit suggests what would happen "if there were no Mount Morris Dam" and instructs visitors that the dam "tamed" the "rage" of the Genesee River. The exhibit includes a retelling of how the dam defeated Hurricane Agnes. "The dam proved its value in Tropical Storm Agnes in June 1972 by saving an estimated $210 million in damage."[78] Absent from this and other public displays, as well as local celebrations of flood control technology, however, are the critical questions such as those raised by White.[79] Policy experts may have known that levees are not foolproof, but many residents of the Twin Tiers would only learn this when the Susquehanna flooded again.[80]

THE DISASTER RELIEF ACT OF 1974

Richard Nixon and the Creation
of Emergency Management

In September 1972, John C. Whitaker wrote a memo to his boss, John Ehrlichman, outlining plans to "reverse the trend of an expanding federal role in the management of disaster relief operations." He wanted to implement a new disaster policy that reduced the "reliance of state and local government, individuals and businesses" on federal money to repair and restore their property.[1] In November, immediately after his landslide reelection, Nixon restricted the benefits available under the Agnes Relief Act and ordered secretary of agriculture Earl Butz to cancel the Farm and Home Administration (FHA) loan program for disaster victims. The president recalled Frank Carlucci from Wilkes-Barre and resisted attempts by members of Congress to extend the time limit for the Small Business Administration (SBA) loan applications. The president vetoed attempts to extend the generous terms of the Agnes Recovery Act to future disasters.[2] Thus, began Nixon's campaign to change the trajectory of American disaster policy and create a new era in which preparation and mitigation at the local level of government was a requirement to receive any assistance from the federal government.

By the end of Johnson's term in office, most of the cost of disaster recovery had shifted from the states to the federal government, and President Nixon set into motion a plan to end this. After his landslide reelection in 1972, Nixon emphasized that local government and states bore the responsibility for disaster mitigation and preparation. Robert Schnabel, who worked in the Office of Emergency Preparedness (OEP), outlined Nixon's disaster philosophy: "The local government does all it can before requesting state help; next the state does all it can before requesting federal help; and as a last resort, the federal government responds."[3] Rather than make the federal government more responsible, Nixon wanted to promote prevention and mitigation at the state and local levels and to shore up the existing system.

This fit into Nixon's call for New Federalism in the form of a philosophy and set of policies meant to return power to the states from what the president saw as an oversized and bureaucratic federal government. Nixon warned that "the further away government is from the people, the stronger the government becomes and the weaker the people become."[4] Highlights of New Federalism included revenue sharing and block grants to allow states and localities greater flexibility on how they spent federal funds. Nixon wanted to rationalize and streamline the federal government, centralizing it under the executive branch but also providing more significant opportunities for local input and control. Nixon was unsuccessful in his attempt to wrest control away from the bureaucracy. He tried a variety of approaches, including outright elimination, consolidation, and a weakening of federal agencies through budget cuts and the executive impoundment of congressional appropriations.[5]

Nixon's plan addressed some of the critical behavioral deficiencies that underlie the tragedy of Hurricane Agnes. Local officials had been unprepared for the disaster, civil defense at the time was virtually nonexistent, and the public placed too much faith in the technological fixes of levees, dams, and NWS satellites. Nixon offered to fund to state and local governments for planning and preparation against disaster. Before the flood, only a few local governments had signed on to the flood insurance program. This legislation added incentives to join but tied eligibility to the local regulation and restriction of floodplain development. The bill challenged the distributive tendency of Congress, where benefits accrue in bills so that members can build support and claim credit for generous policies. It opposed the deeply ensconced welfare state and a belief that the government should take the lead in dealing with social problems.[6] Congress resisted Nixon's reform ideas for more than a year and insisted the government should expand federal relief and shoulder more responsibility for long-term recovery in disaster zones.[7]

From Bill to Act

After Hurricane Agnes, government at all levels launched investigations to discover and correct the failures in the warning system, the civil defense organization, and flood control mechanisms. Due to the high death toll, the extensive property damage, the number of states involved, and the national press coverage, there was heightened congressional interest in Hurricane Agnes, which became a focusing event that encouraged debate about the future direction of disaster policy.[8] Media coverage by Jack Anderson and others detailed the incompetence of disaster officials and led the U.S. Senate to investigate the government's handling of the disaster.[9]

In early 1973, a Senate subcommittee held hearings to examine the governmental response to the Agnes disaster at all levels. Quentin Burdick (D-ND) chaired the committee, whose members included James Buckley (C-NY), Dick Clark (D-IA), Joe Biden (D-DE), and Pete Domenici (R-NM). The youngest senator ever elected by popular vote, Biden turned 30 a few weeks after his 1972 election to the Senate from Delaware. Although elected from Delaware, Biden came from Scranton and provided the citizens of the Wyoming Valley with a reassuring presence. He had a lively personality and effectively used humor to make his points, but he also had a depth of emotion about him. Just weeks after his election, Biden suffered a personal tragedy when his wife and three children were involved in an auto accident that killed his wife and their infant daughter. He nearly resigned from office, but U.S. Senate majority leader Mike Mansfield (D-MT) convinced him to stay and allowed Biden to take his Senate oath in the hospital room where his two sons lay recovering.[10]

The Senate hearings scrutinized government performance in response to Hurricane Agnes and welcomed a platoon of witnesses who called on Congress to centralize the mechanism for delivering disaster relief. Many cited the role of Frank Carlucci as the most effective model for creating a new disaster policy. Hugh Scott, the Senate minority leader, criticized the decentralized disaster system. Scott cited the fact that thirty federal agencies went to the Wyoming Valley, and he complained that "There was no one place where individuals could go for help." Scott suggested a single agency run by a disaster czar much like Frank Carlucci. A "stern federal taskmaster would have been welcome from the beginning," he said. Daniel J. Flood agreed with Scott. He held forth, in his usual dramatic manner, on the need for more planning and coordination by the federal government. He praised the efforts of those agencies and bureaucrats involved. "Everyone knocked their brains out. They did the best they could." Their efforts did not lead to results. "The importance of planning and effective organization cannot be overlooked," Flood told the committee. He also wanted one central agency involved in disasters, what he called a "civil pentagon," to handle a natural disaster. In addition to Scott and Flood, a bevy of federal and state officials testified that there needed to be more federal oversight and coordination after disasters, akin they said to the work that Frank Carlucci performed in Wilkes-Barre.[11]

By the time of the hearings, President Nixon had already terminated the Office of Emergency Preparedness and moved its functions to the Federal Disaster

Assistance Administration located within the Department of Housing and Urban Development. Members of Congress scorned this move and agreed that the Department of Housing and Urban Development (HUD) should not oversee disaster assistance. Senator Schweiker (R-PA) suggested creating a Civil Disaster Division, housed within the U.S. Army Corps of Engineers.[12] Burdick rejected HUD as "too ponderous."[13] Burdick wanted Nixon to restore the Office of Emergency Preparedness within the Executive Office.[14] Senator Jacob Javits (R-NY) warned that Nixon's move eroded the federal capacity to respond to a disaster.[15]

Less formal and more acid-tongued testimony came from Governor Shapp, whose personal animus against HUD was sharpened after his public spat with Romney. Shapp expressed incredulity that Nixon was now proposing to put all federal disaster relief under the aegis of HUD. "The disorganization and discourtesy of HUD employees has become legendary here in the Wyoming Valley and other communities throughout Pennsylvania," Shapp testified. Turning emergency response over to HUD would be, he said, "like turning the operation of a morgue over to the corpse."[16] Despite the objections aired at the hearing, Nixon's reorganization plan stood.

The hearings also featured a debate as to whether the U.S. government should create a create a catastrophic insurance program modeled on the National Flood Insurance Program (NFIP) but instead covering all types of natural disaster. Backed by the federal government and sold by private insurance companies, catastrophic insurance indemnified homeowners and businesses against disaster. The idea attracted the support of a bipartisan coalition of governors, senators, and House members and could be traced back to senator Birch Bayh (D-IN), who offered legislation on this after Hurricane Camille in 1969 and again in 1970. During the 1972 presidential election, senator George McGovern (D-SD) had campaigned against Nixon on a platform that included national catastrophic insurance, and Burdick used his role as chair of the subcommittee to promote catastrophic insurance.[17]

Republicans liked the idea as well. Joseph McDade (R-Scranton) advocated for insurance in order to "return the victims of the flood to the same home, the same farm, the same business, and the same communities they had before the disaster struck." He noted, "Neither the Agnes Disaster Act nor any other legislation has ever proposed to do precisely that."[18] Scott said insurance spread the cost and but still placed the burden of insurance premiums on those most likely to use it. Senator Buckley (C-NY) agreed to the idea of passing costs onto those who were most likely to need it, as did Pete Domenici (R-NM).[19] Optimistic about the passage of the new insurance program, supporters introduced several bills in the

House and Senate, signing on as cosponsors and earning supportive editorials from the *Washington Post* and other newspapers.[20]

When the 93rd Congress convened in January 1973, Daniel Flood wasted no time in introducing HR 499, a bill to create a central disaster agency and a catastrophic insurance program.[21] The House Committee on Banking and Currency pigeonholed the bill, but Flood was undeterred. He found more congressional cosponsors and introduced the bill again in February, April, May, and July. Each time, however, the House Committee on Banking refused action on it.[22] The bill ran afoul of a powerful interest group consisting of bankers, insurance companies, and real estate brokers, which lobbied against adding surcharges to mortgages in order to pay for the additional insurance coverage. They claimed existing policies were adequate and expressed fear that even with federal subsidies, catastrophic insurance might bankrupt their industry.[23] These powerful interests, with the support of the Banking Committee, stifled attempts to create a new government program, while supporting changes to the NFIP offered by President Nixon.

Nixon easily defeated proponents of catastrophic insurance because natural disasters engender no permanent national interest group, like the realtors or insurance industry, both of which opposed catastrophic insurance.[24] Supporters of catastrophic insurance found themselves championing an issue that lacked salience, a national interest group, and the attention of the national media. By 1980, many of the leading proponents of catastrophic insurance left government altogether, thus disbanding the coalition of lawmakers that might have sustained the idea.

The 1976 presidential election removed key advocates for catastrophic insurance from the political scene. Senator Schweiker (R-PA) and Senator Bayh (D-IN), both vocal supporters of expanding the federal insurance program and creating a centralized federal disaster agency, pursued failed bids for the White House in 1976 and left the Senate in 1980. Schweiker served as secretary of health and human services under President Reagan from 1981 until 1983 before becoming a lobbyist for the insurance industry.[25] Bayh lost his 1980 reelection bid to political newcomer Dan Quayle, who represented the rising conservative trend in American politics. Shapp, the anti-Nixon proponent of full equity for disaster victims, also succumbed to presidential ambition. He spent much of 1974 on organizing 1976 presidential bid, but he was forced to withdraw from the primaries after he received fewer votes than "no preference" in the Florida primary. Shapp left politics altogether in 1978 and wrote an unpublished autobiography. He then wrote a musical about politics but failed to get it on Broadway before his death in 1994.[26]

Turnover in Congress was also high in this period and led to discontinuities in disaster policy. The Watergate scandal led the Republicans to widespread defeat in 1974, and seventy-five new members were elected to the House of Representatives. These lawmakers rewrote the rules of Congress and thereby erased decades of institutional memory, upended long-established rules of behavior, and terminated the seniority system, which had empowered the longest-serving members of the House.[27] Watergate also removed Scott, one of the highest-ranked Republicans in the government, who retired from office in 1976.[28]

Lacking legislative continuity and with the support of the insurance, banking, and real estate lobbies, the Flood Disaster Protection Act effectively nullified the attempt of reformers to pass catastrophic disaster insurance.[29] Carlucci lamented this and believed that in the aftermath of Hurricane Agnes, "the time was ripe for a program providing disaster insurance to all Americans."[30]

President Nixon proposed the Disaster Preparedness and Assistance Act of 1973. "A major objective of the bill is to consolidate responsibility for disaster assistance, reduce the number of federal agencies involved," and to "strengthen the role of state and local and private institutions in meeting this important challenge," the president stated in his message to Congress. Rather than increase the federal role, Nixon crafted legislation to reinforce the idea that the responsibility for disasters lies with state and local government. He did not expand disaster aid but rather trimmed away the benefits that he had made available to the victims of Agnes.[31]

He imposed new mandates for receiving disaster aid, which included the new regulation that states and localities must plan for disaster.[32] As an incentive, the legislation provided upward of $250,000 to aid state and local government, but these localities also had to pledge to prepare plans detailing how they would avoid recurrence of losses.[33] Nixon also moved on his pledge to have state and local government shoulder more responsibility by turning over to them the management of temporary housing and repairs.[34]

Senator John Sparkman (D-AL) introduced Nixon's bill in the Senate. His cosponsor was Senator Domenici (R- NM), the ranking Republican on the Public Works Committee.[35] Thomas Dunne, from the SBA, testified in favor of the bill, reminding Senators that responsibility for dealing with disaster begins at the local level.[36] Conservative members of Congress supported Nixon's plan but also stressed that they were not removing federal assistance. Domenici noted that the federal government would still supply resources to the states but that the states would then make the decisions about how best to use them. Nixon's ideas met with the approval of Congressman Ogden Reid of New York, who commented that thousands of people in the state suffered "needlessly" because the "state government was not prepared in advance to deal with the emergency."[37]

Despite support in the Senate, Nixon's proposal languished in Congress for nearly a year due to opposition from the National Governor's Association and the National League of Cities. These organizations objected to limits on the generous benefits that had been available in disaster legislation after Hurricanes Camille and Agnes. They found a champion for their cause in Burdick who held the legislation up in committee until Nixon's allies made some concessions.[38] They agreed to the condition that the federal government assumes 100 percent of the cost of repairing public facilities and pay the full cost of housing for people who are displaced after a disaster. Nixon, who had eliminated loan forgiveness provisions, accepted a proposal for an Individual and Family Grant (IFG) that provided aid to individuals and families in the aftermath of a major disaster.[39] Nixon also agreed to the provision allowing predisaster assistance to states when a disaster was imminent rather than force states to apply for assistance after a major disaster struck.[40]

The bill was still in the Public Works Committee in April 1974, when a weather system running from Alabama to Ohio generated 148 tornadoes that killed 315 people in a twenty-four-hour period. This extraordinary weather event prompted the committee to move the bill to the floor vote, where it quickly passed.[41] In signing the Disaster Relief Act of 1974 (PL 93-288) on May 22, 1974, Nixon remarked that this bill "truly brings the new federalism to our disaster prepared-ness and assistance activities."[42]

The significance of the Disaster Relief Act of 1974 is debatable; some analysts see it as a continuation of practices set into motion by the Disaster Relief Act of 1950, whereas others see it as a significant departure from prior disaster legis-lation.[43] On the surface, there seemed to be much in the legislation that rein-forced the Johnson-era natural disaster entitlements for victims of the disaster. The federal share of disaster relief and rebuilding remained high, the benefits remained undiminished, and the declaration of a major disaster remained in the hands of the president. However, a closer look at the Nixon-era accomplishments show that they left an indelible imprint on disaster policy.[44]

The Disaster Relief Act of 1974 marked the beginning of the regulatory phase of disaster assistance, an era in which the federal government limited federal costs and forced individuals and communities to assume some of the responsibility of living in disaster-prone areas.[45] The legislation contained the provisions requiring states and localities to take steps to mitigate future disasters.[46] Moreover, com-munities to have plans and contingencies for disaster, which laid the founda-tion of the professionalization of emergency management.[47] In fact, this may be Nixon's greatest policy success.[48]

During the 1972 floods in Corning, Elmira, and Wilkes-Barre, the local gov-ernment was ill-prepared and lacked the human or financial resources to cope

FIGURE 21. Xenia, Ohio, in 1974, after a superstorm spawned tornadoes in a number of states. Courtesy of the National Oceanic and Atmospheric Administration/Department of Commerce: United States Airforce, Wright Patterson Air Force Base.

with the disaster. Most municipalities relied on a vastly underfunded civil defense system aimed at preparing for nuclear war rather than natural disaster.[49] Nixon's policies provided funding for new research into disasters and new educational curriculum on disaster training, and they provided on-site seminars on disaster preparedness.

The Disaster Relief Act of 1974 created the Federal Disaster Assistance Administration (FDAA), which assumed the functions of the now-abolished OEP. Many people criticized Nixon for taking the leading disaster agency away from the White House and placing it within HUD, but Thomas Dunne, who supervised the FDAA, claimed that separating that agency from the White House had in fact honed its ability to respond to natural disasters. Unlike the former OEP, the FDAA did not have to deal with issues such as the threat of nuclear war or the oil shortage crisis, issues that had been the responsibility of the OEP. The FDAA had one mission, which was working with state and federal agencies on programs to prevent or mitigate disasters.[50] In order to enhance disaster preparation, the FDAA provided grants of up to $240,000 to states for creating warning systems, planning evacuations, and creating community-based disaster planning.[51]

In preparation for the elimination of the OEP, Nixon reorganized the Office of Civil Defense in 1972 and mandated a "dual use" policy mandating that civil defense offices prepare for both natural and human-made disasters.[52] President Nixon moved civil defense out of the U.S. Department of the Army and into the DOD and renamed it the Defense Civil Preparedness Agency (DCPA). DCPA was, from its outset, meant to shore up the obvious problems with local civil defense organizations and place more responsibility for disaster preparation on the states.[53]

The repurposed agency was responsive to the needs of local authorities for training to deal with local, regional and even statewide natural disasters and played a role in the development of the profession of emergency management.[54] The DCPA held on-site training for local and state officials, which included disaster scenarios. The training included making an inventory listing potential hazards for a given area, assessing the local capacity to deal with these hazards, identifying deficiencies, and developing a response plan. Few local executives undergo it without resolving that civil preparedness needs more of their attention.[55] Thousands of individuals went through training for dealing with natural disasters at the DCPA Staff College in Battle Creek, Michigan, which, starting in 1974, granted college credit to participants through an agreement with Michigan Technical University. These credits brought a sense of professionalism to the program. The agency also expanded money in researching disasters and preparing insight into how to best cope in the aftermath.[56]

The DCPA launched a bimonthly publication, *Foresight*, which is delivered to forty-five thousand subscribers, including included federal, state, and local officials, public libraries, colleges, and radio and television stations. In addition to the magazine, the DCPA sponsored public service radio and film productions and created a museum exhibit on natural disasters to educate the public about preparation.[57] These efforts laid the groundwork for the creation of the new profession of emergency management.

St. Joseph's College in Emmetsburg, Maryland, became the National Emergency Training Center (NETC), whose mission was to "train and educate the nation's emergency management community." To date, the institute has provided thousands of courses and trained hundreds of thousands of local disaster personnel who became the first generation of emergency management experts.[58] Funding transformed the states' disaster response programs. For example, federal money provided to officials in New York allowed them to draft a comprehensive emergency management plan that led to a new disaster agency, the Office of Disaster Preparedness, which was centered in Albany, the state capital, and included six regional directors who promoted disaster planning and mitigation within their regions.[59]

The DCPA provided training, and after the bill became law, disaster experts, researchers, community leaders, and elected officials tapped into resources from either the DCPA or the FDAA to support mitigation, planning, response, and recovery. Funding underwrote the consulting work of Robert Schnabel, the former director of preparedness at the OEP; Joe Sartori, who guided Elmira through its crisis; and William Wilcox, who oversaw the rebuilding in Pennsylvania after the flooding; all of whom shared their disaster expertise with state and local officials in the years following Hurricane Agnes.[60]

The Disaster Relief Act of 1974 altered the trajectory of disaster policy in the United States. Between legislation in 1950 and the election of Nixon in 1968, the main thrust of federal disaster policy had been to increase aid, the number of benefits available, and the criteria for who could receive federal assistance. Before 1968 there no incentive for state and local governments to better plan and prepare for disaster, as the existing law was a disincentive to better planning because many officials feared that if they did too much, they would not be eligible for the generous federal disaster benefits.[61] By mandating preparation in order to receive federal benefits and being provided with money to plan, the Disaster Relief Act of 1974 changed the course of U.S. disaster policy and strengthened the capacity of local and state governments to deal with a disaster. It also effectively planted the seeds for the growth of emergency management as a profession, which was amplified and strengthened in the Robert T. Stafford Disaster Relief and Emergency Assistance Act in 1988.[62]

The Disaster Relief Act of 1974 began a new era in disaster policy, but also served as the final act for a number of the individuals who had been active in the Hurricane Agnes disaster and recovery. Within a decade, many of the elected officials involved in dealing with Hurricane Agnes had left politics, and some had died. Moreover, the legislation was one of the last significant actions by Nixon before his August resignation from office due to the Watergate scandal.

The Watergate break-in occurred the same week in 1972 when Hurricane Agnes was forming in the Atlantic Ocean, and the investigation into that break-in shadowed the administration from 1972 until 1974. On August 9, 1974, after eighteen months of wrangling in the courts over the release of audio tapes of conversations recorded in the Oval Office, Nixon was ordered by the Supreme Court to release the tapes that proved he had attempted to obstruct the investigation into the break-in. Rather than face the humiliation of impeachment and trial by an already hostile Congress, Nixon became the first president to resign from office. He spent the rest of his life attempting to reform his image and restore his reputation.[63]

Modern Emergency Management

President Nixon rejected the call for a centralized, all-hazards, independent federal agency operating out the White House. His own experience with Hurricane Agnes led him to vest executive authority to oversee disaster operations in HUD, since that agency housed the NFIP, had responsibility for postdisaster housing, and oversaw the newly formed FDAA. Perhaps because the FDAA was outside the White House and more insulated from political pressure, the National Governors Association (NGA) lobbied against this change. The governor's association launched the Emergency Preparedness Project in 1977 to review disaster policy and to make recommendations for improvement. In a report issued in February 1978, it called for a comprehensive all-hazards agency and a consolidation of all disaster services into one organization under the direction of an individual with direct access to the president.[64]

President Jimmy Carter, a former Georgia governor, was in sympathy with the recommendations of the NGA. From his first day in office, President Carter faced an assortment of natural and human disasters, including a blizzard that swept across the Midwest and into western New York, extreme cold that destroyed much of the citrus crop in Florida, and the gravest natural gas shortage in U.S. history.[65] Displeased with the disaster system he had inherited from President Nixon, Carter ordered the Office of Management and Budget (OMB) to conduct a thorough analysis of federal preparation and response to natural, accidental and wartime civil disasters.

The OMB called for consolidation of all existing agencies into one, a recommendation enthusiastically supported by the director of the FDAA, William Wilcox. Wilcox had overseen disaster relief for the state of Pennsylvania after Hurricane Agnes and was an advocate for centralizing the agencies involved in disaster relief and recovery.[66] The OMB's report dovetailed with recommendations from the NGA.[67] Carter responded by issuing an executive order to create a Federal Emergency Management Agency (FEMA). Carlucci, the flood czar who oversaw recovery in Wilkes-Barre, believed the inspiration for FEMA came from his experiences in the Agnes crisis, which he shared with Carter's staff when they were designing FEMA.[68]

FEMA brought together agencies from the Department of Commerce, HUD, and the General Services Administration.[69] The agencies came from diverse cultures and did not always work in harmony. FEMA was not a fully centralized disaster agency. Several programs remained outside of the agency, including those overseen by the Department of Agriculture, the Federal Highway Authority, and the SBA.[70] FEMA oversaw over one hundred different programs related to disaster, preparation, response, and recovery, and reported to twenty separate congressional

FIGURE 22.   President Jimmy Carter, who enhanced federal disaster response by creating the Federal Emergency Management Agency (FEMA), meets with Senator Birch Bayh, a longtime advocate for disaster victims. Courtesy of the National Archives (photo 182837).

committees. Carter's first director of FEMA was John Macy, a career bureaucrat who held many positions across the federal spectrum before running FEMA.[71]

Carter's plan brought into FEMA the civil defense elements separated by Nixon and located in the Department of Defense and was at least in this way a regressive movement. By combining civil defense and natural disasters into one agency, FEMA's all-hazards approach included military and natural disasters and threatened to repeat the problems associated with the civil defense programs of the 1950s.[72] Remembering Hurricane Agnes, Dunne argued for retaining two distinct agencies, one for disasters and one for military emergencies. He was rightly concerned that one agency might fail to meet its dual mission requirements. As it turned out, the broader military concerns of the Reagan presidency overshadowed FEMA's mission to assist in a natural disaster, as did the War on Terror under President George W. Bush.[73]

President Ronald Reagan saw only a few significant disasters as president. In the absence of any dramatic need for disaster relief, David Stockman of the OMB called for budget cuts to FEMA and the elimination of most, if not all, disaster relief programs offered to individuals. Stockman wanted to end what some called the "Agnes syndrome," describing victims who showed up at government offices expecting an immediate payment for property lost in the disaster. Stockman objected to the federal government footing the bill for the array of entitlements provided to disaster victims in the form of temporary housing, food stamps, unemployment compensation, mental health care, legal aid services, low-interest loans, free rent, expedited income tax refunds, and short-term assistance with mortgage payments. Stockman believed states should run and pay for these services themselves. He was distressed that farmers, members of the business community, and individuals all received low-interest loans through the SBA.[74]

Congress rejected Stockman's Nixonesque plan to remove benefits.[75] However, it passed new legislation in 1988, in the form of the Robert T. Stafford Act. The Stafford Act reinforced the ideas of the 1974 Disaster Act by restating the principle that local and state political units must retain responsibility for natural disasters. "It is the intent of the Congress, by this Act, to provide an orderly and continuing means of assistance by the federal government to state and local governments in *carrying out their responsibilities* to alleviate the suffering and damage which result from such disasters."[76] Emphasizing the role of states and cities to look after themselves in disaster fit neatly in President Reagan's agenda. Under Reagan, whose administration saw new Cold War tensions with the U.S.S.R, FEMA became a tool of military preparedness rather than natural disaster management.[77] FEMA was now focused more on planning for the aftermath of a nuclear war than on natural disasters. Reagan proposed in 1982 to give the agency $4.2 billion to develop and prepare a program to "provide for the survival of a substantial proportion of the population in the event of a nuclear attack,"[78] and signaled his intent to orient FEMA toward national defense rather than disasters by appointing Louis Giuffrida to direct it.

While Stockman attacked the expense of disaster aid, FEMA was building a 112,544 square foot bunker in West Virginia to house Congress in the case of nuclear attack.[79] FEMA's new mandate did not sit well with the Democratic members of Congress, many of whom lampooned the idea of surviving a nuclear attack and instead wanted a nuclear freeze. Eventually, Giuffrida left FEMA under charges of malfeasance and cronyism.[80] President Reagan's second appointment, General Julius Becton, focused the agency on nuclear war and admitted that natural disasters such as earthquakes, hurricanes, and floods were at the bottom of his priorities.[81]

Natural disasters also held a low priority in the White House under President George H. W. Bush. President Bush made no significant appointments to FEMA in his first year in office, nor did he move to fill positions after Reagan appointees resigned, which left gaps in the senior staffing. Bush appointed Robert Morris as acting director of FEMA in 1989.

Morris faced two critical disasters: in September 1989, Hurricane Hugo cut a swath of damage from Puerto Rico and the Virgin Islands to Florida and South Carolina. The storm led to the death of eight-five people and caused $15 billion in damage. A month after Hugo, an earthquake struck California, killing sixty-three and causing nearly $10 billion in damage. FEMA's focus on military preparation made the agency ill-prepared to deal with the natural hazard crisis. Senator Fritz Hollings of South Carolina went on television and called the disaster team responders "the sorriest bunch of bureaucratic jackasses" he had ever seen.[82] Months after Hurricane Hugo, FEMA remained mired in bureaucratic red tape and was incapable of assisting the neediest populations. A similar set of problems occurred after the earthquake; this time both the press and the public blamed president George H. W. Bush.[83] Bush responded by appointing Wallace Stickney.

Even if FEMA had not been overly concerned with military affairs in the 1980s, there would still have been problems in aid delivery.[84] Bush's problems with Hugo were similar to those in the Agnes disaster and resulted from vertical and horizontal fragmentation, both of which are all too common in extreme events.[85] As President Woodrow Wilson once wryly noted, federalism allows for the "division of authority and concealment of responsibility."[86] This was proven when multiple agencies representing several levels of government failed to coordinate their activities. After the debacle of Hurricane Hugo, Stickney, sounding a bit like George Lincoln after the OEP's inept response to Hurricane Camille in 1969, claimed that FEMA had learned its lesson from Hugo. However, Stickney's agency failed again when Hurricane Andrew slammed into Florida in August 1992. The storm killed twenty-six people and caused $27 billion in damage. Moreover, the hurricane drove a million people from their homes. In the immediate aftermath, chaos ensued in Florida, leaving storm victims without food, water, or medical supplies.

When Stickney failed to assume control, President Bush reached back into Nixon's playbook by circumventing his natural disaster agency and sending a disaster czar to Florida in the guise of secretary of transportation Andrew Card, who went to South Florida with thousands of military personnel to coordinate rescue and recovery operations. Stickney's rejoinder to his critics was that under the Stafford Act, the federal role was supportive rather than central to disaster recovery, which was an accurate but politically unacceptable assessment. In fact, after George H. W. Bush lost his reelection bid later that fall, some political insiders suggested that his dismal handling of the natural disaster crisis was to blame.[87]

Future president William Jefferson Clinton paid close attention to the bad press and poor performance FEMA has received under his predecessor, and after his election to the White House, he remade it as a cabinet-level agency and appointed James Lee Witt to direct it. Witt was the first FEMA director to have a

FIGURE 23. James Lee Witt, the first professional emergency manager appointed to run FEMA, pictured here with vice president Albert Gore, Jr. Courtesy of the National Archives (photo 5698265).

background in emergency management, having served as the head of the Arkansas emergency services department under then-governor Clinton. Witt's appointment satisfied the press but also had political overtones, since the director was an Arkansas crony of the president. Nonetheless, Witt's term as director of FEMA was widely praised, especially by those who worked for him. He came to power at a time when the fall of the Soviet Union and the increasingly global orientation, along with the development of a market-based economy in the People's Republic of China, made the Cold War irrelevant. This in turn allowed Witt to focus his agency almost exclusively on disaster mitigation, prevention, response, and recovery. He used this opportunity to hire professionals and improved the agency's profile nationwide.[88]

The election of George W. Bush in 2000 ended the harmony that FEMA had with the press and public. Dubbed "Bush 43," he was very much like his father, "Bush 41," in his disinterest in disaster policy. Following the terror attacks on September 11, 2001, Congress made FEMA an adjunct of the newly created Department of Homeland Security (DHS), which emphasized training and preparation against terrorist attacks.[89] Bush created the new Cabinet Department in March 2003 and drew into it twenty-three existing federal agencies, including FEMA.[90] Under Bush, FEMA reached its nadir when it failed to provide for the public during the crisis created by Hurricane Katrina in 2005. FEMA's disorganized and dysfunctional response made the disaster into a tragedy that included the death of over 1,800 people and $80 billion in damage.[91] In the face of widespread public criticism and facing political fallout that eventually lost his party control of the House and Senate in 2006, President Bush belatedly signed into law the Post-Katrina Emergency Reform Act of 2007which reorganized FEMA and emphasized preparedness and readiness. Under the new legislation, FEMA became an independent agency whose director reported to the secretary of homeland security.[92]

FEMA continues to be the political tool of the president. Having the agency so closely associated with the White House has kept it attentive to the president's political needs and electoral calculations. Much in the same way Johnson and Nixon had used the OEP, FEMA has been a political tool of the White House. Presidents are cognizant that a failure to enact generous disaster relief benefits, an appearance of ineptitude, or a failure to visit a disaster-wracked region will lead to a political backlash.[93] President Clinton drew lessons from Nixon's response to Hurricane Agnes in 1972, and proved himself more generous in making disaster declarations and delivering federal dollars to states and communities across the United States than his predecessors in the Oval Office. His FEMA director, Witt, unabashedly testified to Congress that disasters were political events and required a political response.[94] Clinton was not alone in understanding the politics of disaster. A study of disaster declarations from 1981 until 2004 found that during presidential election years, swing states or states that might vote for either candidate receive twice as many disaster declarations as their more partisan counterparts.[95]

The ideals of Nixon's disaster policies remain imperfectly realized. Emergency management has become a profession that has better prepared local first responders for disaster, but FEMA has returned to the mixed-use objectives of preparing for military and natural disasters, and with uneven results. Meanwhile, playing politics with natural disaster has continued since the presidency of Nixon as presidents have co-opted the agency to achieve their own political goals, sometimes at the expense of sound public policy. Even though they have become better prepared for a disaster, local and state governments have not fully met the standards of reducing risk by removing people from the floodplain, with predictable and tragic results.

Déjà Vu

For Stacey Gould, it was déjà vu. On Thursday, September 8, 2011, she stood by as flood water submerged her two-story home. Turning to a nearby reporter, she asked, "In 2005, we had a 100-year flood, and in 2006, we had a 500-year flood, what year flood is this?"[96] Stacey was one of the thousands of people living along the Susquehanna River who faced a reprise of Hurricane Agnes when Tropical Storm Lee stalled over the twin tiers of New York and Pennsylvania on September 6. Much like Hurricane Agnes, this storm arrived after a wet spring and summer and just a fortnight after remnants of Hurricane Irene had swept through the area, delivering 6–8 inches of rain.[97] Lee added 10–11 inches of rain to already saturated ground. Creeks and streams overfilled then spilled into the surrounding floodplain, causing flash flooding throughout the region. A major disaster awaited those in the Susquehanna River Basin as severe flooding washed out roads, destroyed sewer systems, knocked out power, and invaded villages, towns, and cities, caused a billion dollars in damage and killed seventeen people.

Thomas Libous, the state senator who represented Binghamton, New York, a city of 45,000 on the Susquehanna River, feared that the flood walls would give out. If that happened, he fretted, "We will have a mini New Orleans," referring to Hurricane Katrina in 2005.[98] At 10 a.m. on September 8, the river invaded Binghamton and coursed through the streets, rising halfway up lamp posts in a downtown plaza. Binghamton was soon sealed off from the outside world.[99] Mayor Matt Ryan called the situation "dire." Residents were fortunate that Ryan issued an evacuation order in the dawn hours of September 8, thereby saving lives.[100]

The state was better prepared in 2011 and Governor Andrew Cuomo much more involved and more evident in the disaster than his predecessor Rockefeller had been during Hurricane Agnes in 1972.[101] Governor Cuomo helicoptered over the Southern Tier and pleaded with residents to heed the evacuation order. "The Susquehanna is going to get higher . . . this should be taken seriously."[102] He warned residents that "By the time it looks that bad, you won't be able to leave, so leave and leave now."[103] Echoing Cuomo were area congressional representatives Richard Hanna and Maurice Hinchey, who urged "residents to heed warnings from local law enforcement and public officials and prepare for flooding to develop as rivers and creeks continue to rise.[104] Despite the warning and precautionary evacuation, emergency responders still had to rescue those holdouts who had failed to leave their homes because they were unaware of the call to evacuate or did not understand the nature of the threat.[105] Some were plucked from rooftops by helicopter and others were saved by motorboat.[106]

The situation in the Northern Tier of Pennsylvania mirrored events in New York. As had occurred in 1972, the National Weather Service (NWS) experienced problems calculating the height of the river and when it would crest. During the crisis, it predicted that the Susquehanna would crest at 40 feet near Wilkes-Barre, but instead, the river climbed nearly three feet higher.[107] After Tropical Storm Lee, the NWS blamed the inaccurate river forecast on a broken river gauge.[108] Even with advanced technology, however, one forecaster acknowledged limits to the science of forecasting, "We knew flooding would occur but didn't know how much."[109]

According to Jim Brozena, the executive director of the Luzerne County Flood Protection Agency, the levees in Wilkes-Barre reached "their extreme limits."[110] "This is a scary situation," said Stephen Bekanich, the Luzerne Country director of emergency management. Wilkes-Barre mayor Tom Leighton called a mandatory evacuation for all the areas that had been flooded by Hurricane Agnes forty years earlier. The mayor told residents to prepare for a 72-hour evacuation and advised them to take along clothing, food, and prescription medications.[111] Officials evacuated half the city's 40,000 residents and asked businesses to close by midday. By 4 p.m. Thursday, September 8, Wilkes-Barre was "a ghost town." Across the region, more than 70,000 people were told to get to higher ground.[112]

Structural changes to the riverine system after Hurricane Agnes increased the velocity of the river and transferred problems downstream. The flooding caused by Tropical Storm Lee differed from the floods of Hurricane Agnes because it brought water into areas that had never flooded, and it was deeper and farther into areas that had prior flooding. Municipalities that had not been flooded since the great floods of 1935 and 1936 took the brunt of flooding: Nichols, Tioga Center, Owego, Johnson City, Vestal, and the city of Binghamton. Downriver from Wilkes-Barre, which was protected by new floodwalls, the Susquehanna swamped those areas without flood barriers such as Pittston, Tunkhannock, Edwardsville, Plymouth Township, and Nanticoke.[113] The higher levees built after Hurricane Agnes in 1972, Wilkes-Barre was spared from flooding, but West Pittston, a town of 4,800 people that was not protected by a flood wall, bore the brunt of the flooding in the Wyoming Valley.[114]

After consulting with FEMA, President Obama declared a major disaster for New York and Pennsylvania and sent vice president Joe Biden to Pennsylvania to survey the damage there. Biden, whose first year in the U.S. Senate in 1973 was spent, in part, investigating Hurricane Agnes and its aftermath, returned to the Wyoming Valley on September 16, 2011.[115] Obama's FEMA director was Craig Fugate, who was appointed to that position by the president in 2009. Like former director Witt, Fugate was a specialist in emergency management. During Fugate's tenure at FEMA, he restored faith in the agency by ably demonstrating his leadership skills in dealing with crises such as Tropical Storm Lee, and politicians and the press alike praised the actions of his agency.[116]

Under guidelines established in the Robert T Stafford Act in 1988, FEMA is responsible for overseeing and coordinating disaster assistance, which now included an array of benefits that may have made victims of Hurricane Agnes envious. For example, the Individuals and Households Program provided as much

FIGURE 24.   Senator Joseph Biden investigated disaster relief after Hurricane Agnes in 1973. Pictured here in 2011 when, as vice president, Biden comforted victims of Tropical Storm Lee. Courtesy of the Federal Emergency Management Agency/Liz Roll.

as $30,200 to replace property damaged or destroyed by natural disaster. FEMA had a revolving fund of money to cover repairs for public and private structures, and along with the SBA, it issued low-interest loans to individuals and businesses whose flood insurance did not cover their loss, with caps of 8 percent interest rate.[117] In addition to direct federal assistance, New York and Pennsylvania now provide financial and technical assistance to victims of disaster, although much of the funding for these programs originated with the federal government.[118] Unlike their counterparts, who waited months for Congress to take action, victims of Tropical Storm Lee had much quicker access to the broad array of state and federal benefits. One method of comparing the benefits available to flood victims in 1972 and those in 2011 is to reflect on the fact that in 1972, Howard Robison issued a one-page list of benefits for disaster victims, but in 2011, senator Kirsten Gillibrand of New York issued a thirty-six-page booklet listing benefits.[119]

More benefits have meant more paperwork. As Tunkhannock, Pennsylvania, mayor Norm Ball said with some resignation, "It's quite a process; I've dealt with it before."[120] Managing the rules and regulations created by the NFIP, which was now overseen by FEMA, falls on local government officials. Thomas Balskiewicz of West Pittston in the Wyoming Valley lamented, "In Luzerne County, there are 76 municipalities. Many of the communities are staffed by one person that handles all administrative functions. Typically, salaries are low, and turnover is high. Most do not have the technical expertise or training to properly administer the flood insurance Program."[121] Because of this, a year after Tropical Storm Lee, residents of West Pittston discovered that they had run afoul of the FEMA-run program. Many residents had remodeled or rebuilt their homes without obtaining permits or following the stringent FEMA guidelines, and as a result, the agency threatened to remove the flood insurance program entirely.[122]

The flooding spawned by Tropical Storm Lee drew instant comparisons with Hurricane Agnes, which had become the benchmark by which all floods are measured in the Twin Tiers. Theodore Champney, who worked for the NWS in Binghamton, New York, said Tropical Storm Lee was worse than anything he had seen in his years of working for the weather service. Josie Uravage of Wilkes-Barre, Pennsylvania, called it "the worst disaster since Tropical Storm Agnes in 1972." James ("Jim") Brozena, the executive director of the Luzerne County Flood Protection Authority, echoed this sentiment and drew a closer parallel by noting that residents of the Wyoming Valley had in 1972 and again in 2011 been lulled into thinking they were safe behind their dikes and levees and had forgotten the dangers of flooding. Like the civil defense personnel in 1972, Brozena found that local emergency managers and first responders were not well prepared for the disaster. "A lot of people working in flood protection and emergency services had no prior experience with floods."[123]

Tropical Storm Lee showed the need to enhance local awareness and knowledge of flood hazards. After Lee, some communities launched new local-federal partnerships to address flood preparedness.[124] This led to new programs to raise flood awareness. Without this knowledge, people are left unprepared and devastated by the unexpected. Josie Uravage bought a house a mile from the Susquehanna River on West Main Street in Plymouth Township, Pennsylvania, in 2003. Since it was a mile from the river, it never occurred to her that it would be in a flood zone, but she learned the hard way that it was when her house flooded in 2004, 2005, 2006, and again in 2011.[125]

The Tioga County government erected 48 "Communal Visual Landmark Flood Signs" that warn residents of the historical high-water mark in that area.[126] These signs are tangible reminders that flooding has occurred, and may occur again. Nationally, FEMA has adopted a similar flood awareness campaign called the High Water Mark Initiative, which allows local officials to apply to have signs placed in their cities to indicate the high mark of historical flooding. Harrisburg, Pennsylvania was one of the first test communities, and the signs, which are scattered around the city, show where and how high floodwater reached during Hurricane Agnes in 1972.[127] Such knowledge may affect income from property tax revenue if people or businesses decide not to locate in areas that are at risk for flooding.

Partnerships between the National Weather Service and cell phone carriers are also making individuals more aware of flooding. Despite the saturation of weather news through the NWS National Warning System (NAWAS), which covers 95 percent of the United States and territories and twenty-four-hour access to weather forecasts on television, cable, Internet, and weather apps on smartphones, residents in the Twin Tiers were caught off guard when Tropical Storm Lee struck.[128] Officials found that "Many residents and business owners complained to officials that they did not have a proper warning or were not sufficiently prepared for the storm. Many stated they heard emergency vehicles in the streets, but the message announcing evacuation procedures was garbled and difficult to understand." Misunderstanding the situation meant residents did not evacuate or move valuable property to higher ground.[129]

To better instruct the public, the NWS and several U.S. wireless service carriers partnered to add push notifications to smartphones. This program follows a successful project launched in Canada,[130] which allows emergency management the ability to send out alerts to people within a specific radius of a disaster. This more specific, personal alert system, seems to address the problem of general alerts broadcast to the entire public, which had been ignored or misunderstood.[131]

Developments in disaster policy from Hurricane Agnes in 1972 to Tropical Storm Lee in 2011 show an improvement in how governments manage disaster. The rise of emergency management as a profession, utilization of new technology, and enhanced cooperation between government agencies has made a significant difference over the last half-century. The new emphasis on shaping the individual response to disaster is encouraging. However, all of this policy has been driven by the continually, and perhaps even rising, risk of flooding that resulted from prior government policy that allowed populations to move into areas of risk. Perhaps the twenty-first century will be the century in which Americans take stock of the antecedents to disaster and the culpability of past policy.

Epilogue

INTO THE FUTURE

Imagine the Susquehanna River as it was before flood control projects and levees, before the logging and coal industry denuded the countryside surrounding the river, before the advent of railroads, automobiles, and floodplain development. The river supported aquatic plants and animals and the terrestrial creatures that fed on them. Native Americans and later European settlers found an abundance of resources including the river itself, timber, fertile fields caused by flooding, and coal. Dwellings along the river were situated above the floodplain to avoid the expectable flooding. Annual flooding and a greater flood every decade or so fertilized the soil near the river and helped promote wetlands and woodlands that absorbed excess water. Floods dug the riverbed deeper and built higher banks that kept water mostly within the floodplain.

This changed in the nineteenth century as intensive logging and mining reshaped the land beside the river and efforts at farming and industry destroyed wetlands and woodlands. Visiting Elmira, New York, in the 1840s, writer and poet Nathanial Parker Willis shuddered at the ugliness along the river there and expressed his desire that Congress should buy all the riverfront property along the Susquehanna Basin, clear it, and turn it back into public space.[1] His ideal was not to be as, development increased in the twentieth century, when local, state and federal policy encouraged more building on the flood plain and constructed levees and dams to protect these buildings, thereby lulling citizens into believing they were safe from flooding. Cities crowded what was once a floodplain, and development along the river meant more roads, sewers, and underground utilities, which further destroyed habitats.[2]

Federal disaster relief, initiated in 1950, subsidized riverfront development as government relief payments eased the financial burden caused when the Susquehanna flooded. Attempts to dissuade people from building or rebuilding in the vicinity of the river, such as the National Flood Insurance Program (NFIP), proved unsuccessful. After Congress waived mandates and kept flood insurance premiums low, insurance payouts covered property damage and people merely rebuilt. Changes in the Stafford Act in the 1990s were made to encourage those owning homes or businesses that had experienced repetitive flooding to sell out and relocate.

The Volkmer Amendment to the Stafford Act created a government fund to buy out private homes and businesses located in persistent flood zones. The federal government offered 75 percent of the cost of buying the property and requested that the state or local government pay the final quarter of the cost. People who offered to sell there received the preflood market rate for their property. This proved successful, and in just five years, the Hazard Mitigation Program bought more than twenty thousand homes and businesses along the Mississippi River. In some cases, the program bought entire towns.[3] This was not popular in the Susquehanna River Basin, however, where people continued to demand that the government build higher or longer dikes and levees to protect them from flooding.

As late-twentieth-century deindustrialization removed manufacturing from cities such as Corning, Elmira, and Wilkes-Barre, local governments sought economic revitalization through redevelopment. Their efforts added new infrastructure in the form of roads, pavement, parking lots, buildings, sewers, and other utilities, which in turn removed more woodlands and wetlands. Concrete and asphalt replaced nature, absorbing less water and allowing more to enter streamlets and creeks feeding the river, which led to new flooding along the river. The cycle of development and risk to life and property persisted in this region throughout the twentieth century.[4]

Changes in the policy toward the Susquehanna River began after the first decade of the twenty-first century. After Tropical Storm Lee in 2011, Scott Cuppett of the New York Department of Environmental Conservation pointed to the poor choices made after Hurricane Agnes in 1972, which, he claimed, continued to put "people and investments . . . in harm's way." "The only sure way to reduce flooding is to keep our assets out of these areas while creating a more resilient watershed that can absorb and retain rainfall from intense storms," added Cuppett.[5] In other words, it was to stop development and revert to natural systems to absorb water and restore the Susquehanna to its predeveloped state.

Following Tropical Storm Lee, neither the U.S. Army Corps of Engineers nor the state of Pennsylvania showed interest in adding to or creating new flood walls along the Susquehanna River, the policy that had been preferred in the twentieth century.[6] Instead, the state obtained grants from FEMA, which, along with an additional $8.5 million grant from HUD, it used to purchase houses and businesses in the Wyoming Valley. Hundreds of people, tired of the perpetual flooding, sold their homes to the local government, which then cleared them off the floodplain and began to restore the river and floodplain to a natural state. Most towns and cities planned to use the new green space for sports facilities, parks, and historical monuments in order to give the riverfront back to the public.[7]

After spending billions to build infrastructure and billions more to restore flooded property, leaders in government are beginning to embrace the idea of a managed retreat from the riverfront. "By purchasing severely flood-prone properties and turning these high risk areas into open space, we can protect the community from future flooding," said U.S. Senator Kirsten Gillibrand in a joint press release with Senator Charles Schumer of New York.[8] After Tropical Storm Lee, the State of New York. in conjunction with federal authorities and local governments initiated the purchase of hundreds of properties near Binghamton. Perhaps the most ambitious plan was set for Sidney, New York, where the mayor and local authorities decided to clear away the entire neighborhood that sat on the floodplain and move the people to a new development on what was once farmland.[9]

This process is painful for cities in the Twin Tiers, a region still suffering from the lingering effects of deindustrialization. Once the local government buys the property, it is removed from the tax roll.[10] The cost of maintaining the renatured property falls on the local government. Mayor Tom Blaskiewicz of West Pittston noted this Catch-22, "If we raze the homes, our tax base is reduced, and on top of that, the maintenance of the properties falls on the borough, a cost that any small town with an already reduced tax base would find it difficult to pay for."[11] Local governments, especially those already stressed by years of economic decline, are incapable of doing this work alone. Just as their ability to combat natural disasters required the intervention of regional partnerships, state intervention, and federal resources; they will need this assistance if they are to continue with this program. One solution might be to develop public-private partnerships. The local governments might purchase the land but transfer it to an organization such as the Land Trust which would take on the responsibility for maintenance. These programs have been successful elsewhere and could mitigate the hardship small towns and cities bear in this process.[12]

Yet, this fundamental rethinking may only be the beginning. An even more radical idea is being advanced by environmentalist urge the removal of existing levees and dams along the Susquehanna. This idea was inspired by efforts in New England, where over 125 dams have been removed and the local rivers revitalized. To critics who suggest that the Susquehanna River is much larger than any of the restored New England rivers, environmentalists remind them that the Delaware River runs 330 miles from the Catskill Mountains to the Delaware Basin without structural barriers. The river is as federally designated wild and scenic river and manages flooding by natural rather than artificial means. Already the State of Pennsylvania leads the nation in removing old dams and implementing the policy of allowing smaller rivers to revive and develop natural flood barriers.[13]

Over the next century, the Union of Concerned Scientists predicts calamitous flooding, especially in the northeast which will become wetter and make flooding more frequent and intense.[14] It is this climate crisis that has awakened citizens and the government to the need for human adjustment to the natural rhythm of the river and for the managed retreat off the floodplain. It is not wholly inconceivable that in the future the Susquehanna River might bear a strong resemblance to its pre-developed past and satisfy Nathaniel Parker Willis' prophetic desire that the floodplain and rivers be stripped of buildings and returned to the community.[15]

Notes

INTRODUCTION

1. "Kate Fleisher, Chronology of a Catastrophy," *Star Gazette*, July 2, 1972, 30.
2. Bill O'Brien, "Living Walk Like Dead," *Democrat and Chronicle*, June 26, 1972; *Star-Gazette, The Great Flood of '72 in the Twin Tiers* (Elmira, NY: *Star-Gazette*, n.d.).
3. Quoted in Stranahan, *Susquehanna*, 129.
4. Rita McCall, "Souchik: "I Knew We Were in for Big Trouble . . . an Uncontrollable Situation,"" *Citizen's Voice*, June 23, 1992; Nicholas Souchik, "The Day 'Agnes' Made the Sirens Wail." *Sunday Independent*, June 24, 1973, sec A.
5. Nixon is quoted in Jack Brubaker, *Down the Susquehanna to the Chesapeake* (University Park, PA: Pennsylvania State University Press, 2002), 60.
6. Robert Dyment, "When the Next Big Flood Hits: Lessons from Hurricane Agnes," *Popular Mechanics* 139 (June 1973), 122–125.
7. Richard Nixon, "Remarks Proposing Additional Emergency Disaster Relief Following Tropical Storm Agnes," July 12, 1972, online at Gerhard Peters and John T. Woolley, The American Presidency Project https://www.presidency.ucsb.edu/node/254630.
8. Until 1970, the NWS was known as the National Weather Bureau.

1. AMERICAN DISASTER POLICY THROUGH 1972

1. "Dear Mr. President," September 10, 1972, Box 65, Folder 22, Joseph M. McDade Congressional Papers, McHugh Special Collections, University of Scranton (hereafter McDade Papers). The names of the petitioners have been removed to protect their privacy.
2. Gareth Davies, "Dealing with Disaster: The Politics of Catastrophe in the United States, 1789–1861," *American Nineteenth Century History* 14, no. 1 (2013): 53–72, https://doi.org/10.1080/14664658.2013.768422.
3. Disaster Relief Act of 1966, online at https://www.gpo.gov/fdsys/pkg/STATUTE-80/pdf/STATUTE-80-Pg1316.pdf; Richard Nixon, "Statement on Signing the Disaster Relief Act of 1970," December 31, 1970, online at Gerhard Peters and John T. Woolley, The American Presidency Project, https://www.presidency.ucsb.edu/node/240834.
4. Grover Cleveland: "Veto Message," February 16, 1887, online at Gerhard Peters and John T. Woolley, The American Presidency Project, http://www.presidency.ucsb.edu/ws/?pid=71489; see also David A. Moss, *When All Else Fails: Government as the Ultimate Risk Manager* (Cambridge, Mass.: Harvard University Press, 2004), 254.
5. Barton's concern had racist undertones; see Marion Moser Jones, "Race Class and Gender Disparities in Clara Barton's Late Nineteenth-Century Disaster Relief," *Environment and History* 17, no. 1 (February 2011): 107–131, http://www.jstor.org.ezproxy.naz.edu/stable/25799117; Marian Moser Jones, *The American Red Cross from Clara Barton to the New Deal* (Baltimore: Johns Hopkins University Press, 2013).
6. Stephen Skowronek, *Building a New American State: The Expansion of National Administrative Capacities, 1877–1920* (Princeton: Princeton University Press, 2002); Gerald Grob, *Mental Illness and American Society, 1875–1940* (Princeton: Princeton University Press, 1983), 7–29.

7. Gareth Davies, "The Emergence of a National Politics of Disaster, 1865–1900," *Journal of Policy History* 26, no. 3 (July 2014): 305–326, https://doi.org/10.1017/S089803 0614000141.

8. Davies "The Emergence of a National Politics of Disaster," 316–317.

9. Disaster policy was event-driven, as new legislation followed from specific disasters. Thomas Birkland first used this concept to explain disaster policy in *After Disaster: Agenda Setting, Public Policy, and Focusing Events* (Washington, D.C.: Georgetown University Press, 1997); Bruce Clary, "The Evolution and Structure of Natural Hazards Policies," *Public Administration Review* 45 (January 1985): 20–28, http://links.jstor.org/sici?sici=0033-335 2%28198501%2945%3C20%3ATEASON%3E2.0.CO%3B2-%23; Roy S. Popkin, "The History and Politics of Disaster Management in the United States," in *Nothing to Fear: Risks and Hazards in American Society*, edited by Andrew Kirby, 104 (Tucson: University of Arizona Press, 1990).

10. Peter May, *Recovering from Catastrophes: Federal Disaster Relief Policy and Politics* (Westport, Conn.: Praeger, 1985), 19. Bryan Jones and Frank R. Baumgartner developed the idea that policy movement occurs through a punctuated equilibrium of rapid change followed by little or no development, see their *Agendas and Instability in American Politics* (Chicago: University of Chicago Press, 1993).

11. Philip L. Fradkin, *The Great Earthquake and Firestorms of 1906: How San Francisco Nearly Destroyed Itself* (University of California Press, 2006); Popkin, "History and Politics of Disaster Management," 104.

12. Patrick S. Roberts, *Disasters and the American State: How Politicians, Bureaucrats, and the Public Prepare for the Unexpected* (repr., New York: Cambridge University Press, 2016), 75.

13. For a discussion of the racist nature of federal relief see Pete Daniel, *Deep'n as It Come: The 1927 Mississippi River Flood* (New York: Oxford University Press, 1977); John Barry, *Rising Tide: The Great Mississippi Flood of 1927 and How It Changed America* (New York: Simon and Schuster, 1998); Robyn Spencer, "Contested Terrain: The Mississippi Flood of 1927 and the Struggle to Control Black Labor," *Journal of Negro History* 79, no. 2 (Spring 1994): 170–181, DOI: 10.2307/2717627; Jason David Rivera and DeMond Shondell Miller, "Continually Neglected: Situating Natural Disasters in the African American Experience," *Journal of Black Studies* 37, no. 4 (March 2007): 503–533, DOI: 10.1177 /0021934706296190.

14. David Butler, "The Expanding Role of the Federal Government: 1927–1950," in *Emergency Management: The American Experience, 1900–2010*, edited by Claire Rubin, 51–82 (Boca Raton, Fla.: Taylor and Francis, 2012).

15. Michele Landis Dauber, *The Sympathetic State: Disaster Relief and the Origins of the Welfare State* (Chicago: University of Chicago Press, 2013); Sidney M. Milkis and Michael Nelson, *The American Presidency: Origins and Development, 1776–1998* (Washington, D.C.: CQ Press, 1999), 270–271.

16. Historians of public policy continue to debate whether the New Deal was a turning point for federal disaster policy or merely the culmination of preexisting trends. Michele Landis Dauber, *The Sympathetic State: Disaster Relief and the Origins of the American Welfare State* (Chicago: University of Chicago Press, 2013) argues that the New Deal was the culmination rather than a turning point and that the origins of federal disaster policy should be moved back into the nineteenth century. Gareth Davies finds little evidence that the nineteenth century was an incubator for the twentieth-century disaster policy and points to the weak administrative state, the lack of sustained congressional interest in the subject, and a public that had little expectation of federal assistance; see Davies, "Dealing with Disaster" and his review of Dauber in *The Historian* 77 (2015): 116–118.

17. George Haddow, Jane Bullock, and Damon P. Coppola, *Introduction to Emergency Management*, 3rd ed. (Burlington: Elsevier, 2007), 2; Clary, "The Evolution and Structure of Natural Hazards Policies," 24; Butler, "The Expanding Role of the Federal Government," 51.

18. Surplus Property Law of 1917; *Subcommittee on Natural Disaster Relief, A Subcommittee Report on Natural Disaster Relief* (Washington, D.C.: Government Printing Office, 1955), 3–4; U.S. Congress, "Alleviation of Damage from Flood or Other Catastrophe," S. Rpt, 435, 80th Cong., 1st sess., 1947; *Congressional Record*, 80th Cong., 1st sess., 1947: 8300–1; *Congressional Record*, 81st Cong., 2d sess., 1950: 896.

19. Bruce Lindsay and Justin Murray, *Disaster Relief Funding and Emergency Supplemental Appropriations Congressional Research Service*, July 15, 2009, http://assets.opencrs.com/rpts/R40708_20090715.pdf.

20. Gareth Davies, "Pre-Modern Disaster Politics: Combating Catastrophe in the 1950s," *Publius: The Journal of Federalism* 47, no. 2 (2017), DOI: 10.1093/publius/pjx016.

21. John F. Kennedy, "Executive Order 11051—Prescribing Responsibilities of the Office of Emergency Planning in the Executive Office of the President," September 27, 1962, online at Gerhard Peters and John T. Woolley, The American Presidency Project, https://www.presidency.ucsb.edu/node/235997; Clark F. Norton, *Emergency Preparedness and Disaster Assistance: Federal Organization and Programs* (Washington, D.C.: Congressional Research Services, 1978), 19; *New Dimensions of Civil Emergency Preparedness, 1969–1973* (Washington, D.C.: Office of Emergency Preparedness, 1973), 3–5.

22. Elizabeth Tower, *Anchorage, From its Humble Origins as a Railroad Construction Camp* (Anchorage: Epicenter Press, 1999), 97; William Anderson, *Disaster and Organizational Change: A Study of the Long Term Consequences of the 1964 Alaskan Earthquake* (Ohio State Disaster Research Center, 1969), 19–23; Thomas A. Birkland, *Lessons of Disaster: Policy Change after Catastrophic Events* (Washington, D.C.: Georgetown University Press, 2006), 132.

23. "LBJ and Senator Russell Long on Hurricane Betsy," University of Virginia Miller Center, https://millercenter.org/the-presidency/educational-resources/lbj-and-senator-russell-long-on-hurricane-betsy.

24. Kent Germany, "LBJ and the Response to Hurricane Betsy," University of Virginia, Miller Center, http://whitehousetapes.net/exhibit/lbj-and-response-hurricane-betsy.

25. Gareth Davies, "The Historical Presidency: Lyndon Johnson and Disaster Politics," *Presidential Studies Quarterly* 47(2017):529–551, https://doi.org/10.1111/psq.12384.

26. OEP Director Buford Ellington warned Johnson that his actions were opening the door to a new entitlement; see Natalie Schuster, "This 'Who Shot John Thing': Disaster Relief as Entitlement in the 20th Century," *Federal History* 5 (2014): 84–107; Gareth Davies coined the term "responder in chief" to address the presidential role in disasters after Johnson; see Davies, "Taming Disaster: Fatalism and Mastery in American Disaster Management, 1800–2013" (January 2014), http://americanstudiesglasgow.blogspot.com/2014/01/taming-disaster-fatalism-and-mastery-in.html.

27. Keith Bea, "The Formative Years: 1950–1978," in *Emergency Management: The American Experience 1900–2010*, edited by Claire Rubin (Boca Raton, FL: Routledge, 2012), 83–114, https://doi.org/10.1201/b11887. Lyndon Johnson, "Statement by the President upon Signing Natural Disaster Act 1966," November 6, 1966, online at Gerhard Peters and John T. Woolley, The American Presidency Project https://www.presidency.ucsb.edu/node/238500; Rivera and Miller, "A Brief History," 5–14.

28. Kenneth J. Bagstad, Kevin Stapleton, John R D'Agostino, *Ecological Economics* 63, no. 2–3 (2007): 285–298, https://econpapers.repec.org/RePEc:eee:ecolec:v:63:y:2007:i:2–3:p:285–298.

29. Robert M. Collins, "The Economic Crisis of 1968 and the Waning of the 'American Century'" *American Historical Review* 101, no. 2 (1996): 396–423, https://doi.org/10.1086/ahr/101.2.396; President Eisenhower favored flood insurance but despite passage, Congress failed to fund the Flood Insurance Act of 1956, see The American Institute for Research, The Pacific Institute for Research and Evaluation, and Deloitte and Rouche, LLP, *A Chronology of Major Events Affecting the National Flood Insurance Program, prepared for the Federal Emergency Management Agency*, under Contract no. 282-98–029 (October 2002), http://www.dhs.gov/xlibrary/assets/privacy/privacy_pia_mip_apnd_h.pdf.

30. Richard Nixon, "Address to the Nation on Domestic Programs August 8, 1969," *Public Papers of President Nixon* (Washington, D.C., 1969), 637–638.

31. "Record of Major Nixon Legislative Proposals and Action Taken in the Second Session of 92d Congress," *New York Times*, October 20, 1972.

32. Stephen Wayne, "Expectations of the President," in *The President and the Public*, edited by Doris A. Graber (Philadelphia: Institute for the Study of Human Issues, 1982). Some scholars see a correlation between the rising expectations of the electorate and the string of troubled presidencies that the United States experienced from the late 1960s to the present. See Hank C. Jenkins-Smith, Carol L. Silva, and Richard Waterman, "Micro and Macro Models of the Presidential Expectations Gap," *Journal of Politics* 67, no. 3 (2005): 690–715, https://doi.org/10.1111/j.1468–2508.2005.00335.x; Richard Neustadt, *Presidential Power: The Politics of Leadership from FDR to Carter* (New York: John Wiley and Sons, 1980).

33. "Recovery Commander George Arthur Lincoln," *New York Times*, August 23, 1969.

34. Philip Shabecoff, "US Panel Issues Oil Price Study," *New York Times*, May 4, 1971; Grace Lichtenstein, "A U.S. Agency here Bows Out, 2d Steps into Wage-Price Scene," *New York Times*, November 13, 1971. https://search-proquest-com.ezproxy.naz.edu/docview/119129888?accountid=28167.

35. Judith Howard and Ernest Zebrowski, *Category 5: The Story of Camille. Lessons Unlearned from America's Most Violent Hurricane* (Ann Arbor: University of Michigan, 2010); Roger Pielke, Chantal Simonpietri, and Jennifer Oxelson, "Thirty Years after Hurricane Camille: Lessons Learned, Lessons Lost," http://sciencepolicy.colorado.edu/about_us/meet_us/roger_pielke/camille/report.html; "The U.S. Unprepared for Big Disasters," *Washington Post*, January 11, 1970; questions of racial bias surfaced early; see "Red Cross Actions Dehumanizing to Negro," *New York Times*, January 10, 1970.

36. Mark M. Smith, *Camille, 1969 Histories of a Hurricane*, Mercer University Lamar Memorial Lectures; No. 51. (Athens, University of Georgia Press, 2011), 2–4.

37. Office of Emergency Preparedness, *A Year of Rebuilding: The Federal Response to Hurricane Camille* (Washington, D.C.: Government Printing Office, 1970), 7; Mark M. Smith, *Camille 1969: Histories of a Hurricane* (Athens: University of Georgia Press, 2011), 2.

38. Tom Casey, Memorandum September 2, 1969, Box 1, Folder 1, Records of the Disaster Study Group, 1971-1972, Records Group 396. Office of Emergency Preparedness, 1951–1973. National Archives, College Park, Maryland (hereafter OEP Records).

39. Nixon saw disaster in political terms. In 1970 he was more worried that a Texas drought would lead Hispanics to move north than in the economic effect on Texas ranchers. President Richard M. Nixon and George A. Lincoln, April 13, 1971, Miller Center, Secret White House Tapes, https://millercenter.org/the-presidency/secret-white-house-tapes/1-74.

40. Another aspect of the Southern Strategy was the nomination of Clement Haynsworth to the Supreme Court in 1969. Senator Bayh led Democrats on the Judiciary Committee in rejecting Haynsworth's nomination. Democrats claimed their opposition was due to improprieties evinced by Judge Haynsworth when he was on the Court of Appeals. However, Haynsworth, a southern and conservative judge, was targeted by labor unions and civil

rights leaders, both critical constituencies of the Democratic Party. *Congress and the Nation: A Review of Government and Politics*, Volume 3, 1969–1972 (Washington, D.C.: Congressional Quarterly Services, 1973), 292–295; Nixon was not the first to see the political implications of disaster, presidents since Eisenhower have been cognizant of the political value of disaster actions; see Richard Sylves, *Disaster Politics and Policy: Emergency Management and Homeland Security*, 2nd revised edition (Washington, D.C.: CQ Press, 2014), 218–219.

41. "Forecasters Need Better Equipment," *Mississippi Press*, August 22, 1969; Francis Lewine, "Better Storm Prediction Equipment Urged by Agnew," *Times-Picayune*, August 27, 1969.

42. Charles Sullivan, "Camille: The Mississippi Gulf Coast in the Coils of the Snake," *Gulf Coast Historical Review* 2, no. 2 (January 1987): 49–77; Smith, *Camille 1969*, 50.

43. "The South: Welcome in Mississippi," *Time*, September 19, 1969, 21.

44. Sullivan, "Camille," 70.

45. Smith, *Camille 1969*, 32.

46. "S.B.A. Insists Few Negro Areas Were Hit by Hurricane Camille," *New York Times*, January 1, 1970.

47. Smith, *Camille 1969*, 45.

48. Memo Wilfred H. Rommel to Richard T. Burress RE: Disaster Relief Legislation; July 22, 1969, Box 1, Folder: 9/1/1969-10/31/1969, White House Central Files: Subject Files: DI (Disasters), Richard Nixon Presidential Library and Museum, Yorba Linda, CA (hereafterWHCF-DI). Rommel noted that the Department of Treasury did not like the new reliance on federal credit after a disaster.

49. Andrew Morris, "Hurricane Camille and the New Politics of Federal Disaster Relief, 1965–1970," *Journal of Policy History* 26, no. 3 (2014): 406–428, https://doi.org/10.1017/S0898030614000189.

50. The term "disaster safety net" is used by Ted Steinberg, *Acts of God: The Unnatural History of Natural Disaster in America*, 2nd ed. (New York: Oxford University Press, 2000), 176.

51. "Hurricane Kills at Least 50; Record Winds Whip Gulf Coast," *Washington Post*, August 19, 1969.

52. 91st Congress, "Conference Report to Accompany H.R. 6508," 14.

53. Stewart McClure noted Muskie's grandstanding; see "Stewart E. McClure: Chief Clerk, Senate Committee on Labor, Education, and Public Welfare (1949–1973)," Oral History Interviews, Senate Historical Office, Washington, D.C. (hereafter Stewart McClure).

54. David Moss, "The Peculiar Politics of American Disaster Policy: How Television Has Changed Federal Relief" in *The Irrational Economist: Making Decisions in a Dangerous World*, (eds.) Erwann Michel-Kerjan and Paul Slovic (New York: Public Affairs Books, 2010), 151–160.

55. Robert C. Maynard, "Bitter Exchanges Mark Camille Relief Hearing," *Washington Post*, January 8, 1970; Robert C. Maynard, "Racial Bias Hindered Relief Effort After Hurricane Camille, Probe Told," *Washington Post*, January 9, 1970; The Red Cross was also single out for bias, Jon Nordheimer, "Red Cross Actions After Storm Called 'Dehumanizing' to Negro," *New York Times*, January 10, 1970.

56. United States Congress Senate Committee on Public Works Special Subcommittee on Disaster Relief, *Federal Response to Hurricane Camille: Hearings, Ninety-First Congress, Second Session* (Washington D.C.: Government Printing Office, 1970), 134; Gordon Brown, "Bayh Urges Speedy Aid in Disasters," *Washington Post*, January 15, 1970.

57. United States Congress Senate Committee on Public Works Special Subcommittee on Disaster Relief, *Federal Response to Hurricane Camille: Hearings, Ninety-First Congress,*

Second Session (Washington, D.C.: U.S. Govt. Print. Off., 1970), 134; J.Y. Smith, "Virginia Officials Rap Federal Relief Efforts," *Washington Post*, February 3, 1970.

58. Memo, P.H. McIntire to Tom Casey, "Trip Report to VA. Hearing on Disaster Relief," Box 6, Folder: 2-1-70 - 2-3-70, RG 396 (Office of Emergency Preparedness), National Archives, College Park, Md. (hereafter OEP Records).

59. Tom Herman, "Hurricane Camille Recovery Effort by U.S. Assailed," *Wall Street Journal*, January 5, 1970.

60. Lincoln was a career military man who had been a master of logistics in the U.S. Army; see "Recovery Commander: George Arthur Lincoln," *New York Times*, August 23, 1969; On Bayh, see Gordon Brown, "Bayh Urges Speedy Aid in Disasters," *Washington Post*, January 15, 1970; Memorandum Carl Gidland to General Lincoln, RE: Counter Bayh Activity, February 26, 1970, Box 5, Folder 1, RG 396, OEP Records. Some of this memo appeared in a later Office of Emergency Preparedness publication praising the "heroic" effort of the Federal Government see the United States. Office of Emergency Preparedness, *A Year of Rebuilding: The Federal Response to Hurricane Camille* (Washington, D.C.: Office of Emergency Preparedness, 1970).

61. Acts of God, of course, are outside the power of government to control, which exculpates any government inaction.

62. S.3619 A Bill to Create, within the Office of the President, an Office of Disaster Assistance, March 20, 1970, 6.

63. Ibid., 40. One White House staffer liked the idea of all-risk insurance. Fred LaRue wrote a memo on January 20, 1970, and said the idea had "practical and political appeal." See Fred LaRue, RE: Summary of Comments of White House Study Session on Disaster Legislation and Camille, January 20, 1970, Box 1, Folder Disasters 1/1/1970-3/31/1970 (WHCF-DI).

64. Richard Nixon, "Message to Congress on Disaster Relief Act of 1970," in *Federal Response to Hurricane Camille, Hearing before the Special Committee on Disaster Relief*, 1480.

65. Ibid., 1481.

66. Office of Emergency Preparedness, *A Year of Rebuilding*, 3; *Federal Response to Hurricane Camille: Hearings Before the Special Committee on Disaster Relief of the Committee on Public Works*, three volumes (Washington, D.C.: Government Printing Office 1970). Peter J. May claims Bayh's bill was passed in place of the bill offered by the administration, but a careful look at the proposed and final version finds that this is an overstatement. Peter J. May, *Recovering from Catastrophes: Federal Disaster Relief Policy and Politics* (Westport, CT: Greenwood Press, 1978), 26.

67. Bayh's interest in natural disaster is addressed by Stewart McClure see "Stewart E. McClure: Chief Clerk, Senate Committee on Labor, Education, and Public Welfare (1949–1973)," Oral History Interviews, Senate Historical Office, Washington, D.C., https://www.senate.gov/artandhistory/history/resources/pdf/McClure7.pdf; this point is also made in Andrew Morris, "Hurricane Camille and the New Politics of Federal Disaster Relief, 1965–1970," 411.

68. Office of Emergency Preparedness, *Disaster Preparedness; Report to the Congress.* (Washington, 1972); David Moss, *When All Else Fails*, 256.

69. "Major Congressional Action," *Congressional Quarterly Almanac*, February 6, 1970, 754–756; Cathy Davis, "Major Disaster Assistance Legislation" (PhD Diss., Ball State University 1971), 38; Stewart McClure suggested that the House was responsible for removing the disaster insurance from the bill.

70. Richard Nixon: "Statement on Signing the Disaster Relief Act of 1970," December 31, 1970, online at Gerhard Peters and John T. Woolley, *The American Presidency Project*, http://www.presidency.ucsb.edu/ws/?pid=2875. Emphasis added.

71. Cathy Davis, "Major Disaster Assistance Legislation," 27–28; Keith Bea, "The Formative Years: 1950–1978," 97.

2. AGNES MAKES LANDFALL

1. Dorothy Smith (wife of Bill Smith), interview with the author, September 30, 2006 (hereafter cited as Dorothy Smith).

2. Sarah Krazinksi, "A Flood of Animal Tales," *Chemung Valley Reporter*, June 19, 1997; "Bill Smith Sows Crop Protest," Bill Smith Folder, Booth Memorial Library, Chemung Historical Society (hereafter cited as Smith Folder, Booth Library).

3. Placemat from Smithome Farms Restaurant in the Biography File, Booth Memorial Library, Chemung Historical Society; "Weather Reports and Forecasts," *New York Times*, June 15, 1972.

4. "Hurricane Agnes: The Most Costly Storm," *Weatherwise* 25, no. 4 (August 1972), 174–184, https://doi: 10.1080/00431672.1972.9931598.

5. Dudley Clendinen, "A Surprise Punch: Anatomy of a Storm," *Tampa Bay Times*, June 25, 1972.

6. "Storm Surge Overview," NOAA, http://www.nhc.noaa.gov/surge/.

7. "Nixon Rests in Florida," *Washington Post*, June 19, 1972; "Around the Nation: 18 Storm Dead," *Washington Post*, June 21, 1972.

8. National Weather Service Bulletin, Box 83, Folder June 21–July 14, 1972, Records Group 10770 Department of Environmental Conservation, Series: Hurricane Agnes Damage Files, New York State Archives (hereafter cited as Hurricane Agnes Damage Files).

9. "Wilkes-Barre Business Area Flooded," *New York Times*, June 25, 1972. Kai T. Erikson, *Everything in Its Path: Destruction of Community in Buffalo Creek Flood* (New York: Simon and Schuster, 1976); Charles Michael Ray, "40 Years after Killer Flood, A Reshaped City Reflects," NPR, June 8, 2012, http://www.npr.org/2012/06/08/154576917/disastrous-s-d-flood-caused-national-wake-up-call.

10. Bart Barnes, "Wide-Ranging Floods Stagger DC Area: D.C. Area Is Hit By Heavy Flood," *Washington Post*, June 24, 1972.

11. Wallace Shugg, "The Great Patapsco Flood of 1972," *Maryland Historical Magazine* 96, no. 1 (Spring 2001): 53–67; Betsy Stein, "Floods Won't Surprise County Again," *Columbian Flier*, June 19, 1997, http://www.ellicottcity.net/tourism/history/floods/hurricane_agnes/pages/a11_jpg.htm.

12. "As Agnes Departs," *Baltimore Sun*, June 23, 1972.

13. "Memories of 1972 Storm Whose Rains Soaked State Are Still Vivid," *Richmond Times-Dispatch*, June 21, 1997.

14. Laurence McQuillan, United Press International, June 23, 1972, Box 7, Folder 75, Records Group 15 Nelson Rockefeller Gubernatorial Series 10: Counsel and Office: Robert R. Douglass Papers, Rockefeller Archive Center (hereafter cited as Robert R. Douglass Papers).

15. Cf. Boone, *Richmond Flood*, n.p. n.d.

16. Forty years after Agnes, the development of regional disaster or mutual assistance pacts between governors remains an area of disaster policy that could be improved.

17. Franklin S. Adams, "Hurricane Agnes: Flooding vs. Dams in Pennsylvania," *Bulletin of the Atomic Scientists* 29, no. 4 (1973): 30–34, https://doi.org/10.1080/00963402.1973.11455470.

18. Herman Dieck, *The Johnstown Flood* (University Park: Pennsylvania State University Press, 2009), 25–26; David McCullough, *The Johnstown Flood* (New York: Simon and Schuster, 1987); Erikson, *Everything in Its Path*. Many dams filled during the Agnes event, which threatened communities along the Susquehanna River Basin.

19. "Conowingo Dam Crest Nears," *Baltimore Evening Sun*, June 24, 1972; Marvin Mandel (Governor of Maryland in 1972) telephone interview, September 14, 2009 (hereafter cited as Marvin Mandel); "Danger at Conowingo Dam Passes," *Baltimore Sun*, June 25, 1972; Michael Clark, "Clean Up Begins in Ellicott City," *Baltimore Sun*, June 25, 1972; Fred Rasmussen, "Hurricane Agnes Roared Across the State," *Baltimore Sun*, June 22, 1997.

20. Robert Dyment, "When the Next Big Flood Hits: Lessons from Hurricane Agnes," *Popular Mechanics* 139 (1973): 122.

21. Susan Q. Stranahan, *Susquehanna, River of Dreams* (Baltimore: Johns Hopkins University Press, 2014), 128–129.

22. John H. Brubaker, *Down the Susquehanna to the Chesapeake* (University Park: Pennsylvania State University Press, 2002), xi–xiii.

23. Henry Diamond to Nelson Rockefeller, "First Hundred Days," October 8, 1970, Folder "DEC State Environmental Plan," Box 2, Department of Environmental Conservation, Records Group 20138, Series 99: State Environmental Plan Files, New York State Archives.

24. Sandy Marvinney, "DEC Efforts in Hurricane Agnes Flood Disaster Saves Lives and Property," *NY State Environment* 2 (August 1972): 1, 12; George Koch, "Travel Voucher," June 21, 1972, Box 83, Folder Flood Emergency Travel Vouchers, Hurricane Agnes Damage Files; "Report of Flood Emergency, June 21–24, 1972," Box 83, Folder Misc. Flood Correspondence R.A. Cook, Hurricane Agnes Damage Files (hereafter cited as Hurricane Agnes Damage Files).

25. "Olean Is Facing Greatest Flood," *Olean Times Herald*, June 22, 1972; Bert Freed, "Rains Claim 4th Life; Olean Braces for Flood as Portville Evacuates," *Buffalo Evening News*, June 22, 1972.

26. "Upstate Hit Hard," *New York Times*, June 24, 1972.

27. Dale Anderson, "Residents along Genesee River Told to Evacuate" *Buffalo Evening News*, June 23, 1972; Peter Stutz, "Dam Saved Million$," *Democrat and Chronicle*, October 18, 1972; Laurence McQuillan, UPI, Douglass Papers.

28. Nuala McGann Dresher, *Engineers for the Public Good: A History of the Buffalo District US Army Corps of Engineers* (Washington, D.C.: Government Printing Office, 1982), 255.

29. Mike Shore, "Dam Operators Walked Tightrope," *Times Union*, October 19, 1972.

30. Mark Schreiner, "A Storm Named Agnes" *New York State Conservationist* 51 (1997): 14.

31. "High Water Still Plagues Tier," *Elmira Star-Gazette*, June 22, 1972.

32. Rockefeller Declaration, Box 132, Howard W. Robison Papers, #3394, Division of Rare and Manuscript Collections, Cornell University Library (hereafter cited as Robison Papers).

33. "What Disaster Declaration Means," *Times Union*, June 23, 1972.

34. Gene Grey, "Placid Chemung Raged Like a Beast," *Sunday Telegram*, July 2, 1972.

35. *The Flood and the Community* (Corning, N.Y.: Corning Glass Works, 1976), 23.

36. *The Flood and the Community*, 27.

37. *The Flood and the Community*, 42; Thomas P. Dimitroff and Lois S. Janes, *History of the Corning-Painted Post Area: 200 Years in Painted Post Country*, revised ed. (Corning, NY: Whitehouse Publications, 1991), 289.

38. Terry Dillman, "Flood Warnings at Corning: A Gap in Communications," *Times Union*, July 1, 1972.

39. Dimitroff and Janes, *History of the Corning-Painted Post Area*, 291.

40. Ethel Kneeland (Painted Post resident), interview by author, July 7, 1985.

41. "Obituaries," *Leader*, June 29, 1972, 12; "Flood Toll Rises: It's an 'Emergency,'" *Democrat and Chronicle*, June 24, 1972.

42. Corning Museum of Glass, "Stories from the Flood of '72: John Fox," May 31, 1972, https://www.youtube.com/watch?v=1-3_xlwkgh8. Ethel Kneeland. The woman who suffered the heart attack, Edith Griffin, later discovered that her sister had a lively time in her attic drinking wine and eating crackers with one of her guests. Her daughter, Sister Raymond Joseph, had also survived the flood unscathed.

43. "Corning Death List," *Rochester Democrat and Chronicle*, June 26, 1972, 9A; Garth Wade, "Legacy of Sorrow: 18 in Steuben Could Not Escape Rising Water," *Star Gazette*, June 19, 2012, 1A-7A. In 1972 the child was listed as Brian; in 2012 his name is listed as Bryan.

44. Bob Rolfe, "Say Lindley Gauges' Failure Cut Hours from Area Flood Warning" *Corning Leader*, October 13, 1972.

45. Joseph Sartori, Jr. (Elmira City Manager, 1972), interview by author, January 21, 2008, (hereafter cited as Joseph Sartori).

46. Ibid.

47. Ibid.

48. Ibid.

49. To evacuate or not is a dilemma even today, Binghamton, New York Mayor Matt Ryan faced criticism from residents for his call to evacuate in 2011 ahead of Tropical Storm Lee. Michael Gormley, "Binghamton Region Flood Damage Assessed," *Democrat and Chronicle*, September 10, 2011, http://en.occa.mard.gov.vn/Crawl-Content/Binghamton-region-flood-damage-assessed-Rochester-Democrat-and-Chronicle/2011/9/10/62004.news.

50. Charles E. Hughes, *Tioga County, PA Flood!* (Utica, N.Y.: Dodge Group Press, 1972); William G. Williams, "Town by Town: Chronicle of Misery," *Sunday Times*, June 25, 1972; *The Flood of 1972 A Special Edition of the Pennsylvania Mirror*, 4–8; "Lock Haven Flooding Worse Yet," *Patriot and Evening News*, June 28, 1972.

51. Lew Powell, "Swenson Recalls Hours of Anxiety," *Patriot and Evening News*, June 28, 1972; Cal Turner, "Disaster Hits Wormleysburg in Still of Night," *Patriot and Evening News*, June 28, 1972.

52. Cal Turner, "Agnes Had Us Fooled," *Patriot and Evening News*, June 28, 1972.

53. Albert Kachik, National Weather Service hydrologist, interviewed by author, September 25, 2008 (hereafter cited as Albert Kachik).

54. David Krantz, *The Trouble with Agnes* (Wilkes-Barre, Pa.: D. L. Krantz, 1973), 60–63; population figures from Population and Housing Unit Counts, Pennsylvania, http://www.census.gov/prod/cen1990/cph2/cph-2-40.pdf.

55. Stranahan, *Susquehanna*, 130–133.

56. Krantz, *Trouble with Agnes*, 84.

57. Clint Morse, "General Townend Reviews Flood," *Wyoming Valley Observer*, July 16–22, 1972.

58. Richard E. Meyer, "Anguish of 1 Family Same for Thousands," *Sunday Times*, July 2, 1972.

59. Carl J. Romanelli and William McGuff, *The Wrath of Agnes a Complete Pictorial and Written History of the June 1972, Flood in the Wyoming Valley* (Wilkes-Barre, Pa.: Media Affiliates, 1973), 18–20.

60. Jean Hronich, "The Day the River Turned Violent," *Citizen's Voice*, June 23, 1982, B3; "Thousands Flee to Higher Ground as Raging River Breaches Dikes," *Times Union*, June 23, 1972.

61. Romanelli and McGuff, *Wrath of Agnes*, 23; Robert Burke, "Wilkes-Barre Reeling under River's Wrath," *Scranton Times*, June 24, 1972; Gene Coleman, "River Apparently Stabilizing; Evacuation Efforts Continuing," *Sunday Times*, June 25, 1972.

62. Susan Stranahan, *Susquehanna River of Dreams*, 117, 134.

63. Robert Dyment, "When the Next Big Flood Hits."

64. Larry Beaupre and Dick Cooper, "Downtown Elmira . . . It's Like a War Zone," *Times Union*, June 26, 1972. Papers in Pennsylvania suggested their cities took on the appearance of "war-torn European cities"; see Romanelli and McGuff, *Wrath of Agnes*, 38.

65. Laurence McQuillan, UPI, RAC; "Nixon Urges Action on Flood Aid Funds," *Leader*, July 18, 1972.

66. Letters: "Kurt Waldheim to Richard Nixon, June 26, 1972," "Nicolai Ceausescu to Richard Nixon, July 5, 1972," and "Maithripala Senanayake to Richard Nixon, June 30, 1972"; Folder July 1, 1972–December 1, 1972, Box 3, White House Central Files: Subject Files: DI (Disasters), National Archives Richard Nixon Papers Project (hereafter cited WHCF-DI).

67. "Dapper Dan Congressman on the Spot," *US News and World Report*, March 6, 1978, 18; "Dapper Dan's Toughest Scene" *Time*, February 20, 1978, 22; "Agnes Isn't over for Daniel Flood," *Sunday Independent*, June 24, 1973, see Daniel Flood Vertical File, Luzerne County Historical Society.

68. Myra McPherson, "Dan Flood on the Spot: The Congressman's Show Goes On," *Washington Post*, March 17, 1978.

69. George Crile, "The Best Congressman"; Marjorie Hunter, "Daniel John Flood," *New York Times*, January 31, 1978.

70. Crile, "Best Congressman": 60–66; William Kashatus III, "'Dapper Dan'"; Adam Clymer, "Looking Out for The Folks Back Home and One's Self," *New York Times*, March 5, 1978.

71. Crile, "Best Congressman," 62; "Agnes Isn't over for Dan Flood."

72. Libby Brennan, "Flood Recalls Cutting Red Tape," *Sunday Independent*, June 27, 1982, in Daniel Flood Vertical File, Luzerne County Historical Society; Crile, "Best Congressman," 63.

73. "James Fred Hastings," Biographical Directory of United States Congress, http://bioguide.Congress.gov/scripts/biodisplay.pl?index=H000327; "Area Checked by Hastings," *Olean Times Herald*, June 26, 1972, 4; "State-Federal Agencies Prepare Aid Missions," *Buffalo Evening News*, June 24, 1972.

74. Joe Sartori.

75. Box 124, Folder: Agnes Overview, Howard W. Robison Papers.

76. Letter: Marina Nickerson to Richard Nixon, July 31, 1972; Box 14, Folder Natural Disasters by State, WHCF DI.

3. WHO'S IN CHARGE?

1. Joe Sartori; Bob Clark, "A Friend in Need—That's Elmira College," *Star-Gazette*, August 19, 1972; Larry Beaupre and Dick Cooper, "Rough Start for Elmira's New Manager," *Times Union*, June 26, 1972.

2. "William Wilcox, Directory Community Affairs to Governor Milton Shapp, August 7, 1972," Box 61, Folder 1 Flood–Flooding, General Files, 1971–1979, MG-309.9, Milton Shapp Papers, Pennsylvania State Archives, Harrisburg (hereafter cited as Milton Shapp Papers).

3. "Wilkes-Barre Rebound on Eighth Anniversary of Giant Flood of 1972," *Sunday Independent*, June 22, 1980, Agnes Vertical File, Luzerne County Historical Society; Robert P. Wolensky and Kenneth C. Wolensky, "Local Governments Problems with Disaster Management: A Literature Review and Structural Analysis," *Policy Studies Review* 9, no. 4 (Summer 1990): 703–725. https://doi.org/10.1111/j.1541–1338.1990.tb01074.x; Robert Wolensky, *Power, Policy, and Disaster: The Political-Organizational Impact of a Major Flood* (Stevens Point: University of Wisconsin-Stevens Point, Center for the Small City, 1984), 86.

4. United States Congress, Committee on Public Works, Subcommittee on Water Resources, *Disaster Preparedness and Assistance Legislation: Hearings, Ninety-third Congress, First Session, on H.R. 7690 and Related Bills* (Washington, DC: Government Printing Office, 1974), 83.

5. Rolfe, "Doubts Persist," 3; "Lack of Warning Cited," *Rochester Democrat and Chronicle*, October 20, 1972. Horizontal fragmentation or the lack of coordination and communication between governments on the same level often occurs during disaster; thus, what happened in New York and Pennsylvania was not unique, see Richard T. Sylves, *Disaster Policy and Politics: Emergency Management and Homeland Security*, 2nd ed. (Washington, D.C.: CQ Press, 2014), 13.

6. Joe Sartori.

7. Sylves, *Disaster Policy and Politics*, 156. Sylves explains that state and local officials sometimes exaggerate the cost of a disaster to meet eligibility requirements under federal law.

8. United States and Office of Emergency Preparedness, *Disaster Preparedness; Report to the Congress* (Washington, D.C., 1972), 11.

9. Paul Beers, *Pennsylvania, Politics Today and Yesterday: The Tolerable Accommodation* (University Park: Penn Pennsylvania State University Press, 1980), 363.

10. Joseph Persico, *The Imperial Rockefeller: A Biography of Nelson A. Rockefeller* (New York: Simon and Shuster, 1982), 39.

11. Cable Neuhaus, "Is There Life after the Governorship?" *Pennsylvania Illustrated*, (October 1979): 46–48; Paul Beers, *Pennsylvania, Politics Today and Yesterday: The Tolerable Accommodation* (University Park: Pennsylvania State University Press, 1980), 369.

12. Associated Press, June 23, 1972, Box 7, Folder 75, Records Group 15, Nelson Rockefeller Gubernatorial Series 10: Counsel and Office: Robert R. Douglass Papers, Rockefeller Archive (hereafter cited Douglass Papers). Rockefeller was vacationing in New Mexico when he heard about the flooding and contacted the White House to ask for assistance, President Richard Nixon's Daily Diary June 23, 1972; White House Central Files, Staff Member and Office Files, Richard Nixon Presidential Library and Museum, Yorba Linda, Calif. (hereafter President's Daily Diary).

13. Michael Sinclair, "Few Happy with Rocky's Tour," *Olean Times Herald*, June 29, 1972.

14. The task force consisted of Theodore Parker, Commissioner Department of Transportation, Abe Lavine, Commissioner Social Services, Edward Logue, President and CEO, Urban Development Corporation, Joseph Swindler, State Public Service Commissioner, Neal L. Moylan, Commissioner of Commerce, Donald J. Wickam, Commissioner of Agriculture, Box 98, Folder "Hurricane Agnes and Federal Disaster Relief," Division of the Budget, Research and Federal Relations Unit, Records Group 1591.98, New York State Archives.

15. Jerry Allan, "State Officials Tackle Massive Flood Clean Up," *Buffalo Evening News*, June 29, 1972.

16. Having been elected governor of New York in 1958, Rockefeller eyed the presidency with the expectation that it would be the apex of his political career. During summer 1972, the governor was trying to buoy his chances by collecting political IOUs as head of Nixon's reelection effort in New York.

17. Michael Sinclair, "Few Happy with Rocky's Tour," *Olean Times Herald*, June 29, 1972.

18. Letter to Nelson A. Rockefeller, July 11, 1972, Governor Nelson A. Rockefeller Papers, Office Records, Microfilm Reel 21, Disaster Files, Agnes July 19–31, 1972, Rockefeller Archives; Ted Parker response, July 26, 1972, ibid.

19. Joseph Persico, *The Imperial Rockefeller: A Biography of Nelson A. Rockefeller* (New York: Simon and Shuster, 1982), 39; See flood requests in Box 7, Folder 75, Robert R.

Douglass Papers, Rockefeller Archives; "Press Release, June 24, 1972," Folder "Hurricane Agnes and Federal Disaster Relief," Box 3, Division of Budget, Research and Federal Relations Unit, Series Issue Files ca. 1960–1972, New York State Archives.

20. Paul B. Beers, *Pennsylvania Politics Today and Yesterday: The Tolerable Accommodation* (State College: Pennsylvania State University Press, 1980), 369.

21. "Dems Accord on Budget Falls Apart," *Pittsburgh Post-Gazette*, June 30, 1972.

22. The context of 1972 is told with aplomb by Theodore H. White, *The Making of the President 1972* (New York: Harpers, 1973; reprint, 2010).

23. ABC News June 1972, Tape #1291, Westinghouse Broadcasting Company Collection, Library of American Broadcasting, University of Maryland Hornbake Library, College Park, Md. (hereafter cited as Westinghouse Collection).

24. ABC News June 1972, Tape #1291, Westinghouse Collection.

25. White, *The Making of the President 1972.*

26. The flood made attendance at the convention impossible for Shapp who, along with all of Pennsylvania's top Democratic leaders, withdrew and allowed alternates to attend to the convention in their stead. See "Shapp, Kline, Key Legislators to Skip Democratic Conclave," *Scranton Times*, July 1, 1972.

27. "Governor's News Conference, June 29, 1972," Box 49, Folder 8, Records Group, MG 309.14, Milton Shapp Papers.

28. William H. Jones and Nancy Scannel, "Nixon Vows More Flood Funds; Orders Agencies Cut Red Tape," *Washington Post*, June 27, 1972; William H. Jones and Nancy Scannel, "Nixon Asks $100 Million More to Aid Agnes Flood Victims," *Washington Post*, June 28, 1972.

29. Lee is quoted in Beers, *Pennsylvania Politics*, 369.

30. Douglas Smith, "Shapp Prods U.S. on Flood Debates," Box 43, Folder Disasters, Richard S. Schweiker Papers (1771), Historical Collections and Labor Archives, Special Collections Library, Pennsylvania State University (hereafter cited as Richard Schweiker Papers).

31. "Testimony of Governor Milton Shapp before the House Banking and Currency Committee, July 20, 1972," Box 50, Folder 7, Milton Shapp Papers; the term "Greatest Generation" was widely used after the 1990s publication of Tom Brokaw's *The Greatest Generation* (New York: Random House, 1998).

32. "Letter to Milton Shapp, June 28, 1972," "Letter from Addison, New York, to Milton Shapp," Box 50, Folder 7, Milton Shapp Papers.

33. Franklin L. Kury, *Clean Politics, Clean Streams: A Legislative Autobiography and Reflections* (Lehigh, Pa.: Lehigh University Press, 2011), 122.

34. "Statement by Governor Milton J Shapp, before the Joint Special Session of the General Assembly for Flood Relief, August 14, 1972," Box 11, Folder 7, "Flood Relief Bill, Milton Shapp Papers; Jane Shoemaker, "Generous Legislators Fattening Up Appropriations," *Olean Times Herald*, October 14, 1972, 6; Robert Wolensky, *Better Than Ever! The Flood Recovery Task Force and the 1972 Agnes Disaster* (Stevens Point: University of Wisconsin, Stevens Point, 1993), 11; Robert Wolensky, *Power, Policy and Disaster*, 39.

35. Eleanor Stuart, River Road South Corning resident, interviewed by Mary Lu Walker and Peter Voorheis, 2003; John and Susan Peck, 72 Catherine Street, Corning, N.Y., interviewed by Mary Lu Walker and Peter Voorheis; Dimitroff and Janes, *History of Corning–Painted Post Area*, 309.

36. *Public Papers of the Presidents of the United States: Richard Nixon, 1972* (Washington, D.C.: Government Printing Office, 1974): B-10.

37. "Henderson Requests New Flood Aid Plan," *Leader*, July 10, 1972.

38. "Nelson Rockefeller to William Smith, September 8, 1972," Microfilm Reel 20, Records Group 15.37, Nelson A. Rockefeller Gubernatorial Papers, Office Files, Rockefeller Archives. Hereafter Rockefeller Office files.

39. "Nelson Rockefeller to Stanley Steingut, Assembly Minority Leader, September 1, 1972," Box 20, Folder 459, Rockefeller Gubernatorial Files, Ann C. Whitman Papers, Rockefeller Archives Center (hereafter cited as Ann Whitman Papers).

40. Jim O'Hara, "Major Reforms Urged to Avoid Another June '72," *Star Gazette*, February 10, 1973. Smith was anticipating the all-hazards approach that FEMA took in 1979.

41. "Henderson Requests New Flood Aid Plan," *Corning Leader*, July 10, 1972.

42. Michael Whiteman to Nelson Rockefeller, June 11, 1973, Ann C. Whitman Papers.

43. Reid quoted in Rolfe, "Central Disaster Unit Urged."

44. "Michael Whiteman to Nelson Rockefeller, June 6. 1973," Ann Whitman Papers.

45. Anthony Klotz, "Howard W. Robison," *Citizens Look at Congress* (Washington, D.C.: Grossman Publishers, 1972), 1.

46. George Hinman warned Rockefeller about taxes; see Memorandum, George Hinman to Nelson Rockefeller, April 13, 1971, Box 8, Folder 205: George Hinman RE: Rochester Businessmen's Protest on Budget: The Future, Rockefeller Gubernatorial Series 34,Ann C. Whitman Papers, Rockefeller Archives (hereafter cited as Ann Whitman Papers): on Hinman, see Eric Pace, "George Hinman, 91, Is Dead: Longtime Rockefeller Advisor," *New York Times*, September 25, 1997, http://www.nytimes.com/1997/09/25/nyregion/george-hinman-91-is-dead-longtime-rockefeller-adviser.html.

47. *McKinney's Session Laws of New York*, 1973 (St. Paul, Minn.: West Publishing, 1974), 64–65.

48. William Farrell, "Rockefeller Sees Fund-Share Rise," *New York Times*, January 10, 1973.

49. Statement of WC Hennessey to US Senate Public Works Committee Hearings on Tropical Storm Agnes, Elmira NY, June 1–2, 1973, Box 83, Folder Rich Testimony Senate Subcommittee Disaster Relief, Department of Environmental Conservation, Hurricane Agnes Damage Files.

50. "Former State Senator Named Top 'Big Flats Citizen,'" *Star Gazette*, July 1, 2007.

51. "Bill Smith Sows Crop Protest, Recaps High NY Senate Ranking," *The Scene*, July 8, 1973. Smith Collection Booth Library; "Farmer Smith Plows Senate," *Elmira Star Gazette*, September 7, 1962; Bob Rolfe interviewed by author, June 22, 2006 (hereafter cited as Bob Rolfe).

52. William E. Farrell, "Upstate Senator Urges Legislature to Reject a Rise in Lulus," *New York Times*, April 24, 1969.

53. "Testimonial Dinner to Honor Senator Smith," *Chemung Valley Reporter*, March 5, 1987. Granted, the employees who were fired probably had a different point of view.

54. A drunken driver killed Smith's daughter just months after the Agnes flooding, and his initial call for stricter drunk driving laws in New York were, much like his ideas for natural disaster reform, largely ignored.

55. Elected officials are not rewarded for spending money on prevention or mitigation, but studies have found a strong correlation between the dispensation of post-flood relief spending and public attitudes toward elected officials; see Andrew Healy and Neal Malhotra, "Myopic Voters and Natural Disaster Policy," *American Political Science Review* 103 no. 3 (August 2009): 387–406. https://doi.org/10.1017/S0003055409990104.

56. The classic study of how business elites dominate U.S. politics is William Domhoff, *Who Rules America: The Triumph of the Corporate Rich* (New York: McGraw Hill, 2013).

57. Matkowsky, "*Max Rosenn*"; Wolensky, *Better than Ever*, 16–17. Before the advent of federal assistance, it was often the case that businessmen would be granted broad powers to assist after a disaster. See Kenneth Green and Eric Ireland, "A Case Study of Disaster-Related Emergent Citizen Groups: An Examination of 'Vested Interests' as a Generating Condition," University of Delaware Disaster Research Center, 1977.

58. Leonard I. Garth, "Honorable Max Rosenn: Conscience and Role Model of the Court," *University of Pennsylvania Law Review*, 154 (May 2006): 1041–1044.

59. Ibid.

60. Robert Paul. Wolensky, "The Aftermath of the Great Agnes Disaster: An Analysis of Emergent Groups and Local Government Officials in the Wyoming Valley of Pennsylvania" (Dissertation, Penn State University, 1975), 52; Wolensky, *Better than Ever*, 19.

61. William Scranton and Judge Max Rosenn, "Agnes' Aftermath," *The Nation*, 215 (August 21, 1972): 4.

62. Wolensky, *Better than Ever*, 21.

63. Ibid., 23.

64. Ibid., 25.

65. Ibid, 29–30.

66. Robert Wolensky and Kenneth Wolensky, "Born to Organize," *Pennsylvania Heritage* 25, no. 3 (Summer 1999): 32–39.

67. "Joe Calls Corning Tune," *Star-Gazette*, October 1, 1972.

68. Bob Rolfe.

69. Terry Dillman, "Putting It Back Together," *Times Union*, June 27, 1972.

70. Bob Rolfe "Corning Mourns Joe Nasser: For 23 Years He was 'Mr. Mayor' to His Hometown," *Corning Leader*, March 28, 1988.

71. Dillman, "Flood Warnings at Corning."

72. Lillian Brown, "Nasser: Weather Service Gave No Warning," *Leader*, July 15, 1972; Bob Rolfe, "Says Weather Service Word Too Late, Was Inaccurate," *Corning Leader*, July 18, 1972.

73. Some lauded Nasser in Corning for his willingness to defy the leaders of CGW; see Bob Rolfe, "Corning Mourns Joe Nasser."

74. Margaret B.W. Graham and Alec T. Shuldiner, *Corning and the Craft of Innovation* (New York: Oxford University Press, 2001).

75. Jeffrey J. Matthews, *Alanson B. Houghton: Ambassador of the New Era* (Lanham, Md.: Rowman and Littlefield, 2004).

76. Alfred E. Clarke, "Amory Houghton of Corning Glass Works," *New York Times*, February 22, 1981.

77. George James, "Arthur Houghton Jr., 83, Dies; Led Steuben Glass," *New York Times*, April 4, 1990.

78. Monica Langley, "Corning Glass Heir Campaigns in Style for Seat in Congress," *Wall Street Journal*, October 27, 1986; Leslie Eaton, "The Town That Glass Built Hits a Bump, and 1,000 Lose Their Jobs," *New York Times*, July 16, 2001, B1; William C. Symonds, "Corning Back from the Brink," *Business Week*, October 18, 2004, 96–102. The Houghton Library at Harvard is named for this family.

79. *The Flood and the Community*, 81; Erin Kelly, "Houghton's Legacy: Kindness, Civility," *Elmira Star-Gazette*, November 26, 2004.

80. Michael Paulson, "The Apprentice in Public Ministry," *Boston Globe*, March 7, 2005; Bob Rolfe, Houghton Family, http://freepages.genealogy.rootsweb.ancestry.com/~houghton family/p247.htm#i15198. Ammo was elected to the House of Representatives a dozen years after the flood, serving from 1987 until 2005. Later in life, he considered becoming a missionary to Zimbabwe and eventually, after retiring from business and politics in 2004 he became a full-time servant of the Episcopal Diocese of Massachusetts.

81. Robert J. Cole, "What Agnes Left Behind," *New York Times*, July 2, 1972, 133, 144; David Dyer and Daniel Gross, *The Generations of Corning: The Life and Times of a Global Corporation* (New York: Oxford University Press, 2001), 313.

82. Jerry Gale (Corning resident), interviewed by MaryLu Walker and Peter Voorheis, 2003.

83. "Houghton Asks Senate for Special Flood Aid," *Leader*, July 18, 1972; "Text of Houghton's Talk to Senate Unit," *Leader*, July 19, 1972; Editorial, *Star-Gazette*, July 20, 1972; Amory Houghton (CEO, Corning Glass Works), author interview, September 20, 2006 (hereafter Amo Houghton).

84. Joe Sartori, "George Lincoln to Nelson Rockefeller, September 30 1972," Reel Microfilm 20, Nelson A Rockefeller, Office Files; Letter, Amory Houghton to Richard Nixon, July 14, 1972,Box 14, Folder: Natural Disasters By State, 1971–1972,WHCF-DI; "Amory Houghton to Nelson Rockefeller, July 14, 1972," Microfilm Reel 21, Nelson Rockefeller Gubernatorial series Office Files; "Nelson Rockefeller to Amory Houghton, November 6, 1972," Folder 409, Diane Van Wie Papers.

85. "Giambrone Statement," *Leader*, July 5, 1972, 11.

86. Lillian Braun suggested the bedlam metaphor in "Command Center Open 24 Hours," *Leader*, June 28, 1972; Tom MacAvoy, author interview, July 6, 2006 (hereafter as Tom MacAvoy); Amory Houghton; Lois Janes, author interview, March 23, 2007 (hereafter as Lois Janes); Thomas Dimitroff, author interview, September 13, 2007 (hereafter as Tom Dimitroff); *The Flood and the Community*, 85.

87. Hardy Green, *The Company Town: The Industrial Edens and Satanic Mills That Shaped the American Economy* (New York: Basic Books, 2012), 52.

88. Statement of S. Roberts Rose, *Hearings to Investigate the Adequacy & Effectiveness of Federal Disaster Legislations PT.4–5* (Washington, D.C.: U.S. Government Printing Office, 1973), 1881–1889; "Stephen Roberts Rose," *Elmira Star-Gazette*, March 4, 2001, https://www.legacy.com/obituaries/star-gazette/obituary.aspx?n=stephen-roberts-rose&pid=87901448.

4. PLAYING POLITICS WITH DISASTER

1. Miller Center Presidential Recordings Program, 001-074, http://whitehousetapes.net/transcript/nixon/001–074.

2. Memorandum; Bill Gifford to Tod Hullin; RE: Subject Operations under the Attached Procedures; April 6, 1972; Box 3, Folder 7/1/71–12/1/72; White House Central Files: Subject Files: DI (Disasters) Richard Nixon Presidential Library and Museum.

3. In 1968 Nixon lost New York by nearly 400,000 votes and Pennsylvania by nearly 200,000; see Dave Leip's *Atlas of U.S. Presidential Elections*, http://uselectionatlas.org.

4. United States and Office of Emergency Preparedness, *Disaster Preparedness; Report to the Congress* (Washington, D.C.: 1972), 167–172; Peter May notes that presidents have the most considerable influence on disaster aid; see Peter J. May, *Recovering from Catastrophes*, 114; Birkland, *Lessons of Disaster*, 106.

5. Johnson's action after Hurricane Betsy is recorded in the previous chapter. Mayor Lindsay was not swift enough to respond to a blizzard that paralyzed New York City in 1969, and many believe this detailed his political career, see Sewell Chan, "Remembering a Snowstorm That Paralyzed a City," *New York Times*, February 10, 2009, http://cityroom.blogs.nytimes.com/2009/02/10/remembering-a-snowstorm-that-paralyzed-the-city/?_r=0.

6. David K. Twigg, *The Politics of Disaster: Tracking the Impact of Hurricane Andrew* (Gainesville: University Press of Florida, 2012), 5–10.

7. Local elections are explored in Glen F. Abney and Larry B. Hill, "Natural Disasters as a Political Variable: The Effect of a Hurricane on an Urban Election," *American Political Science Review* 60, no. 4 (December 1966): 974–981, https://doi.org/10.2307/1953770; Kevin Arceneaux and Robert M. Stein, "Who Is Held Responsible When Disaster Strikes? The Attribution of Responsibility for a Natural Disaster in an Urban Election," *Journal of Urban Affairs* 28, no. 1 (2006): 45–53, https://doi.org/10.1111/j.0735–2166.2006.00258.x. These studies found limited evidence of electoral change in the aftermath of a disaster; David K. Twigg studied how Hurricane Andrew in 1992 shaped subsequent elections in

The Politics of Disaster; Peter May studied the effect of disaster response on elections and found evidence that highly visible candidates benefited from their actions in the aftermath of a disaster. May found that presidential declarations of major disasters under Nixon, Ford, and Carter were affected by whether it was an election year; see May, *Recovering from Catastrophes*, 118, 112; the intersection of elections and disaster policy under Bill Clinton is explored by Rutherford Platt, *Disasters and Democracy*; a study of how presidential disaster declarations assist in electoral politics is provided in Andrew Reeves, "Political Disaster: Unilateral Powers, Electoral Incentives, and Presidential Disaster Declarations," *Journal of Politics* 73, no. 4 (2011): 1142–1151, DOI:10.1017/s0022381611000843.

8. Memorandum: David Parker to H. R. Haldeman; June 23, 1972: Box 3, Folder 7/1/71-12/1/72, WHCF-DI; Donald Janson, "Nixon Views Damage in Pennsylvania," *New York Times*, June 25, 1972.

9. Richard Nixon explains his All-Star Picks, June 30, 1972, Conversation 744–016, Audiotape 744 (NARA Identifier #6852532), Oval Office Recordings, White House Tapes, Richard Nixon Presidential Library and Museum, https://www.youtube.com/watch?v =Vdgq5spx0xQ; W. Dale Nelson, *The President Is at Camp David* (New York: Syracuse University Press, 2000), 69–81.

10. Transcript, Press Conference of Vice President of the United States, Horseheads, New York, June 29, 1972, Box 3, Folder News Summary, WHCF DI.

11. "June 1972," Tape # 1291, Westinghouse Collection, Library of American Broadcasting, University of Maryland Libraries, College Park, Md.

12. United States Government Printing Office, *Public Papers of the Presidents of the United States, Richard Nixon, 1973: Containing the Public Messages, Statements, and Speeches of the President* (Government Printing Office, 1999), B 12.

13. "Flood Relief Money Voted," *Democrat and Chronicle*, June 29, 1972.

14. James Miskel, *Disaster Response and Homeland Security: What Works, What Doesn't* (Westport, Conn.: Praeger, 2006), 60; Letter to Spiro Agnew; July 9 1972; Box 7, Folder 33, RG 3.5 DI Spiro T. Agnew papers, Special Collections, University of Maryland Libraries (hereafter cited as Agnew Papers).

15. "Flash Flood Watch Issued for Western New York," *Times Union*, June 29, 1972; Jimmie Waters, "Agnew Promises Fast Flood Aid," *Star-Gazette*, June 30, 1972; Transcript, Press Conference of Vice President of the United States Horseheads, WHCF DI; Roy Goodearle and Peter Malatesta, Memo to VP, June 28 1972, Box, 2 Folder 91: Uniondale and New York City June 29-30, 1972, Domestic Trips, Agnew Papers.

16. "Tier Hardest Hit by Floods, Agnew Says," *Buffalo Evening News*, June 30, 1972; "Letter to Vice President Agnew," August 29, 1972, Agnew Papers.

17. Memo Spiro T. Agnew to President Richard Nixon, July 10, 1972 Box 33, Folder: "Visit to the Flood-Afflicted Areas," Agnew Papers.

18. Spiro T. Agnew to President Richard Nixon, July 10, 1972, Agnew Papers; Nixon did send a special note to Lincoln Letter: Richard Nixon to George Lincoln, July 19, 1972, Box 3, Folder 7/1/71-12/1/72 Nixon WHCF.

19. Memo: H.R. Haldeman to Clark MacGregor and Chuck Colson, July 26, 1972, Box 35, Folder 2, White House Special Files, Staff Member and Office Files, Nixon Papers.

20. Gordon W. Chaplin, "Shapp Colleagues Shun Aid Criticism," *Baltimore Sun*, June 26, 1972.

21. Memorandum; Des Barker to Chuck Colson: Re: Pennsylvania; July 11, 1972; Box 2, Folder Pennsylvania Floods, White House Staff Files, Desmond Barker, Richard Nixon Presidential Library and Museum, Yorba Linda, CA (hereafter cited as Des Barker Files); "Annotated News Summary," June 26 and 29, 1972; Des Barker Files.

22. "Not So Secret Agents," *Time*, February 26, 1973, http://www.time.com/time /magazine/article/0,9171,910554,00.html.

23. Memorandum, Ken Cole to President Nixon, July 10, 1972, Box 2, Folder "Hurricane Agnes Disaster Relief Proposal," Des Barker Files.

24. Memorandum: John C. Whitaker to Ken Cole Re: Notes for Ziegler's Morning Briefing, July 17, 1972, Box 2, Folder Pennsylvania Floods, Des Barker Files.

25. Richard Nixon, "Message to the Congress Proposing Additional Disaster Relief Measures Following Tropical Storm Agnes," July 17, 1972. The American Presidency Project, http://www.presidency.ucsb.edu/ws/index.php?pid=3498.

26. Profile on Frank Carlucci, "From the Knives of the Congo to Darkest Pentagon," *Times of London*, November 8, 1987; Philip M. Boffey, "Carlucci: Thoughts on Government and Leaving It," *New York Times,* January 3, 1983.

27. Memorandum, Des Barker to Chuck Colson, July 11, 1972, Box 2, Folder Pennsylvania Floods, Des Barker Files.

28. Melvin Small, *The Presidency of Richard Nixon*, American Presidency Series (Lawrence, KS: University of Kansas Press, 1999); Memorandum: Des Barker to Chuck Colson, July 11, 1972; Memorandum, Barker to Colson. Nixon's comment on Colson is quoted in Rick Perlstein, *"Nixonland": The Rise of a President and the Fracturing of America* (New York: Scribner's, 2008), 560.

29. Memorandum, Barker to Colson.

30. Notes, July 11, 1972, 9:30 a.m., Box 6, Folder 7/11/1972, Notes of Meeting with the President: White House Central Files: Staff Members and Office Files, Series: John D. Ehrlichman; Richard Nixon Presidential Library and Museum, Yorba Linda, Calif. (hereafter cited as Ehrlichman files). Shapp's ideas found a home in the administration's expansion of the Flood Insurance Protection Act in 1973 and the Robert T Stafford Disaster Relief and Emergency Assistance Act of 1988.

31. Nelson, *President Is at Camp David*, 72.

32. Richard Nixon, "Remarks Proposing Additional Emergency Disaster Relief Following Tropical Storm Agnes," July 12, 1972, Public Papers of the President; Memorandum, Stephen Bull to President Nixon, July 12, 1972, Box 3, Folder 7/1/71–12/1/72, WHCF DI; Carroll Kilpatrick, "Nixon Seeks $1.7 Billion in Flood Aid," *Washington Post*, July 13, 1972.

33. Memorandum, John C. Whitaker to Ken Cole, July 12, 1972, Box 2, Folder Pennsylvania Flood, Des Barker Files.

34. Memorandum, John C. Whitaker to Ken Cole, July 11, 1972, Box 2, Folder Pennsylvania Floods, Des Barker Files.

35. Carl Bernstein, who was already working with Bob Woodward on the Watergate break-in, wrote a glowing review of the conference; see Carl Bernstein, "Local, U.S. Aides Cut Flood Aid Red Tape," *Washington Post*, July 15, 1972; for his work on the Watergate break-in see Carl Bernstein and Bob Woodward, *All the President's Men* (New York: Simon and Schuster reissue, 2014); George Bevan returned to Corning and called the event "very worthwhile," see "Optimistic on Aid Bill," *Corning Leader*, July 15, 1972.

36. Stanley I. Kutler, *The Wars of Watergate: The Last Crisis of Richard Nixon* (New York: W. W. Norton, 1990); Perlstein, *"Nixonland,"* 676–677.

37. Alfred E. Lewis, "5 Held in Plot to Bug Democrat's Office Here," *Washington Post*, June 18, 1972.

38. Presidential Recordings Program, "The Smoking Gun," Friday, June 23, 1972, 10:04 a.m.–11:39 a.m., http://whitehousetapes.net/transcript/nixon/smoking-gun.

39. Annotated News Summary June 26 and 29, 1972; Ehrlichman meeting notes July 8, 1972; Ehrlichman Files.

40. Richard Reeves, *President Nixon Alone in the White House* (New York: Simon and Schuster, 2002), 589.

41. Notes: July 8, 1972; Ehrlichman Files.

42. Republicans controlled Congress in 1947–1949 and 1953–1955.

43. "Senate Ups Nixon Flood Aid," *Democrat and Chronicle*, June 28, 1972, 1A; Schweiker, "*Washington Report*," Schweiker Papers.

44. *To Provide Additional Relief to Victims of Hurricane and Tropical Storm Agnes, and to Victims of South Dakota Flood Disaster: Hearing, 92d Congress, 2d Session on H.R. 15935, July 20, 1972*, 1972, 2.

45. Nancy Beck Young, *Wright Patman: Populism, Liberalism and the American Dream* (Southern Methodist University Press, 2000), 287.

46. Ibid., 2–4.

47. Ibid., 48–49.

48. Testimony of Governor Milton Shapp before the House Banking and Currency Committee, Milton Shapp Papers, *To Provide Additional Relief*, 11–13.

49. The federal program was the National Flood Insurance Program, created in 1968, which provided government-subsidized flood insurance to those who were deemed eligible by the government. In 1972 the insurance was not widely available, and even when available, it was not widely utilized. See Rutherford Platt, "The National Flood Insurance Program: Some Midstream Perspectives," *Journal of the American Institute of Planners* 42 no. 3 (1976): 303–313, https://doi.org/10.1080/01944367608977733; *To Provide Additional Relief*, 18–22, 49.

50. Peter J. May notes that this debate was typical in the 1960s and 1970s; see May, *Recovering from Catastrophe*, 19.

51. Richard Schweiker, "Disaster Relief Legislation, S 3804 and S 3805," *Congressional Record* July 19, 1972; "State Not Requesting Higher Flood Payments," *Globe-Times*, July 7, 1972, Richard Schweiker Papers.

52. *To Provide Additional Relief*, 1972, 118–119.

53. "Small Business Disaster Loans-1972," *Hearings before the Subcommittee on Small Business of the Committee on Banking, Housing and Urban Affairs of the United States Senate* (Washington, D.C.: Government Printing Office 1972), 33, 26.

54. *Hearings before the Subcommittee on Small Business of the Committee on Banking, Housing and Urban Affairs*, 26, 37; Pennsylvanians castigated Cranston in a number of letters and editorials in Pennsylvania newspapers, see Joseph McDade Papers.

55. *Hearings before the Subcommittee on Small Business of the Committee on Banking, Housing, and Urban Affairs*, 67.

56. Ibid., 69; Senator Abourezk of South Dakota was delighted by the election year attention and remarked that Rapid City was lucky that Nixon's rival was from South Dakota, which meant the state received greater attention from the government than it might have otherwise. See Abourezk testimony, U.S. Senate, Committee on Public Works, Subcommittee on Disaster Relief, To *Investigate the Adequacy and Effectiveness of Federal Disaster Relief Legislation*, part 2 (Washington, D.C.: Government Printing Office, 1973), 236.

57. "Cattaraugus County resolved to Support Nixon's Plan," WHCF-DI; Harry Laughlin to Miss Rosemary Woods, WHCF-DI; Bernard Gallagher, City Manager Wilkes-Barre, to Richard Nixon, August 1, 1972, WHCF-DI.

58. Robert P. Wolensky, *Better than Ever: The Flood Recovery Task Force and the 1972 Agnes Disaster*, 1st edition (Stevens Point, Wis.: Foundation Press, 1993), 23.

59. Ehrlichman Notes, July 10–19, 1972, Ehrlichman Files; Peter May cites this as an example of logrolling in disaster legislation; see May, *Recovering from Catastrophes*, 21.

60. May, *Recovering from Catastrophes*.

61. Schweiker, "Washington Report, August 1972, 2," Folder Disasters, Box 43, Schweiker Papers.

62. "Senate Votes to Increase Disaster Aid," *Washington Post*, August 6, 1972, D2.

63. Robert Diamond, *Nixon: The Fourth Year of His Presidency* (Washington, D.C.: Congressional Quarterly, 1973); "Fact Sheet on Agnes Recovery Act, July 11, 1972," Box 7, Folder Natural Disasters by State, 1971-1972, WHCF: Subject Files, DI 2.

64. "David N. Parker, White House Proposed Schedule August 3, 1972," Box 67, WHCF Subject Files TR.

65. Hurricane politics plays a role in attracting votes is suggested by some of the commentary and polls taken after Hurricane Sandy struck the East Coast in 2012 just days before Barack Obama's reelection bid. See John Cassidy, "How Much Was Obama Helped by Hurricane Sandy?" *New Yorker*, November 4, 2012, http://www.newyorker.com/news /john-cassidy/how-much-did-hurricane-sandy-help-obama.

5. "I HAVE A HUD-ACHE"

1. Agnew praised Gridley's idea at a Nassau County fundraiser see Alan Eysen, "Three Cheers for Agnew in Nassau," *Newsday*, June 29, 1972; Jack Gridley to Richard Nixon, August 21, 1972, Reel 20, Rockefeller Archives.

2. Anthony Koltz, "Howard W. Robison," *Citizens Look at Congress*, Vol. 6 (Washington, D.C: Grossman Publishers, 1972), 20.

3. American antipathy toward government began to rise after the development of the administrative state in the 1960s, see Paul C. Light. *Government's Greatest Achievements: From Civil Rights to Homeland Security* (Washington, D.C.: Brookings Institution Press, 2002); Robert F. Durant and Susannah Bruns Ali, "Repositioning American Public Administration? Citizen Estrangement, Administrative Reform, and the Disarticulated State," *Public Administration Review* 73, no. 2 (March/April 2013): 278–289, https://doi .org/10.1111/j.1540–6210.2012.02646.x.

4. On fragmented responsibility in emergency management, see Richard T. Sylves, *Disaster Policy and Politics*, 13–15; on the problem of miscommunication, see "Statement of J. Merle Herr, Mennonite Disaster Service, Southern Tier, New York State," in United States, *To Investigate the Adequacy and Effectiveness of Federal Disaster Relief Legislation: Hearings, Ninety-Third Congress, First[Second] Session* (Washington, D.C.: U.S. Government Printing Office, 1973), 2095.

5. Tobin quoted in Robert P. Wolensky, *Better Than Ever: The Flood Recovery Task Force and the 1972 Agnes Disaster*, 1st ed. (Stevens Point, Wisc.: Foundation Press, 1993), 6.

6. Hugh Heclo noted the rising tension between civil servants and appointed executives of bureaucracies, see Hugh Heclo, *A Government of Strangers: Executive Politics in Washington* (Washington, D.C.: Brookings Institute Press, 1977).

7. Flood is quoted in Wolensky, *Better Than Ever*, 9.

8. James Emery to T. Norman Hurd, June 20, 1973, Rockefeller Office Disaster Files, Reel 20, Rockefeller Archives (hereafter cited as Reel 20, Rockefeller Archives).

9. Robert Gruenberg, "Romney, Set to Quit, Warns Nixon about HUD, Flood Aid," *Times Union*, August 12, 1972.

10. Douglas Watson, "Hope, Bitterness Vie in Flood Wake," *Washington Post*, July 30, 1972; Garth Wade, "Federal Agencies Shine," *Star Gazette*, October 1, 1972.

11. "Outburst of Complaints Greet Team of White House Flood Fact Finders," *Scranton Times*, July 3, 1972.

12. Political scientists were already aware of this changing dynamic, the classic study of this is Theodore J. Lowi, *The End of Liberalism: The Second Republic of the United States* (New York: W. W. Norton, 1969).

13. "James Emery to T. Norman Hurd," June 20, 1973;"Area Officials Talk Aid," *Evening Tribune*, October 19, 1972.

14. Donald Janson, "Nixon Views Damage in Pennsylvania," *New York Times*, June 25, 1972; "Governor's News Conference, June 29, 1972," Box 49, Folder 8, MG 309.14 Subject Files Floods, Milton Shapp Papers, Pennsylvania State Archives (hereafter Shapp Papers).

15. Letter: State Senator R. Bud Dwyer to Richard Nixon, June 28, 1972 Box 2, Folder Pennsylvania Floods, Des Barker Files; Cable Neuhaus, "Is There Life after the Governorship?" *Pennsylvania Illustrated* 4 (1979): 47–48.

16. Letter: Flood Victim to Vice President Spiro Agnew, March 4, 1973, Box 7, Folder Disasters, Records Group 3.5 White House Central Files, Subject Files: DI (Disasters), Agnew Papers.

17. Members of Congress have no official role at a disaster scene, but their presence has both policy and political implications. They may enhance the response of executive agencies and gain election support through their presence and credit claiming. Peter May covers the era of Agnes well in May, *Recovering from Catastrophes*, 120; Richard Sylves covers the recent history of disaster policy; see Sylves, *Disaster Policy and Politics*, 93–95.

18. William C. Kashatus III, "Dapper Dan' Flood: Pennsylvania's Legendary Congressman," *Pennsylvania Heritage* 21 (Summer 1995): 4–11.

19. George Crile, "The Best Congressman," *Harper's Weekly*, 258 (January 1975): 60–66; "Marjorie Hunter, "Daniel John Flood," *New York Times*, January 31, 1978.

20. Crile, "Best Congressman"; Libby Brennan, "Flood Recalls Cutting Red Tape," *Sunday Independent*, June 27, 1982, Daniel Flood Vertical File, Luzerne County Historical Society, Wilkes-Barre, Pa.

21. Libby Brennan, "Flood Recalls Cutting Red Tape"; Crile, "Best Congressman," 63.

22. Schweiker came closest to achieving his dream of going to the White House in 1976, the year Ronald Reagan invited Schweiker to be his running mate. The 1976 alliance between Reagan and Schweiker came as a surprise to many people because of Reagan's reputation as a conservative and Schweiker's reputation as a liberal Republican. See "A Housewife in Washington," *North Penn Reporter*, November 2, 1971, Folder "Politics," Richard Schweiker Papers.

23. Steven F. Hayward, *The Age of Reagan: The Fall of the Old Liberal Order, 1964–1980* (New York: Three Rivers Press, 2001), 474.

24. Warren Unna, "Intimidation of War Critics Charged," *Washington Post*, February 5, 1970.

25. "No Help," *New York Times*, September 25, 1975; Mark. J. Green, "James L. Buckley," in *Citizens Look at Congress* (Washington, D.C.: Grossman Publishing, 1972), 5.

26. Harvey Ussach and Erma Ferlanti, "James F. Hastings," in *Citizens Look at Congress, Vol. 6* (Washington, D.C.: Grossman Publishing, 1972), 6.

27. *Corning Leader* reporter Bob Rolfe was more skeptical of Hastings's accomplishments, and author interviews with a variety of community leaders indicate that the congressman left a minimal impression on those who knew him; for the quote on his press releases; see "Report Classes Hastings a Quiet Conscientious Congressman," *Olean Times Herald*, October 23, 1972.

28. Hastings's papers are located in the M. E. Grenander New York State Modern Political Archive at the State University of New York at Albany. The papers consist mainly of press clippings (hereafter cited as James F. Hastings Papers); see Harvey Ussach and Erma Ferlanti, "James F. Hastings," 6.

29. Anthony Koltz, "Howard W. Robison," 7, 19.

30. Robison to James F. Hastings, January 5, 1973, Folder State Local Agencies, Box 131, Howard Robison Papers; Letter to Howard Robison, June 23, 1973, Folder Agnes Letters, Box 132, Howard Robison Papers.

31. Koltz, "Howard W. Robison," 8.

32. Jack Anderson, "Profiteers Prey on Agnes Victims, *Washington Post*, December 21, 1972.

33. Jack Anderson, "Agnes Evidence Offered," *Washington Post*, January 1, 1973.

34. This shift is explained by Larry Sabato, *Feeding Frenzy: Attack Journalism and American Politics* (New York: Free Press, 1991).

35. In the early 1970s, homosexuality was categorized as a mental illness by the American Psychiatric Association and was considered deviant by the general public.

36. Patricia Sullivan, "Investigative Columnist Jack Anderson Dies," *New York Times*, December 18, 2005; G. Gordon Liddy claims to have nearly carried out such an execution in *Will: The Autobiography of G. Gordon Liddy* (New York: St. Martins, 1991), 210–214; Anderson is taken to task for his "gross breach of journalistic ethics" in the 1972 election coverage of senator Thomas Eagleton in Larry Sabato, *Feeding Frenzy*, 9.

37. Jack Anderson, "Bureaucratic Havoc in Agnes' Wake," *Washington Post*, December 20, 1972.

38. Notes: News Review, August 1972, Box 6, Folder: Notes of Meeting with the President, White House Staff Files: John D. Ehrlichman, Richard Nixon Presidential Library and Museum, Yorba Linda, Calif. (hereafter cited as Ehrlichman files).

39. Letter: O'Connell to Harry Dent, Special Assistant to the President, August 7, 1972, Box 2, Folder Pennsylvania Flood, Des Barker Files.

40. Notes: John Ehrlichman, August 7, 1972, 10:50 a.m., Ehrlichman files.

41. "Nixon Orders Romney Visit at Flood Site," *Washington Post*, August 8, 1972; "Nixon Sending Romney to Check Flood-Aid Snag at Wilkes-Barre," *New York Times*, August 8, 1972; WDAY TV Editorial, August 7, 1972, #728, Box 20, Folder 13, Joseph McDade Papers.

42. "The Widening Cracks in Nixon's Cabinet," *Time*, June 1, 1970, http://www.time.com/time/magazine/article/0,9171,878269,00.html.

43. Romney's wife Lenore ran for a U.S. Senate seat in 1970 and one of his sons, Mitt, went on to become governor of Massachusetts and the 2012 Republican Party presidential candidate.

44. Stewart Alsop, "George Romney: The G.O.P.'s Fast Comer," *Saturday Evening Post*, May 26, 1962.

45. In 1968 before the primary, Romney suggested that his support of the Vietnam War had been the result of "brain-washing" by the administration. See "Why Romney Dropped Out," *Time*, March 8, 1969; Melvin Small, *The Presidency of Richard Nixon*, American Presidency Series (Lawrence: University of Kansas Press, 1999).

46. Nathan, *The Plot That Failed*, 39; Small, *Presidency of Richard Nixon*, 40, 249, Wendell E. Pritchett, "Which Urban Crisis? Regionalism, Race and Urban Policy, 1960–1974," *Journal of Urban History* 34 (2008): 278–279.

47. Small, *Presidency of Richard Nixon*, 23.

48. "Widening Cracks in Nixon's Cabinet."

49. John Ehrlichman, *Witness to Power* (New York: Simon and Schuster, 1982), 105.

50. Ehrlichman, *Witness to Power*, 104.

51. Notes, August 3, 1972, Ehrlichman files.

52. Thomas E. Cronin, *The State of the Presidency*, 2nd edition (Boston: Little Brown and Co, 1980), 276–286.

53. Letter: James F. Hastings to Richard Nixon, August 8, 1972, Box 3, Folder 7/1/72–12/1/72, WHCF-DI Nixon Papers.

54. Anthony J. Mussari, *Appointment with Disaster, Vol. 1: The Swelling of the Flood-Wilkes Barre, Pennsylvania before and after the Agnes Flood of June 23, 1972* (Northeast Publishers, 1974), 124.

55. "Raps Flood Relief Efforts," *Scranton Tribune*, August 15, 1972; Richard Schweiker, *Washington Report*, August 1972, Richard S. Schweiker Papers.

56. Letter: Lenore Romney to John D. Ehrlichman, August 8, 1972, Ehrlichman files. On Lenore's Senate race see "Lenore Fights Alone," *Look* 34 (October 20, 1970): 111; Lenore Romney, "Men, Women, and Politics," *Look* 35 (April 6, 1971): 11.

57. Ehrlichman, *Witness to Power*, 101.

58. Mussari, *Appointment with Disaster, Vol. 1. Appointment with Disaster*, 124; Robert Wolensky, "The Aftermath of the Great Agnes Disaster: An Analysis of Emergent Groups and Local Government in the Wyoming Valley after the Agnes Disaster" (Ph.D. dissertation, Pennsylvania State University, 1975).

59. Robert P. Wolensky and Kenneth C. Wolensky, "Born to Organize," *Pennsylvania Heritage*, Summer 1999, 32–39.

60. Quoted in Mussari, *Appointment with Disaster*, 132.

61. Robert Wolensky and Kenneth C. Wolensky, "Min Matheson and the ILGWU in the Northern Anthracite Region, 1944–1963," *Pennsylvania History*, October 1993, 469; Robert Paul Wolensky, "The Aftermath of the Great Agnes Disaster," 147; Mussari, *Appointment with Disaster*, 130; Mary Russell, "Romney, Angry Flood Victims Tangle," *Washington Post*, August 10, 1972; Connie Lizdas, "Min Matheson 'Flood Victims Were 'Nasty' to Romney, But It Worked," *Citizen's Voice*, June 23, 1982.

62. Herbert Klein, *Making It Perfectly Clear: An Inside Account of Nixon's Love-Hate Relationship with the Media* (New York: Doubleday, 1980), 306. Romney's intensity and quest for daily exercise continued until his last day on earth, July 26, 1995, the day when his wife Lenore found him dead, collapsed over his treadmill in their Bloomfield Hills, Michigan, home. See "GOP Remembers George Romney," *Ludington Daily News*, July 27, 1995.

63. Mussari, *Appointment with Disaster*, 145–146.

64. Mary Russell, "Romney Visits Flood," *Washington Post*, August 9, 1972.

65. Mussari, *Appointment with Disaster*, 145–146.

66. August 10, 1972, Milton Shapp; Mary Russell, "Shapp Staged Protest in PA; Romney Claims," *Washington Post*, August 11, 1972.

67. Mary Russell, "Romney, Angry Flood Victims Tangle," *Washington Post*, August 10, 1972, 1.

68. "Romney Shapp Clash over Flood Plans," *New York Times*, August 10, 1972; Pro-Publica, "History of Government Bailout," http://www.propublica.org/special /government-bailouts.

69. Romney's remarks echo those of President Grover Cleveland in his veto message on the Texas drought. See Russell, "Romney, Angry Flood Victims"; Jane Shoemaker, "Agnes Victims Shout Down Romney at Wilkes-Barre," *Bethlehem Globe-Times*, August 10, 1972; "Romney, Shapp Clash over Flood Plans," *New York Times*, August 10, 1972.

70. Russell, "Romney, Angry Flood Victims Tangle."

71. Wolensky, *Better Than Ever*, 41.

72. Russell, "Romney, Angry Flood Victims Tangle."

73. "Romney and Shapp Clash over Flood Plan."

74. Thomas Haskell, "The Curious Persistence of Rights Talk in the 'Age of Interpretation,'" *Journal of American History* 74 (December 1987): 984–1012.

75. Archives at all levels of government contain such letters.

76. Political figures like Romney quickly realized that the lapdog journalism of the 1930s–1960s was over and a new breed of watchdog journalists who often operated on a pack mentality was quick to judge and just as quick to pile on to any news story; see Sabato, *Feeding Frenzy*.

77. Letter to George Romney, August 10, 1972, Box 61, Folder 61, Milton Shapp Papers, Pennsylvania State Archives.

78. Richard Ellis, *Presidential Lightning Rods: The Politics of Blame Avoidance* (Lawrence: University of Kansas Press, 1994), 148–170.

79. Nixon's cottage cheese diet is referred to in Small, *Presidency of Richard Nixon*, 216; see also John T. Woolley and Gerhard Peters, *The American Presidency Project* [online], Santa Barbara, CA, http://www.presidency.ucsb.edu/ws/?pid=2349; Notes: August 11, 1972, 11:10 a.m., meeting with Romney, Ehrlichman files; the recording of the meeting is available online through the Nixon Library, "Tape 767, Conversation 20 (767-020a)," https://www .nixonfoundation.org/artifact/tape-767-conversation-20-767-020a/.

80. "Havoc Charge Disputed by Flood Recovery Chief," *Washington Post*, December 23, 1972, A4; perhaps Romney could take solace in the fact that every cabinet secretary associated with the Agnes disaster was ousted when Nixon fired and reshuffled his cabinet after reelection; see Nathan, *The Plot That Failed: Nixon and the Administrative Presidency* (New York: John Wiley and Sons, 1975), 68.

81. Nixon surrounded himself with public relations staffers see Joe McGinnis, *The Selling of the President: The Classical Account of the Packaging of a Candidate* (reprint, New York: Penguin Books, 1988).

82. Ehrlichman files.

83. Notes: August 12, 1972, 1:45 p.m., Ehrlichman files; Dick Kirschten, "Competent Manager," *National Journal*, February 28, 1987, 468–479.

84. Memorandum, Frank Carlucci to John Ehrlichman, September 9, 1972, Box 14, Folder Pennsylvania Flood, , WHCF DI Nixon Papers; Carlucci quoted in "Nixon Aide Begins Job Coordinating Flood Relief," *New York Times*, August 15, 1972; "A Budget Official to Guide Flood Aid," *New York Times*, August 13, 1972; Mary Russell, "Carlucci Cuts Red Tape on Flood Aid," *Washington Post*, September 5, 1972; "The Lingering Legacy of Agnes," *Washington Post*, September 9, 1972; Note: Erhlichman notes—August 12, 1972, 1:45 p.m.; Ehrlichman files.

85. Jack Anderson, "Bureaucratic Havoc in Agnes' Wake," *Washington Post*, December 20, 1972.

86. Ibid.

87. Douglas Kneeland, "McGovern Talks to Discontented Flood Victims in Pennsylvania," *New York Times*, August 22, 1972, 37; William Greider, "McGovern Hears Flood Anger," *Washington Post*, August 22, 1972, A1, A4. Kneeland mentions Galston, Greider Goulstone.

88. "McGovern Sets Plan to Aid Flood Victims," *Star Gazette*, August 29, 1972, Peter Briggs, *Rampage: The Story of Disastrous Floods, Broken Dams, and Human Fallibility* (New York: David McKay Company), 153; WDAY TV Editorial "McGovern Visit" #739, Joseph McDade Papers, "Natural Disaster Insurance," Des Barker Files.

89. John Whitaker, "Schedule Proposal, August 30, 1972," WHCF SMOF-Desmond Barker.

90. Nixon's visit to the Lincoln Memorial is recounted in Reeves, *President Nixon*, 219–220. Nixon's aides had planned the event weeks before in advance but were unsure if the president would agree to go.

91. UPI, "President Flies to Wilkes-Barre with Funds and Encouragement," *New York Times*, September 10, 1972, 67; UPI, "President Makes Surprise Return to Wilkes-Barre," *Washington Post*, September 10, 1972, A3; Ehrlichman, *Witness to Power*, 269; Sara Fritz, "Campaign 72—Pennsylvania Flood Relief Becomes Campaign Issue," Ehrlichman files; Ehrlichman Notes, September 9, 1972, Ehrlichman Files. Nixon was deeply concerned with his image and commissioned a weekly summary of news stories to see how well he was

doing. Much like the visit to the Lincoln Memorial in 1970, the event was planned by aides who did not know if Nixon would agree to go. For example, one does not have an oversized depiction of a $4 million check in the Oval Office without advance notice, which provides evidence that the event was coordinated long before it happened.

92. Letter to McDade, September 5, 1972, Box 65, Folder 23, Joseph McDade Papers.

93. Ibid. Dan Aykroyd did ten impressions of Nixon from 1976 through 1979; see the *Saturday Night Live* archives, http://snl.jt.org/imp.php?i=11; Pat Oliphant's antipathy of Nixon extended to the former president's death in 1994, see Oliphant's cartoon, "Lest We Forget," April 28, 1994, available at the Library of Congress, http://www.loc.gov/exhibits /oliphant/vc007261.jpg.

94. Lee Linder, "Top PA Democrats Win and Party Keeps Control of Senate; Lose House," *Gettysburg Times*, November 9, 1972.

95. One political scientist thought that McGovern's loss in his home state was tied to his lack of attention to the flash flood that killed 238 people in Rapid City in June 1972; see May, *Recovering from Catastrophes*, 121.

96. "Havoc Charge Disputed by Flood Recovery Chief."

97. Garnett D. Horner, "President Hints at Reform," *Milwaukee Journal*, November 9, 1972.

6. "BETTER THAN EVER"?

1. Richard Nixon, "Statement on Signing a Disaster Assistance Supplemental Appropriations Bill, "August 20, 1972, in John T. Woolley and Gerhard Peters, *The American Presidency Project* [online], Santa Barbara, Calif., http://www.presidency.ucsb.edu/ws/ ?pid=3534.

2. Anthony J. Mussari, *Appointment with Disaster*, xv.

3. Malcolm Wilson, "At Village Square Apartments and Commercial Center," October 21, 1974, *Public Papers of Malcolm Wilson, Fiftieth Governor of New York State* (Albany, 1977), 1808–1809; Peg Gallagher "UDC Moving Office Out of Elmira," *Elmira Star-Gazette*, November 1, 1974.

4. Klein's thesis is that the shock of war and disaster allows capitalists to move into an area and to profit from the social disruption; see *The Shock Doctrine*, especially Part 5, "Shocking Times: The Rise of Disaster Capitalism"; Cable Neuhaus, "Five Years after Agnes, Still a Flood of Problems," *Washington Post*, June 26, 1977; Mussari, *Appointment*, 138.

5. James T. Mulder, "Undaunted Victims Rebuild," *Syracuse American Empire Magazine*, June 27, 1982.

6. *After Agnes, A Triumph over Destruction* (Wilkes-Barre, Pa.: *Times Leader*, 1982), 28.

7. George Winner (assistant to Bill Smith), author interview, January 25, 2008 (hereafter cited as George Winner).

8. The Edwardsville council members were Stanley Blockus, Thomas Benesku, Edward Armusk, and Edward Yarmel; see "And Then There Were Cheaters" in *After Agnes*, 24.

9. James M. Naughton, "Agnew Quits Vice Presidency and Admits Tax Evasion in '67; Nixon Consults On Successor," *New York Times*, October 11, 1973; Peter B. Levy, "Spiro Agnew, the Forgotten Americans, and the Rise of the New Right," *Historian* 75, no. 4 (Winter 2013): 707–739.

10. Richard Lyons, "Patman Joins List of Retiring Congressman," *New York Times*, January 15. 1976; "Ex-Rep Hastings Guilty in Kickback Case," *New York Times*, December 18, 1976; "U.S. Is Suing Legislator to Get $50,000 Returned," *New York Times*, March 27, 1977.

11. Rick Miller, "Former Rep. James F. Hastings Remembered as Good Public Servant," Olean *Times Herald*, October 28, 2014, http://www.oleantimesherald.com/news/here_and

_now/former-rep-james-f-hastings-remembered-as-good-public-servant/article
_93f8c928-5eba-11e4-891b-dbb3e20287bb.html.

12. Prosecutors claimed Flood extorted five thousand dollars from the mobile home dealer and accepted a thousand-dollar bribe from another contractor; see Fred Barbash, "Witness Says Flood Got Bribe at Disaster Site," *Washington Post*, January 24, 1979.

13. Paul Nussbaum, "Ex.-Rep. Dan Flood Dead at 90," *Philadelphia Inquirer*, May 29, 1994, A.1; many residents believe that Daniel Flood was the victim of overzealous prosecutors, and William Kashutas makes a strong case for Flood's innocence in *Dapper Dan Flood: The Controversial Life of a Congressional Power Broker* (University Park: Pennsylvania State University Press, 2010).

14. Elizabeth Skrapits, "Flood Honored in W-B," *Citizens' Voice*, October 3, 2010, https://www.citizensvoice.com/news/flood-honored-in-w-b-1.1042163.

15. Naomi Klein, *The Shock Doctrine: The Rise of Disaster Capitalism* (New York: Henry Holt, 2008) popularized the term *disaster capitalism*. An excellent summary of disaster capitalism is available in Steve Fraser, "A History of Disaster Capitalism," *Mother Jones*, April 4, 2013, https://www.motherjones.com/environment/2013/04/history-disaster -capitalism/. Disaster capitalism in the United States is explored in Kevin Rozario, "What Comes Down Must Go Up: Why Disasters Have Been Good for American Capitalism," in *American Disaster*, edited by Steven Biel, 72–102 (New York: New York University Press, 2011); there have also been a few studies of how large-scale disasters shape localities. Perhaps the leading international scholar is J. M. Albala-Bertrand, *The Political Economy of Large Scale Natural Disasters: With Special Reference to Developing Countries* (London: Oxford University Press, 1993). This research confirms the findings of the 1979 study by Wright et al. that not all disasters have a long-term positive effect on the affected communities. See J. D. Wright, P. H. Rossi, S. R. Wright, and E. Weber-Burdin, *After the Clean-up: Long-Range Effects of Natural Disasters* (Beverly Hills, Calif.: Sage, 1979); this contrasts with a study by Jessica Schultz and James R. Elliot that looks at more recent disasters and concludes that disaster positively influenced long-term demographic changes; see their "Natural Disasters and Local Demographic Change in the United States," *Population and Environment* 34 (2012). 293–312, DOI 10.1007/s11111-012-0171-7.

16. Barry Bluestone and Bennet Harrison, *The Deindustrialization of America: Plant Closings, Community Abandonment, and the Dismantling of Basic Industry* (New York: Basic Books, 1982), 4–6.

17. Paul Clark, Irwin Marcus, Carl Meyerhuber, Charles McCollester, et al., "Deindustrialization: A Panel Discussion [with Commentary]," *Pennsylvania History: A Journal of Mid-Atlantic Studies* 58, no. 3 (July 1991): 181–211.

18. Jason E. Lane and Bruce D. Johnstone, eds., *Universities and Colleges as Economic Drivers: Measuring Higher Education's Role in Economic Development* (Albany: State University of New York Press and ProQuest Ebook Central). See also Matthew Daneman, "Rochester's New 'Big 3' Focus on Health Care, Groceries," *Democrat and Chronicle*, June 29, 2014, https://www.democratandchronicle.com/story/money/business/2014/06/28 /university-rochester-wegmans-rochester-general/11445281/; Paul Davidson, "Just Two Cities Are in Recession. Who's Unhappy? Elmira, New York and Danville, Illinois," USA Today, February 25, 2019, https://www.usatoday.com/story/money/2019/02/25/recession -elmira-new-york-danville-illinois-struggle-amid-us-boom/2920710002/. However, this situation may change in Elmira, which in 2018 received approval to open an osteopathic medical school in the downtown area.

19. Anthony J. Mussari, "The Agnes Flood Disaster as an Agent of Community Change in Wilkes-Barre, Pennsylvania 1972" (Ph.D. dissertation, University of Iowa, 1978), 79–81; Thomas Dublin and Walter Licht, *The Face of Decline: The Pennsylvania Anthracite Region in the Twentieth Century* (Ithaca, New York: Cornell University Press, 2005), 118;

Denise Allabaugh, "Crestwood Industrial Park Mirrors Grim Economy," *Citizens' Voice*, November 15, 2010, https://www.citizensvoice.com/news/crestwood-industrial-park -mirrors-grim-economy-1.1063857.

20. Mussari, "The Agnes Flood Disaster," 333; Donald Jansen, "Wilkes-Barre Festive Despite Woes," *New York Times*, December 18, 1972, 45; Greater Wilkes-Barre Chamber of Commerce History, https://www.wilkes-barre.org/history.

21. Mussari, "The Agnes Flood Disaster," 347.

22. *After Agnes a Triumph over Destruction*, 30; Rachel Swarns, "How a Flood Turned around Pennsylvania City's Economy," *Wall Street Journal*, July 14, 1987; "Anniversary Brings Flood of Memories," *Los Angeles Times*, June 28, 1992.

23. Mussari, *Appointment with Disaster*, xii; on Mussari's influence in Wilkes-Barre, see Bill O'Boyle, "Beyond the By-Line: Godspeed, Tony Mussari," *Times Leader*, October 21, 2017, https://www.timesleader.com/news/local/679566/beyond-the-byline-godspeed-tony -mussari.

24. Denise Allabaugh, "Crestwood Industrial Park"; Andrew Maykuth, "Seeking Out Lessons from Cities that Survived Tragedies," *Philadelphia Inquirer*, September 4, 2005.

25. George Hobor, "Surviving the Era of Deindustrialization: The New Economic Geography of the Urban Rust Belt," *Journal of Urban Affairs* 35, no. 4 (2013): 417–434.

26. Matt Connor, "Wagering on Wilkes-Barre," *Slot Manager*, January/February 2007, 10, 12–14.

27. Peter Cameron, "Casino Not a Good Gamble for Everyone in Region," *New Citizens' Voice*, November 14, 2016, https://www.citizensvoice.com/news/casino-not-a-good-gamble -for-everyone-in-region-1.2117432. A recent study of the regional economy by the Brookings Institute confirms that the casino did not bring vitality back to the Wyoming Valley. Of all the areas in eastern Pennsylvania, Luzerne County had the least growth. The report found that Luzerne County and Wilkes-Barre remained steeped in economic decline. Even as other parts of Pennsylvania grew in population, Wilkes-Barre metropolitan area shrank. It lost population, especially young people aged fifteen to twenty-four, and experienced reduced immigration into the area.

28. Andrew Seder, "Major Changes to Area Seen and Felt," *TimesLeader.com*, December 27, 2010; Mark Gudish, "Heart of W-B Needs Infusion of Caring, Cash," *Times Leader*, August 10, 2010.

29. Bill O'Boyle, "45 Years Later, Agnes Still on People's Minds," *Times Leader*, June 18, 2017, https://www.timesleader.com/news/local/663873/45-years-later-agnes-still-on-peo ples-minds.

30. O'Boyle, "45 Years Later"; the lessons of Agnes have not been learned by other communities, which have focused on postdisaster redevelopment as a means to economic success; see "Gov. Andrew Cuomo's Power Play," *New York Times*, October 30, 2014, http:// www.nytimes.com/2014/10/31/opinion/governor-cuomos-power-play.html; "Lessons Learned from How New Jersey Handled Sandy Relief," *News Works*, October 31, 2014, http://www.newsworks.org/index.php/new-jersey/item/74621-lessons-learned-from -how-new-jersey-handled-sandy-relief.

31. Edward Berkowitz, *Something Happened: A Political and Cultural Overview of the Seventies* (New York: Columbia University Press, 2006), 2; Joe Sartori (Elmira City Manager), author interview, January 21, 2008 (hereafter cited as Joe Sartori); "Sperry Rand Unit in Elmira to Close Its Doors," *Wall Street Journal*, January 21, 1972; Edward Burks, "Rand Will Close its Elmira Plant," *New York Times*, January 22, 1972. Remington Rand had once employed over six thousand workers.

32. Charles Robert Jennings details the reconstruction of Elmira in "Urban Renewal as Disaster Recovery Planning: Tropical Storm Agnes in Elmira, New York with reference to Wilkes-Barre, Pennsylvania" (master's thesis, Cornell University, 1994); Heather Wade,

"Elmira," in *Encyclopedia of New York State*, edited by Peter R. Eisenstadt and Laura-Eve Moss (New York: Syracuse University Press, 2005), 499.

33. Statement of S. Roberts Rose, Chairman, Citizen's Advisory Committee, New York State Urban Development Corporation, "To Investigate the Adequacy and Effectiveness of Federal Disaster Relief Legislation, Hearings Before the Special Subcommittee on Disaster Relief, of the Committee on Public Works, United States Senate, 93rd Congress" (Washington, D.C.: U.S. Government Printing Office 1973), 1885, https://hdl.handle.net/2027/uc1.b3603525.

34. Letter, Annette R. Berman to Michael Whitman, Counsel to the Governor, April 9, 1973. Berman owned Viking Sewing Machines.

35. John D. Williams, "Aftermath of a Storm: Flood Damage Gives Urban Renewal Planners Big Chance," *Wall Street Journal*, November 14, 1972, 48.

36. Ibid.

37. The elite reconstruction of Elmira is told in Jennings, "Urban Renewal as Disaster Recovery Planning"; and Wade, "Elmira," 499.

38. Bluestone and Harrison, *The Deindustrialization of America*, 67–68.

39. Andrea R. Morrell, "The Prison Fix: Race, Work, and Economic Development in Elmira, New York" (Ph.D. dissertation, City University of New York, 2012).

40. Timothy W. Kneeland, "Prisons and Sentencing," *Today's Social Issues: Democrats and Republicans* (Santa Barbara, Calif.: ABC-CLIO, 2016), 265–274; Michelle Alexander, *The New Jim Crow: Mass Incarceration in the Age of Colorblindness* (New York: The New Press, 2012).

41. Eric Schlosser, "The Prison Industrial Complex," *Atlantic*, December 1998, https://www.theatlantic.com/magazine/archive/1998/12/the-prison-industrial-complex/304669/; Morrell, "The Prison Fix."

42. Jerry Gray, "Prison Unrest Shakes Elmira's Peace," *New York Times*, June 2, 1991, https://www.nytimes.com/1991/06/02/nyregion/prison-unrest-shakes-elmira-s-peace.html.

43. Morrell, "The Prison Fix"; prisons did not deliver the economic benefits that had been imagined, see John S. Eason; "Prisons as Panacea or Pariah? The Countervailing Consequences of the Prison Boom on the Political Economy of Rural Towns," *Social Sciences* 6, no. 7 (January 2017), DOI: 10.3390/socsci6010007; Elmira is one of the few cities that remained mired in recession long after the 2008 economic meltdown; see Davidson, "Just Two Cities Are in Recession."

44. George Winner was Bill Smith's assistance in 1972 and a native of Elmira. He returned to Elmira in 1972 just weeks before the flood. After Smith retired, Winner won his seat; see George Winner.

45. Mulder, "Undaunted Victims," 9.

46. Charles Bradley (Elmira town supervisor), author interview, August 17, 2006.

47. Charles R Jennings, *Urban Renewal as Disaster Recovery Planning*.

48. Letter, Michael Whiteman to David Blabey, August 24, 1972, "UDC Land Valuation Problem." Box 54, Folder 562: Natural Disaster Relief, Nelson Rockefeller Gubernatorial Series 10, Counsels Office Subseries 4, Michael Whiteman Papers.

49. Malcolm Wilson, "At Village Square Apartments and Commercial Center," October 21, 1974.

50. Thomas P. Dimitroff and Lois S. Janes, *History of the Corning-Painted Post Area: 200 Years in Painted Post Country*, rev. ed. (Corning, N.Y.: Bookmarks, 1991), 294.

51. Office of the New York State Comptroller, *New York Cities: An Economic and Fiscal Analysis, 1980–2010* (n.p., September 2012), http://www.osc.state.ny.us/localgov/pubs/fiscalmonitoring/pdf/nycreport2012.pdf; "From Alpine Highways to Great Salt Lake, Painted Post Finds Solutions for 100 Years," *Insights: A Publication of the Dresser-Rand Corporation* (1999), 3–5.

52. Dresser-Rand History, http://www.dresser-rand.com/company/history/1980_1990 .php, accessed October 8, 2010; "From Alpine Highways to Great Salt Lake," 3–5.

53. United States Census Bureau, "Painted Post, New York," https://factfinder.census .gov/faces/nav/jsf/pages/community_facts.xhtml?src=bkmk.

54. Davis Dyer and Daniel Gross, *The Generations of Corning: The Life and Times of a Global Corporation* (New York: Oxford University Press, 2001), 335–336; "Glass: Shake-Out at Corning; Jane Shoemaker, Corning Glass at Crossroads," *New York Times*, September 14, 1975, 135.

55. Daniel Cuff, "Business People; Top Officer Shift at Corning Glass," *New York Times*, April 13, 1983, D2; Dimitroff, "Corning," *Encyclopedia of New York State*, 398; Dyer and Gross, *Generations of Corning*, 413–414.

56. Lillian Brown, "Corning Officials Hail Approval of UR Grant," *The Leader*, June 1, 1973; Hardy Green, *The Company Town: The Industrial Edens and Satanic Mills That Shaped America* (New York: Basic Books, 2012), 51; Tom Dimitroff, Author Interview, September, 13, 2007 (hereafter cited as Tom Dimitroff); John Kelleher, "Ex-Corning Mayor Dies," *Star-Gazette*, March 22, 1988.

57. Rita Reif, "A New Setting for Corning's Glass Collection," *New York Times*, June 5, 1980.

58. Alan Ehrenhalt, "The Plight of America's Overlooked Industrial Cities" (December 2017).

59. Clark, et al., "Deindustrialization: A Panel Discussion," 209.

60. Rockwell Museum Fast Facts, http://www.rockwellmuseum.org/Museum-Fast-Facts .html. According to Bob Rolfe, Amory Houghton played a significant role in assisting the community through corporate grants; see Bob Rolfe.

7. WITHOUT WARNING AND DEFENSELESS

1. Rue Bucher, "Blame and Hostility in Disasters," *American Journal of Sociology* 62 (1957): 467–475; Neil Malhotra and Alexander G. Kuo, "Attributing Blame: The Public's Response to Hurricane Katrina," *Journal of Politics* 70, no. 3 (August 2009): 387–406; https://doi.org/10.1017/S0003055409990104.

2. Peter Briggs, *Rampage: The Story of Disastrous Floods, Broken Dams, and Human Fallibility* (New York: David McKay, 1973), 147; Bob Rolfe.

3. Lillian Brown, "Nasser: Weather Service Gave No Warning," *Corning Leader*, July 15, 1972.

4. Terry Dillman, "Flood Warnings at Corning: A Gap in Communications?" *Times Union*, July 1, 1972; "Corning Clears Mud as Residents Ask about Flood's Rise," *Buffalo Evening News*, June 26, 1972; Tom Hartley, "Communication Seen as Weak Link," *Star-Gazette*, July 4, 1972, 6; Lillian Braun, "Nasser: Weather Service Gave No Warning," *Leader*, July 15, 1972; Bob Rolfe, "Says Weather Service Warning Too Late, Was Inaccurate," *Leader*, July 18, 1972.

5. Memorandum, Fred Oettinger, Office of Field Services to Robert Cook, State of New York Department of Environmental Conservation Office of Field Services, RE: Activities of Department Program during Flood Recovery, August 21, 1972, Box 83, Folder:, Misc. Correspondence R.A. Cook, Hurricane Agnes Damage Files; Memorandum, Henry Diamond to Governor Nelson Rockefeller, October 8, 1970, RE: First Hundred Days, Box 2, Folder: Environmental Plan, Department of Environmental Conservation, State Environmental Plan Files, New York State Archives; Memorandum from Wolfgang Meybaum to Dick Konsella, September 15, 1972, RE: Leon Markson, Box 83, Folder News Releases Flood Photos, Hurricane Agnes Damage Files; files also contains "DEC Efforts in Hurricane Agnes Flood Disaster Saves Lives and Property," *New York State Environmentalist* 2, no. 2 (August 1, 1972): 1–2.

6. Bob Rolfe, "Doubts Post's Earlier Flood Warning Was Passed to Area, State Unit Told," *Corning Leader*, October 13, 1972; Bob Rolfe, "Says Weather Service Word Too Late, Inaccurate," *Corning Leader*, July 18, 1972.

7. Terry Dillman, "Flood Warnings at Corning"; Lillian Braun, "Nasser: Weather Service Gave No Warning"'; Rolfe, "Says Weather Service Warning Too Late."

8. Sartori quoted in Tom Hartley, "Communication Seen as Weak Link," *Star-Gazette*, July 14, 1972, 3.

9. The term "many hands" was introduced by Dennis Thompson, "Moral Responsibility of Public Officials: The Problem of Many Hands," *American Political Science Review* 74, no. 4 (1980): 905–916, https://doi.org/10.2307/1954312; see also Brad T. Gomez and J. Matthew Wilson, "Political Sophistication and Attributions of Blame in the Wake of Hurricane Katrina," *The Journal of Federalism* 38, no. 4 (January 2008): 633–650, https://doi.org/10.1093/publius/pjn016.

10. "NOAA's National Weather Service Celebrates 135th Anniversary," http://www.nws.noaa.gov/pa/history/135anniversary.php; Kathryn Miles, *Superstorm*, 21; Eileen L. Shea, *A History of the NOAA: Being a Compilation of Facts and Figures Regarding the Life and Times of the Original Whole Earth Agency* (NOAA, 1987), https://www.history.noaa.gov/legacy/noaahistory_1.html.

11. Robert M. White, "The National Hurricane Warning System," *Bulletin of the American Meteorological Society* 53, no. 7 (July 1972): 631–633. Robert White was the brother of Theodore H. White, whose study of the 1960 election of between Kennedy and Nixon created a new genre of political literature, the campaign biography, see Theodore H. White, *The Making of the President 1960* (New York: Harper Perennial, 2009).

12. Matt Schudel, "George Cressman, Modernized Weather Service Forecasting," *Washington Post*, May 9, 2008.

13. *Tropical Storm Agnes June 1972: Post Flood Report Volume I, Meteorology and Hydrology* (Baltimore, MD: U.S. Army Corps of Engineers, 1974); Patrick Hughes, *A Century of Weather Service, 1870–1970* (New York: Gordon and Breach, 1970).

14. "1965—Hurricane Betsy," *Sun Sentinel*, August 23, 2001, https://www.sun-sentinel.com/news/sfl-1965-hurricane-story.html.

15. Peter Briggs, *Rampage: The Story of Disastrous Flood, Broken Dams and Human Fallibility* (New York: David McKay, 1973), 119–121; James Rodger Fleming, *Fixing the Sky: The Checkered History of Weather and Climate Control* (New York: Columbia University Press, 2010).

16. "'Storm Fury' Aims to Modify Hurricane Winds by Seeding," *Commerce Today*, August 9, 1971, 30–32; Joanne Simpson, who was married to Robert Simpson of the National Hurricane Center, directed the program until it ended in 1983. See Miles, *Superstorm*, 53.

17. H. E. Willoughby, D. P. Jorgenson, R. A. Black, and S. L. Rosenthal, "Project STORM FURY A Scientific Chronicle, 1962–1983," *Bulletin of the American Meteorological Society* 66, no. 5 (May 1985): 505–514, https://journals.ametsoc.org/doi/pdf/10.11.75/1520-0477%281985%29066%3C0505%3APSASC%3E2.0.CO%3B2.

18. Ernest Zebrowski and Judith A. Howard, *Category 5: The Story of Camille. Lessons Unlearned from America's Most Violent Hurricane* (Ann Arbor: University of Michigan Press, 2005), 21–22.

19. Ibid., 46–47.

20. "The U.S. Unprepared for Big Disasters," *Washington Post*, January 11, 1970, 13; Tom Herman, "Hurricane Camille Recovery Effort by U.S. Assailed: Senate Inquiry Opens Wednesday," *Wall Street Journal*, January 5, 1970; Office of Emergency Preparedness, *Disaster Preparedness*.

21. Ernest Zebrowski and Judith A. Howard, *Category 5*.

22. Lewine, "Better Storm Prediction System Urged by Agnew."

23. *Hurricane Camille: Report to the Administrator U.S. Department of Commerce* (Washington September 1969); Memorandum, P.H. McIntire to Tom Casey, RE: Trip Report to VA. Folder Hearings on Disaster Relief, February 1, 1970, through February 3, 1970, Box 1, Disaster Study Group, RG 396, Office of Emergency Preparedness, National Archives, College Park, Md.

24. *Federal Response to Hurricane Camille: Hearings Before the Special Committee on Disaster Relief of the Committee on Public Works, United States Senate* (Washington, D.C.: U.S. Government Printing Office, 1970); United States and Office of Emergency Preparedness, *Disaster Preparedness; Report to the Congress* (Washington, D.C, 1972).

25. "Late Alerts on Flood-Hit," *Los Angeles Times*, June 26, 1972; Memorandum, Weekly Report for June 29, 1972, Box 2, Folder 1 Weekly Report, Records of the Weather Bureau ESSA, National Archives, College Park, Md.; George P. Cressman, Director of the National Weather Service, Flood Forecasting and Warning Service Report, July 3, 1972," Box 2, RG Records of the Weather Bureau ESSA, National Archives, College Park; Susquehanna River Basin Commission, *Recommendations for an Improved and Expanded Flood Forecasting System for the Susquehanna River Basin* (SRB, September 12, 1973).

26. Disaster Survey Team on the Events of Agnes, *Final Report of the Disaster Survey Team on the Events of Agnes; a Report to the Administrator*, Natural Disaster Survey Report, 73–1; Natural Disaster Survey Report, 73–1 (Rockville, Md., National Oceanic and Atmospheric Administration, 1973), http://unicorn.csc.noaa.gov/docs/czic/QC877.N3%5 Fno.73–1/95DD0F.pdf, 16.

27. Anthony Mussari, *Appointment with Disaster Volume I: The Swelling of the Flood Wilkes-Barre, Pennsylvania before and after the Agnes Flood of June 23, 1972* (Wilkes-Barre, Pa.: Northeastern Press, 1974), 45; Albert Kachic, NWS hydrologist, author interview, September 25, 2008 (hereafter cited as Albert Kachic); Michael Mark, NWS River Forecast Center hydrologist, author interview, January 24, 2011 (hereafter cited as Michael Mark).

28. Mussari, *Appointment with Disaster*, 24; Lars O. Feese, NWS hydrologist, author interview, January 10, 2011 (hereafter cited as Lars Feese); Myron Gwinner, NWS hydrologist, author interview, January 26, 2011(hereafter cited as Myron Gwinner).

29. Cal Turner, "Agnes Had Us Fooled," *Patriot Evening News*, June 28, 1972.

30. George B. Galloway, "Investigative Function of Congress," *American Political Science Review*, 21 (1927): 47–70.

31. Heinz complained that there was flooding in Pittsburgh nearly five hours before the computer predicted a flood, see "Forecasting Probe Sought," *Democrat and Chronicle*, June 25, 1972, 84; "Weekly Report for June 29, 1972," Weather Bureau, NARA.

32. *Hearings before a Subcommittee of the Committee on Government Operations House of Representatives Ninety-Second Congress* (Washington, D.C.: Government Printing Office, 1972), 1.

33. Ibid., 25–27.

34. Ibid., 17.

35. "Edwin S. Underhill to Rockefeller, October 18, 1972, Microfilm Reel 20, Disaster Files, Office Records on Microfilm, Rockefeller Archive; "Area Flood Hearing Set," *Star-Gazette*, October 7, 1972; Smith held hearings in Elmira and Corning in October 1972.

36. Bob Rolfe, "Warned 3 A.M. on Flood," *Leader*, October 19, 1972.

37. Bob Rolfe.

38. Nicholas R. Hoye, *The Flood and the Community* (Corning: Corning Glass Works, 1976): 140.

39. "Notice Lack Irks Two," *Leader*, July 13, 1972; Bob Bolger and Bob Rolfe, "Elmira Had No Flood Warning Mayor Testifies," *Leader*, October 12, 1972; Lillian Braun, "Nasser: Weather Service Gave No Warning."

40. Ibid.

41. "Why Flood Area Got No Warning," *Times Union*, October 13, 1972.

42. Ibid.

43. Ibid.

44. "Weekly Report for June 29, 1972," Weather Bureau; Cressman, "Flood Forecasting and Warning System Report," July 3, 1972, Weather Bureau; Sharon T. Ashley and Walker S. Ashley, "Flood Fatalities in the United States," *Journal of the American Meteorological Association* 47 (March 2008): 805–818.

45. *Final Report of the Disaster Survey Team on the Events of Agnes: A Report to the Administrator* (Rockville, Md.: U.S. National Oceanic and Atmospheric Administration, 1973), 1–3,15–16. The NWS gave a gold medal to George H. Schielein, an Albany meteorologist who was sent to Rochester to alert officials to the dangers at Mount Morris Dam; medals also went to the members of the Harrisburg River Forecast Office; see "NOAA History," http://www.history.noaa.gov/hallofhonor/lifesaving_1955-2000nws.html.

46. *Final Report of the Disaster Survey Team on the Events of Agnes*, 14.

47. Ibid.

48. *Final Report of the Disaster Survey Team*, 15–16. Scholars in the field of disaster studies have indicated that when governments frame natural hazards as "acts of God," they justify their inaction; see Ted Steinberg, *Acts of God*; after Camille, the Nixon administration insisted that the disaster was the result of an act of God.

49. "Agnes Probe Finds People Performed Well, Need Better Warning Delivery," *Commerce Today* 3 (1973): 32–33.

50. National Advisory Committee on Oceans and Atmospheres, *A Report for the Administrator of NOAA: The Agnes Floods: A Post-Audit of the Effectiveness of the Storm and Flood Warning System of the National Oceanic and Atmospheric Administration* (Washington, D.C.: Government Printing Office: 1972), ii, 2 (italics in the original document), 8–10. Of course, what they meant is the no single agencies had sole responsibility, which displaced both blame and responsibility for the disaster.

51. NOAA Weather Radio, http://www.nws.noaa.gov/nwr/index.php.

52. Weather.Gov on your mobile phone, https://www.weather.gov/wrn/mobile-phone.

53. Joseph Sartori. Press clippings found in Howard Robison Papers.

54. Matthew Dallek, *Defenseless under the Night: The Roosevelt Years and the Origins of Homeland Security* (New York: Oxford University Press, 2016).

55. Amanda J. Dory, *Civil Security: Americans and the Challenge of Homeland Security* (Lanham, Md.: Rowman and Littlefield / Center for Strategic and International Studies, 2003). Stephen Sanswcct, "Unheeded Sentry: Fight for Survival Occupies Civil Defense Program," *Wall Street Journal*, May 20, 1971; United States Defense Civil Preparedness Agency, *Significant Events in United States Civil Defense History*, compiled by Mary Harris (Washington, D.C.: Information Agency Defense Civil Preparedness Agency, 1975), 20–21.

56. Paul Boyer, "From Activism to Apathy: The American People and Nuclear Weapons, 1963–1980," *Journal of American History* 70 (1984): 821–844. The metal signs indicating fallout shelters are still visible in most U.S. cities.

57. Scott Gabriel Knowles, *The Disaster Experts: Mastering Risk in Modern America* (Philadelphia: University of Pennsylvania Press, 2011), 165.

58. Knowles, *Disaster Experts*, 233.

59. John E. Davis made these comments in a public affairs film, *In Time of Emergency* (Washington, D.C.: Office of Civil Defense, 1969), http://www.youtube.com/watch?v=3Bvk47-WSsg; the federal government invested money in studying the community and individual response to natural disasters in hopes of learning how they might respond to a nuclear attack. This research helped created the Disaster Research Center at Ohio State in

the early 1960s and inspired a cadre of academic disaster experts. See Scott Gabriel Knowles, *The Disaster Experts: Mastering Risk in Modern America* (Philadelphia: University of Pennsylvania Press, 2011).

60. National Governors' Association, Center for Policy Research, *Comprehensive Emergency Management: A Governor's Guide* (Washington, D.C.: May 1979), http://training .fema.gov/EMIWeb/edu/docs/Comprehen.

61. "CD Chief Says City Lucky; It Wasn't Ready," *Scranton Times*, June 23, 1972; "Civil Defense Members Need Better Equipment," *Beaver County Times*, June 28, 1972.

62. "Lack of Warning Cited, Flood Emergency Plan Urged," *Democrat and Chronicle*, October 20, 1972; Bob Rolfe, "Doubts Posts; Earlier Flood Warning Was Passed to Area, State Unit told," *Corning Leader*, October 13, 1972; Beck was a rare example of a woman leading civil defense but was aided by her twenty-two years in civil defense work and service in the U.S. Marine Corps; see "'It Sounds Like a Man's Job' But Mrs. Beck Knows Better," *Olean Times Herald*, July 19, 1975.

63. Clippings found in Folder State-Local Agencies, Box 131, Howard Robison Papers.

64. Jack Lisi quoted in "City Officials Fault June Flood Warning," *Hornell Evening Tribune*, October 20, 1972.

65. Newspaper clippings, Folder Agnes—Newspapers, Box 195, Howard Robison Papers.

66. Crile, "Best Congressman," 62; "Agnes Isn't over for Dan Flood."

67. Richard Sylves, *Disaster Policy and Politics: Emergency Management and Homeland Security*, 2nd revised edition (Washington, DC: CQ Press, 2014), 13–17.

68. Ibid.

69. Grushky assumed that role with the retirement of Raymond Barburti in July 1972. See "State Transportation Bureau Names Disaster Office Head," *Journal*, July 13, 1972.

70. Rolfe, "Doubts Persist," 3; "Lack of Warning Cited," *Democrat and Chronicle*, October 20, 1972.

71. *Report of Special New York Senate Committee to Investigate Flood Warning Systems in New York State*, January 31, 1973, 4–5; "Legislation Planned to Let State Agency Give Flood Warnings," *New York Times*, February 10, 1973.

72. "Legislation Planned to Let State Agency Give Flood Warning"; "Flood Warning System Seen Inundated with Snafus," *Star-Gazette*, February 10, 1973, 1; Memorandum, Michael Whiteman to Nelson Rockefeller, June 11, 1973, RE: Senate Bill 3553, Box 45, Folder 415, Assembly and Senate Memos. Rockefeller Archives.

73. *McKinney's Session Laws of New York, Volume 1, 196th Session 1973* (St Paul, Minn.: West Publishing Co), 2333; *Laws of New York State 1973*, 1756–1759; *New York State Legislative Annual 1973*, 320; Memorandum Michael Whiteman to Nelson Rockefeller, June 6, 1973, Box 46, Folder 416, Assembly and Senate Memos, Rockefeller Archives.

74. Dorothy Smith interviewed by author, September 30, 2006 (hereafter Dorothy Smith); William Smith, et al., *Flood Warning Breakdown, Why? Report of New York Senate Select Committee on Interstate Cooperation Subcommittee to Investigate Flood Warning Systems and Flood Damage Following Hurricane Eloise in September 1975*, New York, 1976.

75. "Daughter's Death Began Fight against Drunk Driving," *Star-Gazette*, May 15, 1977; Jeannie H. Cross, "'Cadillac' Smith Bid Farewell," *Times Union*, December 4, 1986.

8. THE RISKY BUSINESS OF FLOOD CONTROL

1. Anthony J. Mussari, *Appointment with Disaster, Vol. 1: The Swelling of the Flood—Wilkes Barre, Pennsylvania before and after the Agnes Flood of June 23, 1972* (Wilkes-Barre, Pa.: Northeast Publishers, 1974), 48–49; Robert P. Wolensky, *Better Than Ever! The Flood*

Recovery Task Force and the 1972 Agnes Disaster, 1972 (Stevens Point, Wisc.: Foundation Press, 1993), 6; John H. Brubaker, *Down the Susquehanna to the Chesapeake* (University Park: Pennsylvania State University Press, 2002), 64.

2. "Sturdy Dikes Save Corning Once More," *Leader*, Thursday, June 22, 1972.

3. A floodplain is the area of low lying ground adjacent to a river that is subject to flooding.

4. See, for example, Rutherford H. Platt, *Disasters and Democracy* (Washington, D.C.: Island Press, 1999), 37–41; geographers have been particularly critical of the engineering solution to flooding, and have pointed out it that is impossible to protect against flooding completely; see, for example, Luna B. Leopold and Thomas Maddock, Jr., *The Flood Control Controversy: Big Dams, Little Dams, and Land Management* (New York: Ronald Press, 1954), 9–14.

5. Todd Shallat, "Building Waterways, 1802–1861: Science and the United States Army in Early Public Works," *Technology and Culture* 31 (January 1990): 18–50.

6. Trudy E. Bell, *The Great Dayton Flood of 1913* (Charleston, SC: Arcadia Publishing, 2008); Trudy E. Bell, "Angry Waters," *New York Archives*, Winter 2013, 12–17.

7. Alfred J. Henry, *The Floods of 1913 in the Rivers of the Ohio and Lower Mississippi Valleys* (Washington, D.C.: Government Printing Office, 1913), 106; Martin Reuss, "The Army Corps and Engineers and Flood Control Politics on the Lower Mississippi," *Louisiana History, The Journal of the Louisiana Historical Association* 23, no. 2 (Spring 1982): 131, http://www.jstor.org.ezproxy.naz.edu/stable/4232166; Jason David Rivera and DeMond Shondell Miller, "A Brief History of the Evolution of United States' Natural Disaster Policy," *Journal of Public Management and Social Policy* 12, no. 1 (Spring 2006): 5–14.

8. Studies of the 1927 flood include John Barry, *Rising Tide: The Great Mississippi Flood of 1927 and How It Changed America* (New York: Simon and Schuster, 1997); Pete Daniel, *Deep'n as It Come: The 1927 Mississippi River Flood* (Fayetteville: University of Arkansas Press, 1996); Arkansas history is highlighted in Nancy Hendricks, "Flood of 1927," *The Encyclopedia of Arkansas History and Culture*, http://encyclopediaofarkansas.net /encyclopedia/entry-detail.aspx?entryID=2202.

9. Reuss, "Politics and Technology in the Corps of Engineers, 1850–1950," 145; Reuss, "The Army Corps of Engineers," 131–132; Matthew Pearcy, "After the Flood: A History of the 1928 Flood Control Act," *Journal of the Illinois State Historical Society* 95, no. 1 (Spring 2002): 172–201; Rivera and Miller, "United States' Natural Disaster Policy," 7.

10. Franklin Roosevelt, "Commonwealth Club Address," September 23, 1932, American Rhetoric Online Speech Bank, http://www.americanrhetoric.com/speeches/fdrcommon wealth.htm; Franklin D. Roosevelt, "Inaugural Address," March 4, 1933, online at Gerhard Peters and John T. Woolley, *The American Presidency Project*, http://www.presidency .ucsb.edu/ws/?pid=14473m.

11. Michele Landis, "Fate, Responsibility, and 'Natural' Disaster Relief: Narrating the American Welfare State," *Law and Society Review* 33 (1999): 257–318.

12. Copp, *Floods of the Chemung Watershed*, 10–13.

13. Quoted in Joseph L. Arnold, *Evolution of the 1936 Flood Control Act* (Washington, D.C.: Government Printing Office, 1988), 51.

14. "New Bills Speeded on Flood Control," *New York Times*, March 26, 1936.

15. Copp, *Floods of the Chemung Watershed*, 15.

16. "Ask State to Press Flood Control Legislation," *New York Times*, April 21, 1936; Arnold, *Evolution of 1936 Flood Control Act*, 60–70; Shallat, "Engineering Policy: US Army Corps of Engineers and Historical Foundations of Power," *Public Historian* 11, no. 3 (Summer 1989): 6–27, DOI: 10.2307/3378610.

17. Susan Q Stranahan, *Susquehanna, River of Dreams* (Baltimore: Johns Hopkins University Press, 1995), 127.

18. "New Bills Speeded," *New York Times*; Adams, "Hurricane Agnes," 33; Stranahan, *Susquehanna*,128; Thomas P. Dimitroff and Lois B. Janes, *History of the Corning–Painted Post Area: 200 Years in Painted Post Country*, rev. ed. (Corning, N.Y.: Bookmarks, 1991), 288; H. Michael Mogil, "The Weather Warning and Preparedness Programs: The National Weather Service and Mass Media," in *Disasters and Mass Media: Proceedings of the Committee on Disasters and the Mass Media Workshop* (Washington, D.C.: National Science, 1980); Harold Kanarek, *The Mid-Atlantic Engineers: A History of the Baltimore District of the Army Corps of Engineers, 1774–1974* (Washington, D.C.: Government Printing Office, 1976), 123–130.

19. Stranahan, *Susquehanna*, 127.

20. Raymond Burby, "Hurricane Katrina and the Paradoxes of Government Disaster Policy: Bringing about Wise Governmental Decisions for Hazardous Areas," *Annals of the American Academy of Political and Social Science* no. 1 (March 2006): 171–191, https://doi .org/10.1177%2F0002716205284676.

21. Vandenberg is quoted in Todd Shallat, "Engineering Policy."

22. Thomas A. Birkland, *Lessons of Disaster: Policy Change after Catastrophic Events* (Washington, D.C.: Georgetown University Press, 2006), 106.

23. Gilbert White, *Human Adjustment to Flooding: A Geographical Approach to the Flood Problem in the United States* (Chicago: University of Chicago Press, 1945).

24. Ted Steinberg addresses moral hazards in Theodore Steinberg, *Acts of God: The Unnatural History of Natural Disaster in America* (Milton Keynes, U.K.: Lightning Source, 2011), 97–103.

25. For more on the life of Gilbert White, see Robert Hinshaw, *Living with Nature's Extremes: The Life of Gilbert Fowler White* (New York: Big Earth Publishing, 2006).

26. Allison Dunham, "Flood Control via the Police Power," *University of Pennsylvania Law Review* 107 (1959): 1098–1132.

27. Ibid.

28. The American Institutes for Research and the Pacific Institute for Research and Evaluation, *A Chronology of Major Events Affecting the National Flood Insurance Program* (2005), https://www.fema.gov/media-library-data/20130726-1602-20490–472/nfip_eval _chronology.txt.

29. Ibid.

30. Gilbert White, *Human Adjustment to Flooding*; William G. Hoyt and Walter B. Langbein, *Floods* (Princeton: Princeton University Press, 1955).

31. The general willingness to recompense citizens who lose property from a flood as well to pay for levees, dams, and floodwalls has encouraged more building on the floodplain; see Steinberg, *Acts of God*, 97–103.

32. The American Institutes for Research and the Pacific Institute for Research and Evaluation, *A Chronology of Major Events Affecting the National Flood Insurance Program*.

33. Leopold and Maddock, *The Flood Control Controversy*, 17; this point is also made in Knowles, *The Disaster Experts*, 256.

34. Dunham, "Flood Control," 1102.

35. Rutherford H. Platt, "The National Flood Insurance Program: Some Midstream Perspectives," *Journal of the American Institute of Planners* 42, no. 3 (1976): 303–313, https://doi.org/10.1080/01944367608977733; the federal government has been reluctant to enforce many of the provisions requiring floodplain management, while also providing generous disaster aid following a flood thereby limiting the impact of the NFIP.

36. Hugh Scott testimony in *To Investigate Adequacy*, 865–867; Kleppe testimony in *To Investigate Adequacy*, 73–74. Howard Robison and Daniel Flood both tried to get the federal government to pay for the relocation of people living along their respective rivers. Three times each they offered bills amending the Uniform Relocation and Assistance and the Real

Property Acquisition Act of 1970 to allow constituents to sell their property at full market value to the government, but House members killed it in committee.

37. Allesandro Jerolleman et al., *Natural Hazard Mitigation* (Boca Raton, Fla.: CRC Press, 2013), 10. These provisions were rarely enforced and rebuilding in the flood zones and full insurance coverage continued due to waivers provided in the aftermath of flood disasters.

38. Haddow and Bullock, *Introduction to Emergency Management*, 4.

39. Richard Nixon, "Statement on Signing the Flood Disaster Protection Act of 1973," December 31, 1973. Online by Gerhard Peters and John T. Woolley, *The American Presidency Project*, http://www.presidency.ucsb.edu/ws/?pid=4093.

40. Memo: "Robert Schnabel, "Coverage of Issues in the PL 91-606 Disaster Study Group, April 27, 1971," WHCF; "Robert Schnabel, Retired Colonel In Air Force," *Washington Post*, September 14, 1981, https://www.washingtonpost.com/archive/local/1981 /09/14/robert-schnabel-retired-colonel-in-air-force/5ff88349-7e9f-4642-b276 -4480573b804d/?utm_term=.8f894ed32c41.

41. Jerolleman et al. *Natural Hazard Mitigation*, 10. These provisions were rarely enforced and rebuilding in the flood zones and full insurance coverage continued due to waivers provided in the aftermath of flood disasters.

42. Nixon, "Statement on Signing the Flood Disaster Protection Act of 1973."

43. Ibid., 62.

44. Ibid.

45. Erwann O. Michel-Kerjan, "Flood Insurance in the United States: Past, Present and Future," *Journal of Economic Perspectives* 24 (Fall 2010): 165–186.

46. Fred B. Power and E. Warren Shows, "A Status Report on the National Flood Insurance Program,. Mid 1978," *Journal of Risk and Insurance* 46, no. 2 (1979): 61–76, doi:10.2307/252069.

47. "Thousands Hit by Storms Rely on Wobbly Insurance," *New York Times*, November 5, 2017.

48. Birkland, *Lessons of Disaster*, 107–109; *Field Hearings before the Committee on Policy Research and Insurance of the Committee on Banking, Finance and Urban Affairs*, House of Representatives (Washington, D.C.: Government Printing Office, 1990), 6; for a recent assessment of the modest success of the NFIP, see Richard T. Sylves, *Disaster Policy and Politics*, 18–20.

49. Rawle O. King, *The National Flood Insurance Program: Status and Remaining Issues for Congress* (Congressional Research Services, February 6, 2013), http://fas.org/sgp/crs /misc/R42850.pdf.

50. "Thousands Hit by Storms," A1.

51. Rutherford H. Platt, *Disasters and Democracy*, 37–41; Erwann O. Michel-Kerjan, "Catastrophic Economics: The National Flood Insurance Program," *Journal of Economic Perspectives* 24 (2010): 165–186.

52. U.S. General Accounting Office, *Challenges Facing the National Flood Insurance Program*, GAO Report GAO-03-606T (Washington, D.C., 2003), 16.

53. Rawle O. King, *CRS Report for Congress: Federal Flood Insurance: The Repetitive Loss Problem* (Washington, D.C., 2005).

54. Eric Lipton, Felicity Barringer, and Mary Williams Walsh, "Flood Insurance, Already Fragile Faces New Stress," *New York Times*, November 12, 2012.

55. Siobhan Hughes, "Flood Insurance Prices Surge," *Wall Street Journal*, August 13, 2013; H2O Partners, "Getting to Know Flood Reform," http://www.youtube.com/watch ?v=tpeqSQr3ngY&list=UUHMck7Qh7gAf7o4qnPu84IA&index=2.

56. Robert Verchick and Lynsey Johnston, "When Retreat Is the Best Option: Flood Insurance after Biggert-Waters and Other Climate Change Puzzles," *John Marshall Law Review* 47 (2013): 711–712.

57. Andrew Simpson, "Senate Approves Bill to Curb Flood Insurance Hikes," *Insurance Journal*, http://www.insurancejournal.com/news/national/2014/03/13/323273.htm.

58. Richard Rainey, "Floods and Insurance: Congress Renews NFIP Debate, Louisiana Braces," *Times-Picayune*, March 14, 2017, http://www.nola.com/environment/index.ssf /2017/03/floods_and_insurance_congress.html.

59. Wolensky, *Better Than Ever!*, 40.

60. Kury was elected a Pennsylvania State senator in 1972, and his constituents lived in flood-prone areas such as Shamokin Dam, Lewisburg, and Milton. See Franklin L. Kury, *Clean Politics, Clean Streams: A Legislative Autobiography and Reflection* (Pittsburgh: Lehigh University Press, 2011), 124.

61. Ibid., 124–128.

62. H.R. 10203 (93rd): Water Resources Development Act, https://www.govtrack.us /congress/bills/93/hr10203/text; Platt, *Disasters and Democracy*, 79; Mary McCarthy and John J Kiefer, "A History of Hazard Mitigation in the U.S.," in Jerolleman and Kiefer, *Natural Hazards Mitigation*, 6; National Wildlife Federation, "Water Resources Development Act," https://training.fws.gov/courses/csp/csp3132/resources/WRDAs/WhatisWRDA.pdf.

63. The Public Works Committee handled a great deal of pork-barrel projects, and this makes it a plumb committee for members of the House seeking reelection; see Richard F. Fenno, *Congressmen in Committees* (Boston: Little Brown, 1973); in 1968 Robison voted against legislation intended to limit the construction of more man-made flood control structures on the Susquehanna River, after which environmental groups and the *New York Times* editorial board chastised him; see Koltz, "Howard W. Robison," 10–12.

64. Cliff Smith, "Citizens Blocked Anti Flood Dams Army Engineers Say," *Times Union*, June 28, 1972.

65. Mike Wines, "How Haggling Led to Tragedy," *Democrat and Chronicle*, June 28, 1972.

66. Wines, "How Haggling Led to Tragedy," "Stalled New York State Flood Projects Could Have Saved Valley from Disaster," *Sunday Independent*, July 23, 1972; H.R.16254 was passed on August 31, 1972, and included a provision to fast-track the Tioga-Hammond Dam complex.

67. "Howard Robison Dies at 71; Served 17 Years in Congress," *New York Times*, October 1, 1987, http://www.nytimes.com/1987/10/01/obituaries/howard-robison-dies-at -71-served-17-years-in-congress.html.

68. Paul E. Kanjorski, "The Dawn of a New Day in Wilkes-Barre," *Citizens' Voice*, June 19, 2009, http://www.citizensvoice.com/opinion/letters/.

69. Mulder, "Undaunted Victims"; Charlie Coon, "There is No Controlling a Flood," *Star-Gazette*, June 24, 2002; Anthony J. Mussari, *Appointment with Disaster*, 143.

70. Rebecca Solnit explores this concept in *A Paradise Built in Hell: The Extraordinary Communities That Arise in Disaster* (New York: Viking, 2009); the sense of community spirit imbues the early histories of Agnes.

71. Paul E. Kanjorski, "The Dawn of a New Day in Wilkes-Barre," *Citizens' Voice*, June 19, 2009, http://www.citizensvoice.com/opinion/letters/; Michal Sisak, "Former Rep. Kanjorski Sings Praises of Levee Raising Project's Results," *Times-Tribune*, September 12, 2011.

72. Both themes are present in Renita Fennick, "The Torrents of '72," Wilkes-Barre, *Times Leader*, June 1997, http://www.leader.net/specials/agnes/flood.htm; Jeff Murray, "1972 Flood: Could it Happen Again?" *Star-Gazette*, June 16, 2012, http://www.stargazette .com/apps/pbcs.dll/article?AID=/201206161615/NEWS01/206160339.

73. On the Golden Age of dam building, see Robert S. Devine, "The Trouble with Dams," *Atlantic Monthly* 276 (August 1995): 64; Fennick, "The Torrents of '72."

74. Paul K. Walker, *The Corps Responds: A History of the Susquehanna Engineer District and Tropical Storm Agnes* (U.S. Army Corps of Engineers, 1976), http://cdm16021

.contentdm.oclc.org/utils/getfile/collection/p16021coll4/id/145/filename/146.pdf; Harold Kanarek, *The MidAtlantic Engineers: A History of the Baltimore District, U.S. Army Corps of Engineers, 1774–1974* (Washington, D.C.: U.S. Government Printing Office, 1976); Naula McGann Drescher and James Robert Martin-Diaz, *Engineers for the Public Good: A History of the Buffalo District, U.S. Army Corps of Engineers* (U.S. Army Corps of Engineers, 1982), http://cdm16021.contentdm.oclc.org/cdm/singleitem/collection/p16021coll4/id/102/rec/17; U.S. Army Corps of Engineers Buffalo District, Mount Morris Dam, 2013, http://www.nab.usace.army.mil/Factsheets/PDFs/PA%20Tioga-Hammond%20Lakes-O&M.pdf.

75. U.S. Army Corps of Engineers, Baltimore District, Pennsylvania Visitor's Center, August 4, 2013.

76. "Mount Morris Dam," video produced by U.S. Army Corps of Engineers, Buffalo District (2007).

77. Ibid.

78. "Mount Morris Dam" (exhibit at the dam), August 2013.

79. Douglas Brinkley, *The Great Deluge: Hurricane Katrina, New Orleans and the Mississippi Gulf Coast* (New York: Harper Perennial, 2007); John Barry, *Rising Tide: The Great Mississippi Flood of 1927 and How It Changed America* (New York: Simon and Schuster 1998); "Lessons from Agnes: Comparing the Flood of 1972 and 2011," http://www.wnep.com/wnep-lessons-from-agnes-comparing-the-floods-of-1972-and-2011–20111114,0,4110877.story; James Haggerty and David Falcheck, "Tropical Storm Irene Damages Northeast Pennsylvania before Heading up East Coast," *Times-Tribune*, August 29, 2011; Josh Mrozinski and Sarah Hofius Hall, "Governor Sees NEPA Devastation," *Times-Tribune*, August 30, 2011; Mark Scolforo, "Wilkes-Barre Flooding Worse Than Agnes in 1972," www.nbc.philadelphia.com, 20011; Steve McConnell, "FEMA Aid Enroute Thanks to Presidential Declaration," *Times-Tribune*, September 14, 2011.

80. "Lessons from Agnes: Comparing the Flood of 1972 and 2011"; Haggerty and Falcheck, "Tropical Storm Irene Damages Northeast Pennsylvania before Heading up East Coast"; Mrozinski and Hall, "Governor Sees NEPA Devastation"; Scolforo "Wilkes-Barre Flooding Worse Than Agnes in 1972"; McConnell "FEMA Aid Enroute Thanks to Presidential Declaration."

9. THE DISASTER RELIEF ACT OF 1974

1. Memorandum, John C. Whitaker to John Ehrlichman, September 12, 1972, RE: Congressional Mandate to Review the Disaster Relief Program, Folder Disaster Materials, Box 130, White House Central Files, Staff Member Office Files, John C Whitaker, Richard Nixon Presidential Library and Museum, Yorba Linda, Calif. (hereafter cited as John C. Whitaker files).

2. Nixon's actions were the total opposite of actions taken by Lyndon Johnson, who expanded benefits during his presidency and extended the time limit for receiving benefits. Richard Nathan, "There Will Always Be a New Federalism," *Journal of Public Administration Research and Theory* 16, no. 4 (October 2006): 499–510, https://doi.org/10.1093/jopart/muj011; Steven Hayward quote on Chamber of Commerce Republican in Steven F. Hayward, *The Age of Reagan: The Fall of the Old Liberal Order: 1964–1980*, reprint edition (New York: Crown Forum, 2009), 232; Robert P. Wolensky, *Better Than Ever! The Flood Recovery Task Force and the 1972 Agnes Disaster, 1972* (Stevens Point, Wisc.: Foundation Press, 1993), 38; Tom Infield, "Agnes: A Legacy of Federal Aid and a Bedrock for Disaster," *Philadelphia Inquirer*, June 27, 1997, A1.

3. Memorandum, Robert Schnabel, RE: Coverage of Issues in the PL 91–606, April 27, 1971, Box 5, White House Central Files: Subject files DI 2 (Disasters), Richard Nixon Library and Museum, Yorba Linda, Calif. (hereafter WHCF-DI 2); Memorandum, George A Lincoln, Director of Office of Emergency Management, to President Richard Nixon,

December 16, 1969, Box 1, Folder: 11/1/1969-3/31/70, WHCF-DI; Memorandum, Wilfred Rommel to Richard Burress, July 22, 1969, Box 1, Folder 9/1/1969-10/31/1969, WHCF-DI 1. Schnabel's ideas reflect constitutional reality and congressional legislation all of which suggests the federal government supplement rather than supplant state and local response to disaster.

4. Richard Nixon, "Annual Message to Congress on the State of the Union," January 22 1971, American Presidency Project, http://www.presidency.ucsb.edu/ws/index.php?pid =3110; on New Federalism see Richard Nathan, *The Plot That Failed: Nixon and the Administrative Presidency* (New York: John Wiley and Sons, 1975), 24; Timothy Conlon, *New Federalism: Intergovernmental Reform from Nixon to Reagan* (Washington, D.C.: Brooking Institute, 1988), 3.

5. Richard Nixon, "Address to the Nation on Domestic Programs," August 8, 1969, *Public Papers of President Nixon* (Washington, D.C.: Government Printing Office, 1969), 637–638.

6. Bill Smith exemplifies the tension between philosophical belief and pragmatic necessity. See also Robert F. Durant and Susannah Bruns Ali, "Repositioning American Public Administration? Citizen Estrangement, Administrative Reform, and the Disarticulated State," *Public Administration Review* 73, no. 2 (March/April 2013): 278–289, https://doi.org/10.1111/j.1540–6210.2012.02646.x; the tension between small government philosophy and big government demands after a disaster is explored by Natalie Schuster, "This 'Who Shot John' Thing: Disaster Relief as Entitlement in the 20th Century," *Federal History* 5 (2014): 84.

7. *To Investigate the Adequacy and Effectiveness of Federal Disaster Relief Legislation: Hearings, Ninety-Third Congress, First[-Second] Session* (Washington: U.S. Government Printing Office, 1973), https://catalog.hathitrust.org/Record/100670675. 1740.

8. Floods are the disaster least likely to lead to policy change; see Thomas Birkland, *Lessons of Disaster: Policy Change after Catastrophic Events* (Washington, D.C.: Georgetown University Press, 2006).

9. Investigations are apt to occur when the normal functions of the state are interrupted when the distress of a precipitating event is high, and when the media is paying attention. All three criteria occurred after the Agnes disaster. See Loch K. Johnson and Erna Gelles, "The Study of Congressional Investigations: Research . . ." *Congress & the Presidency* 2 19 (1992): 137–156, https://doi.org/10.1080/07343469209507897; Senate investigations may also have underlying political motivations. Politics are especially evident when the government is divided government, where one political party controls the White House and the other controls Congress. See Benjamin Ginsberg and Martin Shefter, *Politics by Other Means: The Declining Importance of Elections in America* (New York: Basic Books, 1990).

10. "Joe Biden," *Contemporary Newsmakers 1986*, Gale Research 1987. Biography Resource Center (Farmington Hills, Mich.: Gale, 2009).

11. Flood in *To Investigate Adequacy*, 899–905, 918, 929, and ff.; Republican Pete Domenici opposed the majority and wanted to increase the state responsibility for response, clean-up, and rebuilding. See Bob Rolfe, "Central Disaster Unit Seen as Need," Corning, *Times Leader*, June 2, 1973, 11.

12. Schweiker testimony in *To Investigate Adequacy*, 870–871; Biden comments in *To Investigate Adequacy*, 874.

13. Ibid.

14. Burdick comments in *To Investigate Adequacy*, 875. Throughout the proceeding Chairman Burdick verbally challenged Governor Shapp and Congressman Joseph McRae whenever they criticized OEP.

15. Rolfe, "Central Disaster Unit Seen as Need."

16. *To Investigate Adequacy*, 881, 901, 918, and ff.

17. Daniel Flood noted that if the Wyoming Valley of Pennsylvania had been destroyed not by a flood but by bombs, the Department of Defense "could have a recovery plan operational in an hour." Disaster victims deserved no less a course of action, see "National Disaster Center Proposed," *Times Daily*, April 30, 1973, 2; David A. Moss, *When All Else Fails: Government as the Ultimate Risk Manager* (Cambridge, Mass.: Harvard University Press, 2004), 264.

18. Joseph McDade, Prepared Statement for Senate Public Works Committee, May 1973, Box 3, Folder 25, Joseph McDade Papers.

19. Bob Rolf, "Mandatory Disaster Insurance Is Proposed at Senate Hearing," *Leader*, June 1, 1973, 8.

20. "Senator Urges SBA Forgive Loan Interest," *Time Leader*, December 14, 1972, Richard Schweiker Papers. Birch Bayh, long an advocate for these measures, resigned from the Senate Public Works Committee on August 2, 1972. House members George Danielson, Edward Roybal, and Daniel Flood offered catastrophic insurance bills multiple times. William Greider, "McGovern Invites Audit of His Campaign Funds," *Boston Globe*, August 29, 1972, 1, 10; Milton Shapp, "Testimony Before the House Banking and Currency Committee," General Files, Milton Shapp Papers; General Files, Pennsylvania State Archives, Harrisburg; Richard Schweiker comments are found in *Flood Insurance and Disaster Assistance Hearings before the Subcommittee on Housing and Urban Affairs* (Washington D.C.: Government Printing Office, 1973), 7. In 1973 a dozen bills dealing with federal insurance and a disaster agency were offered in the House; see http://thomas .loc.gov, *Washington Post*, Editorial, "The Lingering Legacy of Agnes," *Washington Post*, September 9, 1972, 18.

21. Howard Robison supported the bill. From Owego, N.Y., Robison was the longest serving member of the New York Republican delegation.

22. The history of the bill and similar attempts by Flood are available at the Library of Congress, Thomas Site, http://thomas.loc.gov/cgi-bin/bdquery/D?d093:499:./list/bss /d093HR.lst:@@@D&summ2=m&; John E Owens, "Extreme Advocacy Leadership in the Pre-Reform House: Wright Patman and the House Banking and Currency Committee," *British Journal of Politics* 15 (1985): 187–205.

23. C. Robert Hall, "Major Disaster Proposals Invite 'Fed' into Areas Now Well Handled," *National Underwriter* (March 21, 1975): 79.

24. David Moss, *When All Else Fails*, 155–156.

25. Robert McFadden, "Richard S. Schweiker, Former Senator, and Reagan Confidant, Dies at 89," *New York Times*, August 3, 2015, https://www.nytimes.com/2015/08/04/us /richard-s-schweiker-reagan-confidant-dies-at-89.html?_r=0.

26. *After Agnes: A Triumph over Destruction* (Wilkes-Barre: *Times Leader*, 1982), 62; "Milton Shapp Dies," A-1.

27. Donald Ritchie, the Historian of the Senate, indicates that the loss of members in that body can leave gaps in the institutional memory; see Christina Bellantoni, "Key Retirements Sap Institutional Knowledge," *Roll Call*, January 19, 2012, http://www.rollcall .com/news/key-retirements-sap-institutional-knowledge-211624–1.html. On losses in the House and Senate in 1974 and the rise of the Watergate Babies see CQ Almanac, "1974 Elections: A Major Sweep for the Democrats," https://library.cqpress.com/cqalmanac /document.php?id=cqal74–1222893.

28. Hugh Scott was untouched by the Watergate scandal and was honored by his Senate colleagues in 1981 when they named a room in the Capitol the "Hugh Scott Room." In 1989 he chaired a Bicentennial Commission for the U.S. Senate. Scott passed away in 1994 in Falls Church, Virginia; David Binder, "Senator Hugh Scott, 93, Dies; Former Leader of Republicans," *New York Times*, July 23, 1994, http://www.nytimes.com/1994/07/23 /obituaries/senator-hugh-scott-93-dies-former-leader-of-republicans.html.

29. "Nixon Proposes Disaster Aid Unit," *New York Times*, May 9, 1973, 17; Lou Cannon, "Nixon Signs Bills on Last Day of '73," *Washington Post*, January 1, 1974, A20. Memo from DWM to Richard Schweiker, "Flood Issues," October 28, 1974, Richard Schweiker Papers. *New Approaches to Disaster Preparedness and Assistance: Message from the President of the United States* (Washington, D.C.: Government Printing Office, 1973); "S.1840. A Bill to Provide for Disaster Assistance and Other Purposes," GAO Resources, http://ftp.resource .org/gao.gov/93-288/0000FB12.pdf; "Disaster Relief Legislation," Remarks by Mr. Burdick, June 12, 1973, *Congressional Record: Proceedings and Debates of the 93rd Congress*, Senate, Bill 1840, S10932, http://bulk.resource.org/gao.gov/93-288/0000FB10; Message to Congress Proposing Disaster Preparedness and Assistance Legislation, May 8 1973, *American Presidency Project*, http://www.presidency.ucsb.edu; "Nixon Proposes Disaster Aid Unit," *New York Times*, May 9, 1973, 17; Lou Cannon, "Nixon Signs Bills on Last Day of '73," *Washington Post*, January 1, 1974, A20. Memo from DWM to Richard Schweiker, Folder Flood Issues, October 28, 1974, Richard Schweiker Papers; Birkland, *Lessons of Disaster*, 159-165.

30. Carlucci quoted in Wolensky, *Better Than Ever!* 84.

31. Ibid.

32. Robert Schnabel, "Coverage of Issues in the PL 91-606."

33. Richard Nixon, "State of the Union Message to Congress on Community Development," March 8, 1973, *American Presidency Project*, http://www.presidency.ucsb.edu /ws/index.php?pid=4134.

34. Disaster Relief Act of 1974, http://www.gpo.gov/fdsys/pkg/STATUTE-88/pdf /STATUTE-88-Pg143-2.pdf.

35. *New Approaches to Disaster Preparedness and Assistance: Message from the President of the United States* (Washington, D.C.: Government Printing Office, 1973); "S.1840. A Bill to Provide for Disaster Assistance and Other Purposes," GAO Resources, http://ftp.resource .org/gao.gov/93-288/0000FB12.pdf; "Disaster Relief Legislation," Remarks by Mr. Burdick, June 12, 1973, *Congressional Record: Proceedings and Debates of the 93rd Congress*, Senate Bill 1840, S10932, http://bulk.resource.org/gao.gov/93-288/0000FB10. "Nixon Lists Plans to Spread Burden of Disaster Relief," *Wall Street Journal*, May 9. 1973, 3; Subcommittee on Disaster Relief of the Committee on Public Works, *To Investigate the Adequacy and Effectiveness of Federal Disaster Relief Legislation*, 93rd Congress, 1st Session, 1973, 861, 863.

36. Dunne remarks are found in *To Investigate the Adequacy and Effectiveness of Federal Relief Legislation*, Part 6, 78.

37. Ogden Reid is quoted in Rolfe, "Central Disaster Unit."

38. Peter May, *Recovering from Catastrophes: Federal Disaster Relief Policy and Politics*, Contributions in Political Science (Westport, Conn.: Greenwood Press, 1985), 26.

39. Richard Sylves, *Disaster Policy and Politics*, 54-55.

40. Ibid.; May, *Recovering from Catastrophes*, 25.

41. *Disaster Relief Act Amendments of 1974: Report of the Committee on Public Works United States Senate to Accompany S 3062* (Washington, D.C.: Government Printing Office, 1974), 2; "Tornado Toll Hits 324 Aid Set for States," *Washington Post*, April 5, 1974, A1; "Five States Struck by Tornadoes Declare Disaster Areas; Death Toll Surpasses 300," *Wall Street Journal*, April 5, 1974, 15; "Disaster Relief," *Congress and the Nation, Volume 4, 1973–1976* (Washington, D.C.: Congressional Quarterly, 1977), 147-149. As recently as the hearings into Hurricane Katrina there were calls for a catastrophic insurance program for all Americans, see Pamela M. Prah, "Disaster Preparedness," *CQ Researcher* (November 18, 2005); Spencer Rich, "Disaster—Loan Veto Upheld by 59-36 Vote in Senate," *Washington Post*, September 26, 1973, 1, 6.

42. Suburban Emergency Management Project, "U.S. 1974 Tornado Outbreak: Super Catalyst for Fed's Disaster Relief Act of 1974," http://www.semp.us/publications/biot

_reader.php?BiotID=582; Richard Nixon, "Remarks on Signing Disaster Relief Act of 1974," *Presidential Documents*, 1974, http://bulk.resource.org/gao.gov/93–288/0000 FB73.pdf.

43. Keith Bea believes that the Disaster Relief Act of 1974 was "not a radical departure from past legislation." See Keith Bea, "The Formative Years: 1950–1978," in *Emergency Management; The American Experience, 1900–2010*, 2nd ed., edited by Claire Rubin (Boca Raton, Fla.: CRC Press, 2012), 103; I argue that Nixon's proposal was significant because it emphasized behavioral adjustments to natural hazards rather than technological ones. See Sylves, *Disaster Politics and Policy*, which notes that the 1974 legislation policy was changed from structural to nonstructural hazard mitigation, 51.

44. David Moss is among those who do not see the Disaster Relief Act of 1974 as a dramatic change from the Johnson era; see David Moss, *When All Else Fails*, 256.

45. May, *Recovering from Disaster*, 19.

46. Sylves, *Disaster Politics and Policy*, 55. McCarthy and Kiefer, "A History of Hazard Mitigation in the U.S.," 1–18.

47. Birkland, *Lessons of Disaster*.

48. Haddow and Bullock, *Introduction to Emergency Management*, 80–82.

49. Anthony Ripley, "Civil Defense Takes a Role in Natural Disaster," *New York Times*, December 10, 1972.

50. Dunne testimony to Congress in *Federal State and Local Emergency Preparedness: Hearings Before the Joint Committee on Defense Production, Congress of the United States, Ninety-Fourth Congress, 2nd Session, June, 28, 29, 30, 1976* (Washington, D.C.: Government Printing Office, 1976), 56; he might also have noted that Harry Truman had located his emergency management in the Housing and Home Finance Agency.

51. Ibid., 60–61.

52. Blanchard, *American Civil Defense*, 16–20; Norton, *Emergency Preparedness and Disaster Assistance*, 57–61; Anthony Ripley, "Civil Defense Takes over Role in Natural Disaster," *New York Times*, December 10, 1972, 106.

53. Nixon's ideas to improve civil defense were first formulated after Hurricane Camille; see Richard Nixon, "Special Message to the Congress on Federal Disaster Assistance," April 22, 1970, online in Gerhard Peters and John T. Woolley, *The American Presidency Project,* http://www.presidency.ucsb.edu/ws/?pid=2479.

54. Defense Civil Preparedness Agency, *Civil Preparedness: Aa New Dual Mission* (Washington, D.C.: DoD, 1973); Defense Civil Preparedness Agency, *Foresight Annual Report* (Washington, D.C.: DoD,1974); Defense Civil Preparedness, *Mandate for Readiness* Annual Report of the Defense Civil Preparedness Agency (Washington, D.C.: DoD, 1975).

55. Defense Civil Preparedness, *Mandate for Readiness* (DoD: Washington, DC, 1975).

56. Defense Civil Preparedness Agency, *Civil Preparedness*; Defense Civil Preparedness Agency, *Foresight Annual Report* (Washington, D.C.: DoD, 1974); Defense Civil Preparedness, *Mandate for Readiness.*

57. Defense Civil Preparedness, *Mandate for Readiness*, 33–34.

58. FEMA, "EMI History," http://training.fema.gov/History/; Alessandra Jerolleman and John J. Kiefer, *Natural Hazard Mitigation* (Boca Raton, Fla.: CRC Press, 2012), 106–110; Haddow and Bullock, *Introduction to Emergency Management*, 165–170; Gabriel Scott Knowles, *The Disaster Experts: Mastering Risk in Modern America* (Philadelphia: University of Pennsylvania Press, 2011), 274.

59. *Disaster and Recovery: Toward A New State System* (Albany, N.Y.: New York State Assembly, Committee on Ways and Means, 1975), 8–9; Legislative Commission on Expenditure, *Disaster Preparedness Programs* (Albany: The Committee, 1984); *Senate Majority Task Force on State and Local Emergency Preparedness* (Albany: New York State Senate, 2002). Pennsylvania followed a similar path, creating the state's Emergency

Management Agency (PEMA) in 1978, see "History of Emergency Management Agency," http://www.co.cambria.pa.us/EMA/Pages/Department%20History.aspx. Anthony J. Mussari, *Appointment with Disaster*, xii. Malcolm Wilson, "At Village Square Apartments and Commercial Center," October 21, 1974, *Public Papers of Malcolm Wilson, Fiftieth Governor of the State of New York, 1973–1974* (Albany: New York State, 1975), 1808–1809; New York State Disaster Preparedness Commission, *New York State Disaster Preparedness Plan* (Albany: New York State Disaster Preparedness Commission, 1982); Legislative Commission on Expenditure, *Disaster Preparedness Programs* (Albany: The Committee 1984); *Senate Majority Task Force on State and Local Emergency Preparedness* (Albany: New York State Senate, 2002). Pennsylvania followed a similar path, creating Pennsylvania's Emergency Management Agency (PEMA) in 1978, see "History of Emergency Management Agency," http://www.co.cambria.pa.us/EMA/Pages/Department%20History.aspx.

60. Scott Gabriel Knowles, *The Disaster Experts*, especially chapter 6, "A Nation of Hazards"; Joe Sartori, "Robert Schnabel, Retired Colonel in Air Force," *Washington Post*, September 14, 1981.

61. This was also the case with Governor Rockefeller, as explained in chapter 3.

62. Patrick S. Roberts, *Disasters and the American State: How Politicians, Bureaucrats, and the Public Prepare for the Unexpected* (New York: Oxford University Press, 2013), 74–76.

63. Nixon himself acknowledged the damning evidence of the June 23, 1972, tapes: "I was aware of the advantage that course of action would have with respects to limiting the possible public exposure of involvement by person's connected to my reelection campaign"; see Richard Nixon, Statement of August 5, 1974, in folder Legislative Subjects, Box 135, Jack Kemp Papers, Library of Congress (hereafter cited as Jack Kemp Papers); on Nixon's attempts to reform his image, see Stanley I. Kutler, *The Wars of Watergate: The Last Crisis of Richard Nixon* (New York: W. W. Norton, 1990; reprint, New York: Random House, 2013), 612–622.

64. Knowles, *The Disaster Experts*, 272–273.

65. Timothy Kneeland, *Buffalo Blizzard of 1977* (Charleston, SC: Arcadia Publishing, 2017), 7–8.

66. Paul Beers, *Pennsylvania Politics Today and Yesterday*, 369; Sadie Gurman, "Obituary: Ernest Kline, Lt. Governor under Shapp," *Pittsburg Post-Gazette*, May 14, 2009; Sally Downey, "William H. Wilcox, 84, Pushed for Change in City," *Philadelphia Inquirer*, June 7, 2004.

67. National Governors' Association, Center for Policy Research, *Comprehensive Emergency Management: A Governor's Guide* (Washington, D.C., May 1979), http://training .fema.gov/EMIWeb/edu/docs/Comprehen; Clark F. Norton, *Emergency Preparedness and Disaster Assistance Federal Organizations and Programs* (Office of Management and Budget Report No. 78–102, April 18, 1978); Phil McCombs, "'Maxi Disaster' Plan," *Washington Post*, December 23, 1978; Carter officials also recruited Agnes veterans Robert Schnabel and Tom Casey when writing the bill.

68. Carlucci was interviewed by Wolensky in 1992; see Robert P. Wolensky, *Better Than Ever!* 83–84. The group also consulted with Robert Schnabel, a former Nixon administrator.

69. Burton Kaufman and Scott Kaufman, *The Presidency of James Earl Carter, Jr.*, second rev. ed. (Lawrence: University of Kansas Press, 2006), 80–85.

70. Jimmy Carter, "Executive Order 12127," March 31, 1979, in John T. Woolley and Gerhard Peters, *The American Presidency Project* (online), Santa Barbara, Calif., http://www .presidency.ucsb.edu/ws/?pid=32127. Included under the FEMA umbrella were the Federal Insurance Administration, National Fire Prevention and Control Administration, National Weather Service Community Preparedness Program, Federal Preparedness Agency of the General Services Administration, and of course the FDAA from HUD. Civil Defense came into the new agency by way of transfer of the Defense Department's Defense Civil

Preparedness Agency. On the problems in centralizing FEMA, see Alvin H. Mushkatel and Louis F. Weschler, "Emergency Management and the Intergovernmental System," *Public Administration Review* 45, Special Issue: Emergency Management: A Challenge for Public Administration (1985): 49–56.

71. Carter in a speech after Hurricane Katrina suggested that he wanted three elements in FEMA: "One was that it would be headed by highly qualified professionals in dealing with disaster. Secondly, that they would be completely independent and not under another agency that would submerge it. And third, that it would be adequately funded." See Jimmy Carter, "Federal Emergency Management Agency Nomination of John W. Macy, Jr., to Be Director," May 3, 1979, in John T. Woolley and Gerhard Peters, *The American Presidency Project*, Santa Barbara, Calif., http://www.presidency.ucsb.edu/ws/?pid=32273; FEMA did not fully consolidate all federal disaster and emergency functions and programs, and federal agencies continued to compete for resources and jurisdiction when disaster struck; see Sylves, *Disaster Policy and Politics*, 57.

72. Federal Emergency Management Agency, "FEMA History," http://www.fema.gov /about/history.shtm.

73. The most significant included flooding in California, a freeze in Florida, and a severe heat wave in the Midwest. Although this latter event inspired scientists to study a climatic phenomenon called El Nino, it caused little political pressure or public outcry.

74. "Agnes syndrome" cited in Henry Allen, "Virginians Rebel Again; Keeping Heads above Water with Pride, Not Federal Funds," *Washington Post*, December 1, 1985, C5.

75. Janes Seaberry, "Budget-Cutters Eye Disaster Relief, Now a Giant Insurance Agency," *Washington Post*, April 4, 1981.

76. "Section 101," Robert T. Stafford Disaster and Relief and Emergency Assistance Act (emphasis added).

77. Patrick F. Roberts, "FEMA and the Prospects for Reputation-Based Autonomy," *Studies in American Political Development* 20 (2006): 57–87; "FEMA History," Federal Emergency Management Agency, http://www.fema.gov/about/history.htm.

78. Bernard Weinraub, "Reagan Asking $4.2 Billion for Buildup of Civil Defense," New York Times, March 30, 1982, https://www.nytimes.com/1982/03/30/us/reagan-asking-4.2 -billion-for-buildup-of-civil-defense.html.

79. Roberts, "FEMA," 64.

80. On natural disasters in the 1980s see the National Climate Data Center, http://www .ncdc.noaa.gov/oa/reports/billionz.html#narrative; on FEMA's change of mission, see Judith Miller, "Civil Defense Notions Change But Skepticism Remains," *New York Times*, April 4, 1982, E6; "Emergency Chief Will Resign," *New York Times*, July 23, 1985, A17; Ronald Reagan, "Nomination of Louis O. Giuffrida to Be Director of the Federal Emergency Management Agency," February 24, 1981, in John T. Woolley and Gerhard Peters, *The American Presidency Project* [online], Santa Barbara, Calif., http://www.presidency.ucsb.edu /ws/?pid=43453; Bernard Weinraub, "Civil Defense Agency: 'Trying to Do Something,'" *New York Times*, April 8, 1982; "House Unit Finds Misconduct at US Emergency Agency," *New York Times*, July 26, 1985.

81. Thomas Birkland and Sarah Waterman, "Is Federalism the Reason for Policy Failure in Hurricane Katrina?" *Journal of Federalism* 38 (Fall 2008): 696, https://doi.org/10.1093 /publius/pjn020; Lt Gen Julius W. Becton, *Becton: Autobiography of a Public Servant* (Annapolis, Md.: Naval Institute Press, 2008).

82. Hollings quoted in Tiffany Sharples, "A Brief History of FEMA," *Time*, August 28, 2008.

83. "Hurricane Relief Is Said to Skip the Poor," *New York Times*, January 13, 1990; Ronald Smothers, "Pain Lingers for Poorer Victims of Hurricane Hugo," *New York Times*, February 3, 1990; "After Andrew," *USA Today*, September 1, 1992.

84. Alvin H. Mushkatel and Louis F. Weschler, "Emergency Management and the Intergovernmental System," *Public Administration Review* 45 (1985): 49–56, https://doi.org /10.2307/3134997; Birkland, "Is Federalism to Blame for Katrina?"; see also S. Schneider, "Who's to Blame? (Mis) Perceptions of the Intergovernmental Response to Disasters," *Publius: The Journal of Federalism* 38, no. 4 (January 30, 2008): 715–738, https://doi.org /10.1093/publius/pjn019.

85. The greatest challenge to the "perfect" response to disaster is knowing and applying the proper sequence of actions needed when disaster is imminent and after it strikes; see Sylves, *Disaster Policy and Politics,* 13; Thomas A. Birkland, *Lessons of Disaster,* 182–189.

86. Woodrow Wilson, *Congressional Government: A Study in American Politics* (New York: Houghton Mifflin, 1885), 318.

87. Thomas Lippmann, "Hurricane May Have Exposed Flaws in New Disaster Relief Plan," *Washington Post,* September 3, 1992; Marianne Means, "Bush and FEMA, Little or No Help to Disaster Victims," *Seattle Post,* September 2, 1992; Robert Davis, "FEMA Chief: Policy Slowed Response in Florida," *USA Today,* September 29, 1992; the idea that G.H.W. Bush's response to Hurricane Andrew may have cost him the election is developed by Roberts, "FEMA," 65.

88. Haddow and Bullock, *Introduction to Emergency Management,* 10.

89. Steven Mufson, "Overhaul of National Security Apparatus Urged; Commission Cites U.S. Vulnerability," *Washington Post,* February 1, 2001.

90. George W. Bush, "Statement on Signing the Homeland Security Act of 2002," November 25, 2002, in John T. Woolley and Gerhard Peters, *The American Presidency Project* [online], Santa Barbara, Calif., http://www.presidency.ucsb.edu/ws/?pid=64224.

91. Douglas Brinkley, *The Great Deluge: Hurricane Katrina, New Orleans, and the Mississippi Gulf Coast* (New York: Harper Perennial, 2006), 618–619.

92. Jeffrey B. Bumgarner, *Emergency Management* (Santa Barbara, Calif.: ABC CLIO, 2008), 10.

93. George W. Bush failed to go to New Orleans in the aftermath of Hurricane Katrina, and images of him looking at the disaster from Air Force One were used to show how distant he was from the storm victims. Bruce Alpert, "George W. Bush Never Recovered Politically from Katrina," *Times-Picayune,* August 8, 2015, http://www.nola.com/katrina/index.ssf /2015/08/bush_katrina_was_a_setback_to.html. Exit polls in 2102 showed that two in five voters were impressed by Obama's response to Sandy and in his bipartisan embrace of Governor Chris Christie. Elections and disaster are covered in Platt, *Disasters and Democracy,* 57–58; David K. Twigg, *The Politics of Disaster: Tracking the Impact of Hurricane Andrew* (Gainesville: University of Florida Press, 2012); Peter May, *Recovering from Catastrophes,* 118, 112; and Andrew Reeves, "Political Disaster: Unilateral Powers, Electoral Incentives, and Presidential Disaster Declarations," *Journal of Politics* 73 (2011): 1142–1151.

94. Thomas A. Garrett and Russell S. Sobel, "The Political Economy of FEMA Disaster Payments," *Economic Inquiry* 41 (July 2003): 496–509.

95. Reeves, "Political Disaster," 1142–1151.

96. Corey Kilgannon, "Flooding Persists in Southern Tier of New York," *New York Times,* September 9, 2011, https://www.nytimes.com/2011/09/10/nyregion/ny-region-in -triage-mode-as-flooding-persists.html.

97. Steve Stanne, "Perfect Storms: How Hurricane Irene and Tropical Storm Lee Slammed New York," *New York State Conservationist,* August 2012, 8–13, http://www.dec .ny.gov/docs/administration_pdf/0812perfectstorms.pdf.

98. Associated Press, "Record Flooding in Binghamton Leaves 'Dire' Situation," September 8, 2011, Syracuse.com, https://www.syracuse.com/news/index.ssf/2011/09 /record_flood_in_binghamton_lea.html. An Albany dealmaker, Libous was convicted of public corruption in 2015, resigned his seat, and then died of prostate cancer in 2016; see

Thomas Kaplan, "Thomas Libous, New York State Senator, Is Convicted of Lying to F.B.I.," *New York Times*, May 22, 2015, https://www.nytimes.com/2015/07/23/nyregion/thomas-libous-new-york-state-senator-is-convicted-of-lying-to-fbi.html.

99. Fox News, "Tropical Storm Lee Drenches Northeast, Prompting Evacuations Due to Flooding," September 9, 2011.

100. Michael Gormley, "Binghamton Assesses Loss: Some Return Home, but Crisis is not Over," *Democrat and Chronicle*, September 10, 2011, 1, 7.

101. Jennifer Burke, *Catholic Courier*, September 9, 2011.

102. Matt Richmond, "Flood Waters in Binghamton 'Worst I've Seen,'" WSKG, September 8, 2011, http://innovationtrail.org/post/flood-waters-binghamton-worst-ive-seen.

103. The Associated Press, "Tropical Storm Lee Flooding Triggers Evacuation of Thousands in Northeast," NOLA.com, September 8, 2011, http://www.nola.com/hurricane/index.ssf/2011/09/tropical_storm_lee_flooding_tr.html.

104. "Hanna, Hinchey Request Federal Emergency Declarations for Broome, Chenango, Delaware, Otsego, Tioga and Tompkins," *Evening Sun*, September 8, 2011, https://www.evesun.com/news/stories/2011-09-08/13034/Hinchey-and-Hanna-request-Federal-Emergency-declarations-for-Broome-Chenango-Delaware-Otsego-Tioga-and-Tompkins-/.

105. Foxnews, "Tropical Storm Lee Drenches Northeast."

106. Kilgannon, "Flooding Persists."

107. Kilgannon, "Flooding Persists."

108. On the broken gauge, see Rubinkam and Scolforo, "Susquehanna Recedes in PA., NY from Highest Levels"; the internal investigation is featured in Bill Marosi and David Ondrejik, *Flood Forecast Challenges in the Middle Atlantic Region during Hurricane Irene and Tropical Storm Lee*, http://frmpw.nfrmp.us/2012/docs/WORKSHOP/Susquehanna/5%20-%20Friday/0915_-_Marosi_-_JacketsHarrisbugAug241012.pdf.

109. Skraptis, "Flood of Memories."

110. Rubinkam and Scolforo, "Susquehanna Recedes in PA., NY."

111. Associated Press, "Tropical Storm Lee Flooding."

112. Matt Flegenheimer, "Northeast is Soaked Again," https://www.nytimes.com/2011/09/09/nyregion/remnants-of-tropical-storm-soak-an-already-battered-northeast.html.

113. Mark Scolforo and Michael Rubinkam, "PA. NY See Water Subside as MD. Awaits the Worst," *San Diego Union-Tribune*, September 9, 2011, http://www.sandiegouniontribune.com/sdut-pa-ny-see-waters-subside-as-md-awaits-the-worst-2011sep09-story.html.

114. Mark Scolforo and Michael Rubinkam, "Wilkes-Barre Flooding Worse than Agnes in 1972," NBCPhiladelphia.com, https://www.nbcphiladelphia.com/news/local/Wilkes-Barre-Flooding-Worse-Than-1972-Hurricane-Agnes-129545508.html.

115. Foxnews, "Tropical Storm Lee Drenches Northeast, Prompting Evacuations Due to Flooding," September 9, 2011, http://www.foxnews.com/weather/2011/09/08/remnants-lee-bring-fresh-flood-worries-to-east/; FEMA Public Affairs, "Pennsylvania Flood Recovery Continues, Officials Meet with Survivors," September 19, 2011, https://www.fema.gov/es/node/35874; the publicity generated by elected officials also enhanced their approval ratings see Ali Carey, "PA Officials Continue to Support Flood Relief Efforts," PoliticasPa, http://www.politicspa.com/pa-officials-continue-to-support-flood-relief-efforts/28568/.

116. Matt Katz, "Christie Praises Obama Administration Response on Irene, *Philadelphia Inquirer*, September 7, 2011, B1; the only sour note was that FEMA and the NOAA had suggested that New York City was in dire danger, when in fact the storm veered away and inundated Vermont giving those residents only minutes of warning rather than hours; see Sarah Wheaton, "Different Leaders, Different Responses," *New York Times*, September 2, 2011.

117. Department of Homeland Security Office of Inspector General, *FEMA Deployed the Appropriate Number of Community Relations Employees in Response to Hurricane Irene and Tropical Storm Lee* (May 2013).

118. Jon Campbell, "About 1,000 Still in Southern Tier Shelters, State Official Says," *Democrat and Chronicle*, September 12, 2011.

119. "A Guide to Disaster Assistance and Relief Funding: How to Navigate the Disaster Assistance Process" (Compliments of U.S. Senator Kirsten E. Gillibrand, September 2011), https://www.grownyc.org/files/gmkt/Gillibrand_Disaster_Relief_Funding_Assistance _Guidebook.pdf.

120. Mark Scoloforo and Michael Rubinkam, "Northeast Turns to Flood Recover after Lee," Weather/NBC News, September 12, 2011, http://www.nbcnews.com/id/44490089/ns /weather/t/northeast-turns-flood-recovery-after-lee/.

121. Pennsylvania State Senate, "Complete Statement of Thomas Blaskiewicz Mayor West Pittston Borough, Pennsylvania before the Senate Environmental Resources & Energy Committee Pennsylvania State Senate on Flooding and Emergency Response," April 25, 2018, http://www.pasenategop.com/environmentalresources/wp-content/uploads/2018/04 /blaskiewicz.pdf.

122. Associated Press, "A Year after Tropical Storm Lee, PA Towns Remain Unprotected," September 8, 2012, TribLIVE, http://triblive.com/news/2565861–74/corps -flood-west-pittston-borough-ago-bloomsburg-lee-pennsylvania-town.

123. Matt Flegenheimer, "Northeast Is Soaked Again, Forcing Evacuations, *New York Times*, September 8, 2011, https://www.nytimes.com/2011/09/09/nyregion/remnants-of -tropical-storm-soak-an-already-battered-northeast.html; Elizabeth Skrapits, "Flood of Memories: The Wrath of Lee," *Citizen's Voice*, September 8, 2014, http://www.citizensvoice .com/news/flood-of-memories-the-wrath-of-lee-1.1748985, Brozena was cited in Bill O'Boyle, "45 Years Later, Agnes Still on People's Minds," *Times Leader*, June 8, 2017, https:// www.timesleader.com/news/local/663873/45-years-later-agnes-still-on-peoples-minds; I would argue that community memory and the celebration of local structural barriers to flooding were part of the process of forgetting.

124. National Research Council, *Levees and the National Flood Insurance Program: Improving Policies and Practices* (Washington, D.C.: National Academies Press, 2013), https://doi.org/10.17226/18309.

125. Skrapits, "Flood of Memories."

126. New York Rising Reconstruction Program, *NYRCR Tioga,*. (New York, 2014), I–14.

127. FEMA High Water Mark Initiative, https://www.fema.gov/high-water-mark -initiative.

128. Mark Jurkowitz, Paul Hitlin, Amy Mitchell, Laura Santhanam, Steve Adams, Monica Anderson, and Nancy Vogt, "The Changing TV News Landscape," Pew Research Center, http://stateofthemedia.org/2013/special-reports-landing-page/the-changing-tv -news-landscape/; Katherine Fry, *Constructing the Heartland: Television News and Natural Disaster* (Cresskill, N.J.: Hampton Press, 2003).

129. New York Rising Reconstruction Program, *NYRCR Tioga* (New York, 2014), I–13.

130. Alert Ready, https://www.alertready.ca/.

131. National Weather Service, "Wireless Emergency Alerts Continue to Save Lives; and We Are Hearing about It," https://www.weather.gov/news/172103-wireless-emergency -alerts.

EPILOGUE

1. Nathaniel Parker Willis, *Letters from under a Bridge: And Poems* (G. Virtue, 1840), 52. I am indebted to Susan Stranahan for bringing this author to my attention, see Stranahan, *Susquehanna River of Dreams*, 80.

2. Nick Malawskey, "Against the Current: How the Eel Returned to the Susquehanna River," *Penn Live*, July 11, 2018, https://www.pennlive.com/news/2018/07/american_eel _susquehanna_river.html.

3. David R. Conrad, Ben McKnight, and Martha Stout, *Higher Ground: A Report on Voluntary Property Buyouts in the Nation's Floodplains, A Common Ground Solution Serving People at Risk, Taxpayers and the Environment* (Washington, D.C.: National Wildlife Federation, July 1998), viii, xi, 12, 30, https://www.nwf.org/Educational-Resources/Reports /1998/07-01-1998-Higher-Ground. Communities that relocated include Valmeyer and Grafton, Illinois, and Rhineland and Pattonsburg, Missouri.

4. Richard T. Sylves, *Disaster Policy and Politics: Emergency Management and Homeland Security*, 2nd ed. (Washington, D.C.: CQ Press, 2014), 146–147.

5. Steve Stanne, "Perfect Storms," http://www.dec.ny.gov/docs/administration_pdf /0812perfectstorms.pdf.

6. Complete Statement of Thomas Blaskiewicz, Mayor, West Pittston Borough, Pennsylvania, http://www.pasenategop.com/environmentalresources/wp-content/uploads /2018/04/blaskiewicz.pdf; Conrad, McKnight, and Stout, *Higher Ground*.

7. "Homeowners Buyout Program Offered to Flood Victims in Wyoming County," September 29, 2016 WNEP, http://wnep.com/2016/09/29/home-buyouts-offered-to-flood -victims-in-wyoming-county/; Luzerne County Action Plan for Disaster Recovery, July 2012, as amended August 27, 2013, http://www.luzernecounty.org/uploads/images /assets/county/departments_agencies/office_of_community_development/Action%20 Plan%20-%20July%202012.pdf; Bill O'Boyle, "Casey's Infrastructure Summit Message 'We all Need Help,'" March 12, 2018, *Times Leader*, https://www.timesleader.com/news/local /696079/caseys-infrastructure-summit-message-we-all-need-help; Elizabeth Skrapits, "Nearly 3 Years Later, Demolition Will Reshape Flood-Ravaged Towns," *Times-Tribune*, July 27, 2014, http://www.thetimes-tribune.com/news/nearly-3-years-later-demolition-will -reshape-flood-ravaged-towns-1.1725728.

8. Kirsten Gillibrand, Press Release, "Schumer-Gillibrand Announce More than $3.3 Million in FEMA Funding."

9. Christopher Flavelle, "America's Last-Ditch Climate Strategy of Retreat Isn't Going So Well," *Bloomberg Businessweek*, May 2, 2018.

10. Louis Jacobsen, "After the Deluge: Cities Along the Susquehanna River Prepare for the next Big Flood," *Planning*, February 2012, 18–23.

11. Bill O'Boyle, "Casey's Infrastructure Message."

12. For New York, see https://www.landtrustalliance.org/what-we-do/our-regional -programs/northeast/new york program/new-york-state-conservation-partnership

13. Michelle Nijhuis, "Movement to Take Down Dams Goes Mainstream," National Geographic, January 29, 201, https://news.nationalgeographic.com/news/2015/01/150127 -white-clay-creek-dam-removal-river-water-environment/; Lisa W. Foderaro, "High Water in Two Big River Systems, With Different Approaches to Flood Control," *New York Times*, June 30, 2006, https://www.nytimes.com/2006/06/30/nyregion/30anatomy.html; Watershed Sciences and Engineering Program, *Imagine A Sustainable Susquehanna* (Bucknell University Center for Sustainability and Environment, November 2015); Kurt Bresswein, "These 16 Gone in 2017: Pennsylvania Leads Nation in Dam Removal," LehighValleyLive, March 11, 2018, https://www.lehighvalleylive.com/news/index.ssf/2018 /03/these_16_gone_in_2017_pennsylv.html.

14. Bill O'Boyle, "45 years later."

15. Flavelle, "Last-Ditch Climate Strategy."

Selected Bibliography

Abney, Glen F., and Larry B. Hill. "Natural Disasters as a Political Variable: The Effect of a Hurricane on an Urban Election." *American Political Science Review* 60, no. 4 (December 1966): 974–981. https://doi.org/10.2307/1953770.

Adams, Franklin S. "Hurricane Agnes: Flooding vs. Dams in Pennsylvania." *Bulletin of the Atomic Scientists* 29, no. 4 (1973): 30–34. https://doi.org/10.1080/00963402 .1973.11455470.

Albala-Bertrand, J. M. *The Political Economy of Large Scale Natural Disasters: With Special Reference to Developing Countries.* London: Oxford University Press, 1993.

American Institute for Research, Pacific Institute for Research and Evaluation, and Deloitte and Rouche, LLP, "A Chronology of Major Events Affecting the National Flood Insurance Program, prepared for the Federal Emergency Management Agency" (October 2002). http://www.dhs.gov/xlibrary/assets/privacy/privacy_pia _mip_apnd_h.pdf.

Anderson, William. *Disaster and Organizational Change: A Study of the Long Term Consequences of the 1964 Alaskan Earthquake.* Columbus, OH: Ohio State Disaster Research Center: 1969.

Arceneaux, Kevin, and Robert Stein. "Who Is Held Responsible When Disaster Strikes? The Attribution for Responsibility for a Natural Disaster in an Urban Election." *Journal of Urban Affairs* 28, no. 1, (2006): 45–53. https://doi.org/10.1111/j .0735-2166.2006.00258.x.

Arnold. Joseph L. *Evolution of the 1936 Flood Control Act.* Washington, D.C.: Government Printing Office, 1988.

Ashley, Sharon T., and Walker S. Ashley. "Flood Fatalities in the United States." *Journal of the American Meteorological Association* 47 (March 2008): 805–818. https:// doi.org/10.1175/2007JAMC1611.1

Bagstad, Kenneth J., Kevin Stapleton, and John R. D'Agostino. "Taxes, Subsidies, and Insurance as Drivers of United States Coastal Development." *Ecological Economics* 63, nos. 2–3 (2007): 285–298. https://econpapers.repec.org/RePEc:eee:ecolec:v:63: y:2007:i:2–3:p:285–298.

Barry, John. *Rising Tide: The Mississippi Flood of 1927 and How It Changed America.* New York: Simon and Schuster, 1998.

Bea, Keith. "The Formative Years: 1950–1978." In *Emergency Management: The American Experience, 1900–2010*, 2nd ed., edited by Claire Rubin, 83–114. Boca Raton, Fla.: CRC Press, 2012.

Beers, Paul. *Pennsylvania Politics Today and Yesterday: The Tolerable Accommodation.* State College: Pennsylvania State University Press, 1980.

Bell, Trudy E. "Angry Waters." *New York Archives* 12, no. 3 (Winter 2013): 12–17. https://www.nysarchivestrust.org/new-york-archives-magazine/magazine -highlights/winter-2013-volume-12-number-3.

Bell, Trudy E. *The Great Dayton Flood of 1913.* Charleston, S.C.: Arcadia Publishing, 2008.

Berkowitz, Edward. *Something Happened: A Political and Cultural Overview of the Seventies.* New York: Columbia University Press, 2006.

Bernstein, Carl, and Bob Woodward. *All the President's Men.* New York: Simon and Schuster; reprint, 2014.

Birkland, Thomas. *After Disaster: Agenda Setting, Public Policy, and Focusing Events.* Washington, D.C.: Georgetown University Press, 1997.

Birkland, Thomas. *Lessons of Disaster: Policy Change after Catastrophic Events.* Washington, D.C.: Georgetown University Press, 2006.

Birkland, Thomas and Sarah Waterman. "Is Federalism the Reason for Policy Failure in Hurricane Katrina?" *Publius: The Journal of Federalism* 38, no. (Fall 2008): 692–714. https://doi.org/10.1093/publius/pjn020.

Bodnar, John. "Public Memory in an American City: Commemoration in Cleveland." In *Commemorations: The Politics of National Identity,* edited by John R. Gillis, 74–89. Princeton: Princeton University Press, 1996.

Boyer, Paul. "From Activism to Apathy: The American People and Nuclear Weapons, 1963–1980." *Journal of American History* 70, no. 4 (March 1984): 821–844. doi:10.2307/1899750.

Briggs, Peter. *Rampage: The Story of Disastrous Floods, Broken Dams, and Human Fallibility.* New York: David McKay, 1973.

Brinkley, Douglas. *The Great Deluge: Hurricane Katrina, New Orleans and the Mississippi Gulf Coast.* New York: Harper Perennial, 2006.

Brokaw, Tom. *The Greatest Generation.* New York: Random House, 1998.

Brubaker, John H. *Down the Susquehanna to the Chesapeake.* University Park: Pennsylvania State University Press, 2002.

Bucher, Rue. "Blame and Hostility in Disasters." *American Journal of Sociology* 62 (1957): 467–475.

Bumgarner, Jeffrey, B. *Emergency Management.* Santa Barbara: ABC CLIO, 2008.

Burby, Raymond J. "Hurricane Katrina and the Paradoxes of Government Disaster Policy: Bringing about Wise Governmental Decisions for Hazardous Areas." *Annals of the American Academic of Political and Social Science* 604, no. 1 (March 2006): 171–191. https://doi.org/10.1177%2F0002716205284676.

Butler, David. "The Expanding Role of the Federal Government: 1927–1950." In *Emergency Management: The American Experience, 1900–2010,* edited by Claire Rubin, 51–82. Boca Raton, Fla.: Taylor and Francis, 2012.

Clary, Bruce. "The Evolution and Structure of Natural Hazards Policies." *Public Administration Review* 45 (January 1985): 20–28. http://links.jstor.org/sici?sici=0033–3352%28198501%2945%3C20%3ATEASON%3E2.0.CO%3B2-%23.

Collins, Robert M. "The Economic Crisis of 1968 and the Waning of the 'American Century.'" *American Historical Review* 101, no. 2 (1996): 396–423. https://doi.org/10.1086/ahr/101.2.396.

Conlon, Timothy. *New Federalism: Intergovernmental Reform from Nixon to Reagan.* Washington, D.C.: Brooking Institute, 1988.

Conrad, David R., Ben McKnight, and Martha Stout. *Higher Ground: A Report on Voluntary Property Buyouts in the Nation's Floodplains, A Common Ground Solution Serving People at Risk, Taxpayers and the Environment, National Wildlife Federation.* Washington, D.C.: National Wildlife Federation,1998.

Cowie, Jefferson. *Stayin' Alive: The 1970s and the Last Days of the Working Class.* New York: New Press, 2010.

Cronin, Thomas E. *The State of the Presidency,* 2nd ed. Boston: Little, Brown and Co, 1980.

Dallek, Matthew. *Defenseless under the Night: The Roosevelt Years and the Origins of Homeland Security.* New York: Oxford University Press, 2016.

Daniel, Peter. *Deep'n as It Come: The 1927 Mississippi River Flood.* New York: Oxford University Press, 1977.

Dauber, Michele Landis. "Fate, Responsibility, and 'Natural' Disaster Relief: Narrating the American Welfare State." *Law and Society Review* 33 (1999): 257–318.

Dauber, Michele Landis. *The Sympathetic State: Disaster Relief and the Origins of the Welfare State.* Chicago: University of Chicago Press, 2013.

Davies, Gareth. "Dealing with Disaster: The Politics of Catastrophe in the United States, 1789–1861." *American Nineteenth Century History* 14, no. 1 (2013): 53–72. https://doi.org/10.1080/14664658.2013.768422.

Davies, Gareth. "The Emergence of a National Politics of Disaster, 1865–1900." *Journal of Policy History* 26, no. 3 (July 2014): 305–326. https://doi.org/10.1017/S0898030614000141.

Davies, Gareth. "Pre-Modern Disaster Politics: Combating Catastrophe in the 1950s," *Publius* 47, no. 2 (2017): 260–281. https://doi.org/10.1093/publius/pjx016.

Davies, Gareth. "Review of Michelle Dauber, The Sympathetic State." *Historian* 77, no. 1 (Spring 2015): 116–118. https://doi.org/10.1111/hisn.12056_11.

Davies, Gareth. "Taming Disaster: Fatalism and Mastery in American Disaster Management, 1800–2013." January 2014. http://americanstudiesglasgow.blogspot.com/2014/01/taming-disaster-fatalism-and-mastery-in.html.

"DEC Efforts in Hurricane Agnes Flood Disaster Saves Lives and Property." *New York State Environmentalist* 2, no. 2 (August 1, 1972): 1–2.

Dieck, Herman. *The Johnstown Flood.* University Park, Pa.: Pennsylvania State University Press, 2009.

Dimitroff, Thomas P., and Lois S. Janes. *History of the Corning–Painted Post Area: 200 Years in Painted Post Country.* Rev. ed. Corning, N.Y.: Bookmarks, 1991.

Domhoff, William. *Who Rules America? The Triumph of the Corporate Rich.* New York: McGraw Hill, 2013.

Dory, Amanda J. *Civil Security: Americans and the Challenge of Homeland Security.* Lanham, Md.: Rowman and Littlefield/Center for Strategic and International Studies, 2003.

Dresher, Nuala McGann. *Engineers for the Public Good: A History of the Buffalo District US Army Corps of Engineers.* Washington, D.C.: Government Printing Office, 1982.

Dunham, Allison. "Flood Control via the Police Power." *University of Pennsylvania Law Review* 107 (1959): 1098–1132.

Durant, Robert F., and Susannah Bruns Ali. "Repositioning American Public Administration? Citizen Estrangement, Administrative Reform, and the Disarticulated State." *Public Administration Review* 73, no. 2 (March/April 2013): 278–289. https://doi.org/10.1111/j.1540-6210.2012.02646.x.

Dyment, Robert. "When the Next Big Flood Hits: Lessons from Hurricane Agnes." *Popular Mechanics,* June 1973, 122–126, 178.

Dymon, Ute J., and Rutherford H. Platt. "U.S. Federal Disaster Declarations: A Geographical Analysis." In *Disasters and Democracy: The Politics of Extreme Natural Events,* edited by Rutherford H. Platt, 47–68. Washington, D.C.: Island Press, 1999.

Ehrlichman, John. *Witness to Power: The Nixon Years.* New York: Simon and Schuster, 1982.

Ellis, Richard. *Presidential Lightning Rods: The Politics of Blame Avoidance.* Lawrence: University of Kansas Press, 1994.

Erikson, Kai T. *Everything in Its Path: Destruction of a Community in the Buffalo Creek Flood.* New York: Simon and Schuster, 1978.

Federal Response to Hurricane Camille: Hearings before the Special Committee on Disaster Relief of the Committee on Public Works, United States Senate. Washington, D.C.: U.S. Government Printing Office, 1970.

Fenno, Richard F. Jr. *Congressmen in Committees*. Boston: Little, Brown & Co., 1973.

Final Report of the Disaster Survey Team on the Events of Agnes: A Report to the Administrator. Rockville, Md.: U.S. National Oceanic and Atmospheric Administration, 1973.

Fleming, James Rodger. *Fixing the Sky: The Checkered History of Weather and Climate Control*. New York: Columbia University Press, 2010.

Fleming, James Rodger. "The Pathological History of Weather and Climate Modification: Three Cycles of Promise and Hype." *Historical Studies in the Physical and Biological Sciences* 37, no. 1 (2006): 3–25. 10.1525/hsps.2006.37.1.3.

Fradkin, Philip L. *The Great Earthquake and Firestorms of 1906: How San Francisco Nearly Destroyed Itself*. Berkeley: University of California Press, 2006.

Fry, Katherine. *Constructing the Heartland: Television News and Natural Disaster*. Cresskill, N.J.: Hampton Press, 2003.

Galloway, George B. "Investigative Function of Congress," *American Political Science Review* 21, no. 1 (1927): 47–70. https://doi.org/10.2307/1945538.

Garrett, Thomas A., and Russell S. Sobel. "The Political Economy of FEMA Disaster Payments." *Economic Inquiry* 41 (July 2003): 496–509.

Garth, Leonard I. "Honorable Max Rosenn: Conscience and Role Model of the Court." *University of Pennsylvania Law Review* 154, no. 5 (May 2006): 1041–1044.

Ginsberg, Benjamin, and Martin Shefter. *Politics by Other Means: Politicians, Prosecutors, and the Press from Watergate to Whitewater*. New York: Norton, 2002.

Gomez, Brad T., and J. Matthew Wilson. "Political Sophistication and Attributions of Blame in the Wake of Hurricane Katrina." *Publius: The Journal of Federalism* 38, no. 4 (January 2008): 633–650. https://doi.org/10.1093/publius/pjn016.

Graham, Margaret B. W., and Alec T. Shuldiner. *Corning and the Craft of Innovation*. New York: Oxford University Press, 2001.

Green, Hardy. *The Company Town: The Industrial Edens and Satanic Mills That Shaped the American Economy*. New York: Basic Books, 2012.

Green, Kenneth, and Eric Ireland. "A Case Study of Disaster-Related Emergent Citizen Groups: An Examination of 'Vested Interests' as a Generating Condition." University of Delaware Disaster Research Center, 1977.

Grob, Gerald. *Mental Illness and American Society, 1875–1940*. Princeton: Princeton University Press, 1983.

Haas, J. Eugene. "Social Aspects of Weather Modification." *Bulletin of the American Meteorological Society* 54, no. 7 (July 1973): 647–657. https://doi.org/10.1175/152 0-0477(1973)054%3C0647:SAOWM%3E2.0.CO;2.

Haddow, George, Jane Bullock, and Damon P. Coppola. *Introduction to Emergency Management*, 6th ed. Waltham, Mass.: Butterworth-Heinemann, 2017.

Hall, C. Robert. "Major Disaster Proposals Invite 'Fed' into Areas Now Well Handled." *The National Underwriter*, March 1975, 79.

Haskell, Thomas. "The Curious Persistence of Rights Talk in the 'Age of Interpretation.'" *Journal of American History* 74, no. 3 (December 1987): 984–1012. https://doi.org /10.2307/1902162.

Hayward, Steven F. *The Age of Reagan: The Fall of the Old Liberal Order, 1964–1980*. New York: Three Rivers Press, 2001.

Healy, Andrew, and Neil Malhotra. "Myopic Voters and Natural Disaster Policy." *American Political Science Review* 103, no. 3 (August 2009): 387–406. https://doi .org/10.1017/S0003055409990104.

Hearings before a Subcommittee of the Committee on Government Operations House of Representatives Ninety-Second Congress. Washington, D.C.: Government Printing Office, 1972.

Hearings before the Subcommittee on Small Business of the Committee on Banking, Housing and Urban Affairs of the United States Senate. Washington, D.C.: Government Printing Office, 1972.

Heclo, Hugh. *A Government of Strangers: Executive Politics in Washington.* Washington, D.C.: Brookings Institute Press, 1977.

Heclo, Hugh. "Political Executives and the Washington Bureaucracy." *Political Science Quarterly* 92, no. 3 (Autumn 1977): 395–424. DOI:10.2307/2148500.

Henry, Alfred J. *The Floods of 1913 in the Rivers of the Ohio and Lower Mississippi Valleys.* Washington, D.C.: Government Printing Office, 1913.

Hinshaw, Robert. *Living with Nature's Extremes: The Life of Gilbert Fowler White.* New York: Big Earth Publishing, 2006.

Hollis, Amanda Lee. "A Tale of Two Federal Emergency Management Agencies." *Forum* 3, no. 3 (2005): 1–14. https://doi.org/10.2202/1540–8884.1095.

Hosler, C. L. "Overt Weather Modification." *Reviews of Geophysics* 12, no. 3 (1974): 523–527. https://doi.org/10.1029/RG012i003p00523.

Howard, Judith, and Ernest Zebrowski. *Category 5: The Story of Camille. Lessons Unlearned from America's Most Violent Hurricane.* Ann Arbor: University of Michigan Press, 2010.

Howe, J. D. "'Legal Moguls': Ski Areas, Weather Modification and the Law." *University of Pittsburgh Law Review* 33, (1971–1972): 59–77.

Hoye, Nicholas R. *The Flood and the Community.* Corning, N.Y.: Corning Glass Works, 1976.

Hoyt, William G., and Walter B. Langbein. *Floods.* Princeton: Princeton University Press, 1955.

Hughes, Charles E. *Tioga County, PA Flood!* Utica, N.Y.: Dodge Group Press, 1972.

Hughes, Patrick. *A Century of Weather Service, 1870–1970.* New York: Gordon and Breach, 1970.

Jenkins-Smith, Hank C., Carol L. Silva, and Richard W. Waterman. "Micro and Macro Models of the Presidential Expectations Gap." *Journal of Politics* 67, no. 3 (August 2005): 690–715. https://doi.org/10.1111/j.1468–2508.2005.00335.x.

Jennings, Charles Robert. "Urban Renewal as Disaster Recovery Planning: Tropical Storm Agnes in Elmira, New York, with Reference to Wilkes-Barre, Pennsylvania." MA thesis, Cornell University, 1994.

Johnson, Loch K., Erna Gelles, and John C. Kuzenski. "The Study of Congressional Investigations: Research Strategies." *Congress & the Presidency* 19, no. 2 (1992): 137–156. https://doi: 10.1080/07343469209507897.

Jones, Bryan, and Frank R. Baumgartner. *Agendas and Instability in American Politics.* Chicago: University of Chicago Press, 1993.

Jones, Marian Moser Jones. *The American Red Cross from Clara Barton to the New Deal.* Baltimore: Johns Hopkins University Press, 2013.

Jones, Marion Moser Jones. "Race, Class and Gender Disparities in Clara Barton's Late Nineteenth-Century Disaster Relief." *Environment and History* 17, no. 1 (February 2011): 107–131. http://www.jstor.org.ezproxy.naz.edu/stable /25799117.

Kanarek, Harold. *The Mid-Atlantic Engineers: A History of the Baltimore District, U.S. Army Corps of Engineers, 1774–1974.* Washington, D.C.: U.S. Government Printing Office, 1976.

Kashutas, William, III. *Dapper Dan Flood: The Controversial Life of a Congressional Power Broker.* University Park: Pennsylvania State University Press, 2010.

Kashatus, William T., III. "'Dapper Dan' Flood: Pennsylvania's Legendary Congressman." *Pennsylvania Heritage* 21 (Summer 1995): 4–11.

King, Rawle O. "The National Flood Insurance Program: Status and Remaining Issues for Congress." Congressional Research Services, February 6, 2013. http://fas.org /sgp/crs/misc/R42850.pdf.

Klein, Herbert. *Making It Perfectly Clear: An Inside Account of Nixon's Love-Hate Relationship with the Media.* New York: Doubleday, 1980.

Klein, Naomi. *The Shock Doctrine: The Rise of Disaster Capitalism.* New York: Henry Holt, 2008.

Kneeland, Timothy W. *Buffalo Blizzard of 1977.* Charleston, S.C.: Arcadia Publishing, 2017.

Knowles, Scott Gabriel. *The Disaster Experts: Mastering Risk in Modern America.* Philadelphia: University of Pennsylvania Press, 2011.

Krantz, David. *The Trouble with Agnes.* Wilkes-Barre, Pa.: D. L. Krantz, 1973.

Kury, Franklin L. *Clean Politics, Clean Streams: A Legislative Autobiography and Reflections* Lehigh, Pa.: Lehigh University Press, 2011.

Kutler, Stanley I. *The Wars of Watergate: The Last Crisis of Richard Nixon.* New York: W. W. Norton, 1990. Reprint. New York: Random House, 2013.

Leopold, Luna B., and Thomas Maddock, Jr., *The Flood Control Controversy: Big Dams, Little Dams, and Land Management.* New York: Ronald Press, 1954.

Levy, Peter B. "Spiro Agnew, the Forgotten Americans, and the Rise of the New Right." *Historian* 75, no. 4 (Winter 2013): 707–739.

Liddy, G. Gordon. *Will: The Autobiography of G. Gordon Liddy.* New York: St. Martins, 1991.

Light, Paul C. *Government's Greatest Achievements: From Civil Rights to Homeland Security.* Washington, D.C.: Brookings Institution Press, 2002.

Lipsitz, George. *Time Passages: Collective Memory and American Popular Culture.* Minneapolis: University of Minneapolis Press, 1990. Reprint, 2001.

Lorditch, Emilie. "Advances in Weather Analysis and Forecasting." *Weatherwise* 69, no. 1 (January/February 2009): 22–27. https://doi.org/10.3200/WEWI.62.1.22–27.

Lowi, Theodore J. *The End of Liberalism: The Second Republic of the United States.* New York: W. W. Norton, 1969.

Malhotra, Neil, and Alexander G. Kuo. "Attributing Blame: The Public's Response to Hurricane Katrina." *Journal of Politics* 70, no. 1 (2008): 120–135. doi:10.1017/ s0022381607080097.

Matthews, Jeffrey J. *Alanson B. Houghton: Ambassador of the New Era.* Lanham, Md.: Rowman and Littlefield, 2004.

May, Peter. *Recovering from Catastrophes: Federal Disaster Relief Policy and Politics.* Westport, Conn.: Praeger, 1985.

Mayer, Matt. "States: Stop Subsidizing FEMA Waste and Manage Your Own Disasters." *Backgrounder*, no. 23 (September 29, 2009): 1–9.

McCarthy, Mary V., and John J. Kiefer. "A History of Hazard Mitigation in the U.S." In *Natural Hazards Mitigation*, edited by Alessandra Jerolleman and John J. Kiefer, 1–18. Boca Raton, Fla.: CRC Press, 2013.

McCullough, David. *The Johnstown Flood.* New York: Simon and Schuster, 1987.

McGann Drescher, Naula, and James Robert Martin-Diaz. *Engineers for the Public Good: A History of the Buffalo District, U.S. Army Corps of Engineers.* Buffalo, N.Y.: The District, 1982.

McGinnis, Joe. *The Selling of the President: The Classical Account of the Packaging of a Candidate.* Reprint. New York: Penguin Books, 1988.

Michel-Kerjan, Erwann O. "Catastrophe Economics: The National Flood Insurance Program." *Journal of Economic Perspectives* 24, no. 4 (Fall 2010): 165–186. 10.1257/jep.24.4.165.

Milkis, Sidney M., and Michael Nelson. *The American Presidency: Origins and Development, 1776–1998.* Washington, D.C.: CQ Press, 1999.

Miskel, James. *Disaster Response and Homeland Security: What Works, What Doesn't.* Westport, Conn.: Praeger, 2006.

Morris, Andrew. "Hurricane Camille and the New Politics of Federal Disaster Relief, 1965–1970." *Journal of Policy History* 26, no. 3 (Summer 2014): 406–426. https://doi.org/10.1017/S0898030614000189.

Mosher, Frederick. *A Tale of Two Agencies: A Comparative Analysis of the General Accounting Office and the Office of Management and Budget.* Baton Rouge: Louisiana State University Press, 1984.

Moss, David. "The Peculiar Politics of American Disaster Policy: How Television Has Changed Federal Relief." In *The Irrational Economist: Making Decisions in a Dangerous World,* edited by Erwann Michel-Kerjan and Paul Slovic, 151–160. New York: Public Affairs Books, 2010.

Moss, David A. *When All Else Fails: Government as the Ultimate Risk Manager.* Cambridge, Mass. Harvard University Press, 2004.

Moss, Mitchell, Charles Schellhammer, and David A. Berman. "The Stafford Act and Priorities for Reform." *Journal of Homeland Security and Emergency Management* 6, no. 1 (2009): 1–21. https://doi.org/10.7916/D86H4T5R.

Mushkatel, Alvin H., and Louis F. Weschler. "Emergency Management and the Intergovernmental System." *Public Administration Review* 45, Special Issue: Emergency Management: A Challenge for Public Administration (January 1985): 49–56. https://doi.org/10.2307/3134997.

Mussari, Anthony J. *Appointment With Disaster, Vol. 1: The Swelling of the Flood—Wilkes Barre, Pennsylvania before and after the Agnes Flood of June 23, 1972.* Wilkes-Barre, Pa.: Northeast Publishers, 1974.

Nathan, Richard. "There Will Always Be a New Federalism." *Journal of Public Administration Research and Theory* 16, no. 4 (October 2006): 499–510. https://doi.org/10.1093/jopart/muj011.

Nathan, Richard P. *The Plot That Failed: Nixon and the Administrative Presidency.* New York: John Wiley and Sons, 1975.

National Advisory Committee on Oceans and Atmospheres. *A Report for the Administrator of NOAA: The Agnes Floods a Post-Audit of the Effectiveness of the Storm and Flood Warning System of the National Oceanic and Atmospheric Administration.* Washington, D.C.: Government Printing Office: 1972.

Natural Disasters: The Oft-Repeated Failures: A Report of the New York State Senate Ad Hoc Committee on Natural Disasters. Albany: New York State Senate, 1979.

Neuhaus, Cable. "Is There Life after the Governorship?" *Pennsylvania Illustrated* 4, (1979): 47–48.

Neustadt, Richard. *Presidential Power: The Politics of Leadership from FDR to Carter.* New York: John Wiley and Sons, 1980.

New Dimensions of Civil Emergency Preparedness, 1969–1973. Washington, D.C.: Office of Emergency Preparedness, 1973.

Newman, Richard S. *Love Canal: A Toxic History from Colonial Times to the Present.* New York: Oxford University Press, 2016.

Nixon, Richard. *Public Papers of President Nixon.* Washington, D.C.: 1969.

Nora, Pierre. "Between Memory and History" ["Les Lieux de Memoire"]. *Representations* 26, (Spring 1989): 7–24. http://www.jstor.org/stable/2928520?origin=JSTOR-pdf.

Norton, Clark F. *Emergency Preparedness and Disaster Assistance: Federal Organization and Programs.* Washington, D.C.: Congressional Research Services, 1978.

Office of Emergency Preparedness. *A Year of Rebuilding: The Federal Response to Hurricane Camille* Washington, D.C.: Government Printing Office, 1970.

Owens, John E. "Extreme Advocacy Leadership in the Pre-Reform House: Wright Patman and the House Banking and Currency Committee." *British Journal of Politics* 15 (1985): 187–205.

Pearcy, Matthew. "After the Flood: A History of the 1928 Flood Control Act." *Journal of the Illinois State Historical Society* 95, no. 1 (Spring 2002): 172–201.

Perlstein, Rick. *"Nixonland": The Rise of a President and the Fracturing of America.* New York: Scribner, 2008.

Persico, Joseph E. *The Imperial Rockefeller: A Biography of Nelson a Rockefeller.* New York: Simon and Schuster, 1982.

Pielke, Roger, Chantal Simonpietri, and Jennifer Oxelson. "Thirty Years after Hurricane Camille: Lessons Learned, Lessons Lost." http://sciencepolicy.colorado.edu/about _us/meet_us/roger_pielke/camille/report.html.

Platt, Rutherford. *Disasters and Democracy.* Washington, D.C.: Island Press, 1999.

Platt, Rutherford. "The National Flood Insurance Program: Some Midstream Perspectives." *Journal of the American Institute of Planners* 42, no. 3 (1976): 303–313. https://doi.org/10.1080/01944367608977733.

Popkin, Roy S. "The History and Politics of Disaster Management in the United States." In *Nothing to Fear: Risks and Hazards in American Society*, edited by Andrew Kirby. Tucson: University of Arizona Press, 1990:101–129.

Power, Fred B., and E. Warren Shows. "A Status Report on the National Flood Insurance Program Mid 1978." *The Journal of Risk and Insurance* 46 (1979): 61–76. doi:10.2307/252069.

Pritchett, Wendell E. "Which Urban Crisis? Regionalism, Race and Urban Policy, 1960–1974." *Journal of Urban History* 34, no. 2 (January 2008): 209–220. https://doi.org/10.1177%2F0096144207308678.

Reeves, Andrew. "Political Disaster: Unilateral Powers, Electoral Incentives, and Presidential Disaster Declarations." *Journal of Politics* 73, no. 4 (2011): 1142–1151. DOI:10.1017/s0022381611000843.

"Report of Special New York Senate Committee to Investigate Flood Warning Systems in New York State," January 31, 1973.

Reuss, Martin. "The Army Corps and Engineers and Flood Control Politics on the Lower Mississippi." *Louisiana History: The Journal of the Louisiana Historical Association* 23, no. 2 (Spring 1982): 131–148. http://www.jstor.org.ezproxy.naz.edu/stable/4232166.

Rivera, Jason David, and DeMond Shondell Miller. "A Brief History of the Evolution of United States' Natural Disaster Policy." *Journal of Public Management and Social Policy* 12, no. 1 (Spring 2006): 5–14.

Rivera, Jason David, and DeMond Shondell Miller. "Continually Neglected: Situating Natural Disasters in the African American Experience." *Journal of Black Studies* 37, no. 4 (March 2007): 503–533. DOI: 10.1177/0021934706296190.

Roberts, Patrick F. "FEMA and the Prospects for Reputation-Based Autonomy." *Studies in American Political Development* 20, no. 1 (April 2006): 57–87. https://doi.org /10.1017/S0898588X06000010.

Roberts, Patrick S. *Disasters and the American State: How Politicians, Bureaucrats, and the Public Prepare for the Unexpected.* New York: Oxford University Press, 2013.

Rosenthal, Donald B. "Bargaining Analysis in Intergovernmental Relations." *Publius* 10, no. 3 (Summer 1980): 5–44. DOI: 10.2307/3329681.

Rozario, Kevin. "What Comes Down Must Go Up: Why Disasters Have Been Good For American Capitalism." In *American Disasters,* edited by Steven Biel, 72–102. New York: New York University Press, 2011.

Sabato, Larry. *Feeding Frenzy: Attack Journalism and American Politics.* New York: Free Press, 1991.

Schneider, Sandra. "Who's to Blame? (Mis) Perceptions of the Intergovernmental Response to Disasters." *Publius: The Journal of Federalism* 38, no. 4 (January 2008): 715–738. https://doi.org/10.1093/publius/pjn019.

Schreiner, Mark. "A Storm Named Agnes." *New York State Conservationist* 51, no. (1997): 14.

Schultz, Jessica, and James R. Elliot. "Natural Disasters and Local Demographic Change in the United States." *Population and Environment* 34 (2012): 293–312. DOI 10.1007/s11111-012-0171-7.

Schuster, Natalie. "This 'Who Shot John' Thing: Disaster Relief as Entitlement in the 20th Century," *Federal History* 5 (2014): 84–107.

Shallat, Todd. "Building Waterways, 1802–1861: Science and the United State Army in Early Public Works." *Technology and Culture* 31, no. 1 (January 1990): 18–50. DOI:10.2307/3105759.

Shallat, Todd. "Engineering Policy: US Army Corps of Engineers and Historical Foundations of Power." *Public Historian* 11, no. 3 (Summer 1989): 6–27. DOI: 10.2307/3378610.

Shugg, Wallace. "The Great Patapsco Flood of 1972. "*Maryland Historical Magazine* 96 (2001): 53–67.

Shughart, William F. "Disaster Relief as Bad Public Policy." *Independent Review* 15, no. 4 (Spring 2011): 529–531.

Skowronek, Stephen. *Building a New American State: The Expansion of National Administrative Capacities, 1877–1920.* Princeton: Princeton University Press, 2002.

Small, Melvin. *The Presidency of Richard Nixon.* American Presidency Series. Lawrence, Kans.: University of Kansas Press, 1999.

Smith, Mark A. *Camille 1969: Histories of a Hurricane.* Athens, Ga.: University of Georgia Press, 2011.

Solnit, Rebecca. *A Paradise Built in Hell: The Extraordinary Communities That Arise in Disaster.* New York: Penguin Books, 2010.

Spencer, Robyn. "Contested Terrain: The Mississippi Flood of 1927 and the Struggle to Control Black Labor." *Journal of Negro History* 79, no. 2 (Spring 1994): 170–181. DOI: 10.2307/2717627.

Steinberg, Ted. *Acts of God: The Unnatural History of Natural Disaster in America,* 2nd ed. New York: Oxford, 2000.

Stranahan, Susan. *Susquehanna, River of Dreams.* Baltimore: Johns Hopkins University Press, 2014.

Sullivan, Charles. "Camille: The Mississippi Gulf Coast in the Coils of the Snake." *Gulf Coast Historical Review* 2, no. 2 (Spring 1987): 49–77.

Sylves, Richard. *Disaster Politics and Policy: Emergency Management and Homeland Security,* 2nd rev. ed. Washington, DC: CQ Press, 2014.

Thompson, Dennis F. "Moral Responsibility of Public Officials: The Problem of Many Hands." *American Political Science Review* 74, no. 4 (1980): 905–916. https://doi.org/10.2307/1954312.

Tower, Elizabeth. *Anchorage: From its Humble Origins as a Railroad Construction Camp.* Anchorage: Epicenter Press, 1999.

Tropical Storm Agnes June 1972: Post Flood Report Volume1I, Meteorology and Hydrology. Baltimore, Md.: U.S. Army Corps of Engineers, 1974.

Twigg, David K. *The Politics of Disaster: Tracking the Impact of Hurricane Andrew.* Gainesville: University of Florida Press, 2012.

United States and Office of Emergency Preparedness. *Disaster Preparedness; Report to the Congress.* Washington, D.C., 1972.

United States Congress Senate Committee on Public Works Special Subcommittee on Disaster Relief. *Federal Response to Hurricane Camille: Hearings, Ninety-First Congress, Second Session.* Washington, D.C.: U.S. Government Printing Office, 1970.

United States Defense Civil Preparedness Agency. *Significant Events in United States Civil Defense History,* compiled by Mary Harris. Washington, D.C.: Information Agency Defense Civil Preparedness Agency, 1975.

Verchick, Robert, and Lynsey Johnson. "When Retreat Is the Best Option: Flood Insurance after Biggert-Waters and Other Climate Change Puzzles." *John Marshall Law Review* 47 (2014): 695. https://dx.doi.org/10.2139/ssrn.2418089.

Walker, Paul K. *The Corps Responds: A History of the Susquehanna Engineer District and Tropical Storm Agnes.* Baltimore: U.S. Army Corps of Engineers, 1976.

Walker, Wallace Earl. "Elmer Staats and Strategic Leadership in the Legislative Branch." In *Leadership and Innovation: A Biographical Perspective on Entrepreneurs in Government,* edited by Jamesson W. Doig and Erwin C. Hargrove, 282–314. Baltimore, Johns Hopkins University Press, 1987.

Waugh, William. "Katrina and the Governors." *Public Organization Review* 9 (December 2009): 343–351. https://doi.org/10.1007/s11115-009-0092-9.

Waugh, William. *Living with Hazards, Dealing with Disasters: An Introduction to Emergency Management.* Armonk, N.Y.: M. E. Sharpe 2000.

Wayne, Stephen. "Expectations of the President." In *The President and the Public,* edited by Doris A Graber, 17–21. Philadelphia: Institute for the Study of Human Issues, 1982.

White, Gilbert. *Human Adjustment to Flooding: A Geographical Approach to the Flood Problem in the United States.* Chicago: University of Chicago Press, 194.

White, Robert M. "The National Hurricane Warning System." *Bulletin of the American Meteorological Society* 53, no. 7 (July 1972): 631–633. http://www.jstor.org.ezproxy.naz.edu/stable/26254520.

White, Theodore H. *The Making of the President 1972.* New York: Harpers, 1973. Reprint, 2010.

Willoughby, H. E., D. P. Jorgenson, R. A. Black, and S. L. Rosenthal. "Project STORM FURY A Scientific Chronicle, 1962–1983." *Bulletin of the American Meteorological Society* 66, no. 5 (May 1985): 505–514. https://journals.ametsoc.org/doi/pdf/10.1175/1520–0477%281985%29066%3C0505%3APSASC%3E2.0.CO%3B2.

Wilson, Malcolm. *Public Papers of Malcolm Wilson, Fiftieth Governor of New York State* (Albany, N. Y.: 1977).

Winter, Jay, and Emmanuel Sivan. *War and Remembrance in the Twentieth Century.* New York: Oxford University Press, 2000.

Wolensky, Robert, and Kenneth C. Wolensky. "Min Matheson and the ILGWU in the Northern Anthracite Region, 1944–1963." *Pennsylvania History* 60, no. 4 (October 1993): 455–474. http://www.jstor.org.ezproxy.naz.edu/stable/27773676.

Wolensky, Robert P. *Better Than Ever! The Flood Recovery Task Force and the 1972 Agnes Disaster, 1972.* Stevens Point, Wisc.: Foundation Press, 1993.

Wolensky, Robert P. *Power, Policy, and Disaster: The Political-Organizational Impact of a Major Flood.* Stevens Point: University of Wisconsin–Stevens Point, Center for the Small City, 1984.

Wolensky, Robert P., and Kenneth Wolensky. "Born to Organize." *Pennsylvania Heritage* 25, no. 3 (Summer 1999): 32–39.

Wolensky, Robert P., and Kenneth C. Wolensky. "Local Governments Problems with Disaster Management: A Literature Review and Structural Analysis." *Policy Studies Review* 9, no. 4 (Summer 1990): 703–725. https://doi.org/10.1111/j .1541–1338.1990.tb01074.x.

Wolensky, Robert Paul. "The Aftermath of the Great Agnes Disaster: An Analysis of Emergent Groups and Local Government Officials in the Wyoming Valley of Pennsylvania." Ph.D. dissertation, Pennsylvania State University, 1975.

Wright, J. D., P. H. Rossi, S. R. Wright, and E. Weber-Burdin. *After the Clean-up: Long-Range Effects of Natural Disasters*. Beverly Hills, Calif.: Sage, 1979.

Young, Nancy Beck. *Wright Patman: Populism, Liberalism and the American Dream*. University Park, Tex.: Southern Methodist University Press, 2000.

Zebrowski, Ernest, and Judith A. Howard. *Category 5: The Story of Camille. Lessons Unlearned from American's Most Violent Hurricane*. Ann Arbor: University of Michigan, 2005.

Index

CPSIA information can be obtained
at www.ICGtesting.com
Printed in the USA
LVHW101032060723
751598LV00014B/177/J